LETTERS AT 3AM

Reports on Endarkenment

Michael Ventura

Spring Publications
Dallas

Also by Michael Ventura . . .

Non-fiction: *Shadow Dancing in the U.S.A.; We've Had a Hundred Years of Psychotherapy—And the World's Getting Worse* (co-authored with James Hillman) • **Fiction:** *Night Time Losing Time; The Zoo Where You're Fed to God* (forthcoming, 1994) • **Poetry:** *The Mollyhawk Poems; Sitting on Moving Steel* • **Films:** *I'm Almost Not Crazy—John Cassavetes: The Man and His Work* (director and writer); *Echo Park* (writer); *Roadie* (co-writer with James "Bigboy" Medlin)

Spring Publications, Inc. • P.O. Box 222069 • Dallas TX 75222

© 1993 by Michael Ventura

First printing 1993. Printed in the United States of America, text on acidfree paper. Cover designed and produced by Margot McLean. Distributed in the United States by the Continuum Publishing Company (through the services of Publisher Resources, Inc.); in Canada by Maxwell Macmillan; in the United Kingdom, Eire, and Europe by Airlift Book Co

All material attributed to Randolph Bourne is taken from *The Radical Will: Randolph Bourne—Selected Writings, 1911–1918*, © 1977, Olaf Hansen (Introduction), Christopher Lasch (Preface), used by permission of the University of California Press

Library of Congress Cataloging-in-Publication Data

Ventura, Michael.
    Letters at 3am : reports on endarkenment / Michael Ventura.
        p.   cm.
    ISBN 0–88214–361–1 (pbk. : alk. paper)
    1. United States—Social life and customs—1971–   2. United States—Social conditions—1980–   I. Title.
E169.O4V46   1993
973.9—dc20   93–23203
                                                      CIP

for Brendan McCambridge

*It is not necessary to understand
the opening of the door
to feel the wind.*

—*Michael Luciano Ventura*

Contents

Part Three: War Is the Health of the State

Part Four: The Witness Tree

Coda

Author's Note

All these pieces were originally written for the *L.A. Weekly* except "An Inventory of Timelessness," which was written for *ZG* (at the suggestion of Rosetta Brooks), and "The Age of Endarkenment," an earlier version of which appeared in *The Whole Earth Review*. (My thanks to Sam Joseph for the word "endarkenment.") A version of "An Inventory of Timelessness" also appeared in *We've Had a Hundred Years of Psychotherapy—And the World's Getting Worse*. Ron Stringer edited most of the "3AM" columns, and I owe him much for his patience and intelligence. Thanks also to Steve Erickson, who edited the pieces on the Gulf War; Kateri Butler, who edited "You, in Particular, Are Going to Die" and "Grand Illusion"; Tom Carson, who edited "The Toy from Hell"; Harold Meyerson, who edited the earthquake piece; and especially Kit Rachlis, who made our paper worth reading again and who edited the Vegas piece and "The Witness Tree." Thanks also to Greg Burke, copy editor supreme; and to Pam Klein and her crew of fact-checkers. And finally: my gratitude to James Hillman and Mary Helen Sullivan of Spring Publications for their faith and care.

Michael Ventura
Los Angeles, 1993

Part One

The Age of Endarkenment

What God on Whose Side?

Take one of the most exciting banner headlines of the century, from *The New York Times*, 10 November 1989: "EAST GERMANY OPENS FRONTIER TO THE WEST FOR MIGRATION OR TRAVEL; THOUSANDS CROSS." This was so thrilling that many ignored two stories on the same page: "GOP Leaders Urge Softer Line About Abortion" and "Evolution Theory's Foes Win Textbook Battle in California." Taken as a whole, the page shows America preoccupied with a religious war as Europe tries to forge the twenty-first century.

The textbook story went like so: "In a concession to evangelical Christians that could affect the teaching of science nationwide . . ." so-called "creationists" had intimidated the entire state of California into denigrating a body of science (evolution research) that involves geology, biology, astronomy and physics—all of which go against creationist beliefs. This as evidence piles up about the miserable ignorance of our kids, especially in science. Analysts in business and government fear that this has become a national-security issue, with America sure to lose its high-tech edge in commerce and the military unless the trend reverses. Yet these super-Christians are superpatriots as well, the first to cry "America first!" Which leaves you with a sect of desperate people trapped in a labyrinth of ironies, selling out the country they love for the god they fear.

This crippling religious war is going on at every level, subverting many areas of American life, but we tend to see it as a matter of separate political or social issues rather than as one of the fundamental struggles of our era. Here's a *Los Angeles Times* item ("Court Signals Change on Religion Cases") dated 10 July 1988: "A Supreme Court majority appears ready to abandon Jefferson's wall of separation between church and state." The piece goes on to detail a ruling that sanctions giving government money where it had never been given before, to church programs teaching kids about sex. The court is assuming, among other things, that Christianists can prevent sexual activity in the young, though a study reported earlier that year (*Los Angeles Times*, 6 February 1988) showed that 43 percent of teens in conservative and evangelical churches have had "sexual relations" by the age of eighteen—26 percent by age sixteen. So it would seem the Supreme Court was acting purely on belief, not on knowledge. And again, what do you get? More super-Americans subverting the Constitution for a Christianism that doesn't attain even *their* stated goals—and, in the process, giving more clout to factions that want to see a stupider, hence a weaker, America.

Fast-forward to the *Los Angeles Times*, 18 April 1990: "Won't Shield Religions From Law, Court Says." But the word "religions," in this case, doesn't refer to mainstream or fundamentalist Christianism. The court ruled against two people of the Native American Church who lost their jobs for using peyote in an ancient religious rite. "In a sweeping opinion, Justice Antonin Scalia went far beyond the case at hand and declared that, when religious rights clash with the government's need for uniform rules, the court will side with the government. . . . Religions that are out of the mainstream are most likely to be affected, because [of] their unconventional practices and lack of political influence." Scalia called this the "unavoidable consequence of democratic government"—although we avoided it pretty good, for two hundred years, till he came along.

Of course, this is the same line of attack being used against American artists as Congress restricts the NEA. The *Times* also reported in that article, "In 1986 a Jewish serviceman was denied the right to wear a yarmulke with his uniform. In 1988 the court said the government may build a road through a sacred Indian burial ground. [*Would they have done that to a sacred Baptist burial ground?*] Last year, the court said Scientologists may not claim a tax exemption for the cost of 'auditing,' a central figure of their religious practice." In short, the

Supreme Court is building up an impressive body of precedents that beliefs that are not Christianist are not protected by the Constitution.

Mainstream and evangelical Christianist institutions are treated very differently. The *Los Angeles Times*, 1 May 1990: "The Supreme Court . . . dismissed a long-running suit challenging the tax exemption of the Roman Catholic Church because of its anti-abortion activities." This, though there is an IRS rule forbidding tax-exempt groups, like churches and religions, from using their funds "to influence legislation." The hypocrisy and intent of the Scalia-Rehnquist court are clear. They are the point men for a movement to equate Christianism with America and to codify that equation into law. Yet this is still a big, hairy land, with dissension always bubbling. The *Los Angeles Times* again, 9 August 1989: "A coven of witches has won tax-exempt status in Rhode Island as a legitimate religious group." And Connecticut (those feisty New Englanders again) last week made abortion a state right.

Which brings us to another aspect of our religious war, and another juxtaposition of heady headlines. The *Los Angeles Times*, 4 December 1989, during the Bush–Gorbachev summit: "SUMMIT SPEEDS WORK ON ARMS, ECONOMICS—A New Era Is Ushered In by Superpowers"; "Prague Facing Crisis, Street Protests Called"; "Entire East German Leadership Resign." And, unnoticed in the hubbub, a Column One feature called "One Step Beyond Organic":

"SANTA BARBARA—To farmer Stephen Moore, the manufacture of fertilizer is an act of faith, an esoteric ritual guided by spiritual forces and arcane philosophy, a mixture of organic agriculture, astronomy and metaphysics." The *Times* goes on to describe, rather calmly, some of the steps in the manufacture of this incredibly effective "biodynamic" compost: "yarrow blossoms aged in a stag bladder, chamomile buried in a cow's intestine, a sheep's skull filled with oak bark and buried beside a stream and dandelions aged in a cow membrane over winter." Biodynamic farmers have many such beliefs and practices—for instance, that certain crops should be planted only when the moon is in Pisces or Scorpio. Yet retailers testify that these supernatural farmers grow "some of the best produce" on the market.

(The biodynamic method, by the way, isn't "New Age," but was founded in Austria in 1924 and is very popular in Europe among thousands of commercial growers. Which is only natural, since these practices go way, way back to pre-Christianist times, when our word "pagan" originally meant "peasant.")

Another Column One piece, dated 13 January 1990, talks about the aftereffects of the Stockton school massacre, in which five Asian immigrant children were killed and twenty-nine other students were wounded. One of the psychologists treating the survivors said, "We have learned that folk medicine and religious rituals may be just as effective [as] the best therapy a psychologist can offer or the best medicine a psychiatrist can prescribe."

For instance, some of the children were seeing ghosts in the schoolyard. With the approval of school officials, a 100-year-old Buddhist monk performed an exorcism. The ghosts disappeared, the *Times* reported. A slightly different kind of ritual was reported in another *Times* article I clipped, but didn't remember to date: "Study Says Cancer Survival Rises With Group Therapy": "Cancer patients who get emotional and social support through group therapy may survive up to twice as long as patients on medical treatment alone, according to a surprising new [ten-year, Stanford–UC Berkeley] study . . . embarked upon . . . in hopes of refuting popular notions that the right mental attitude can help conquer disease." Pause at that: healing energy strong enough to double the length of survival, purely through focused human contact. One of the researchers, reported to be "stunned" by the outcome, said, "I would have bet the mortgage of my home that it would not have come out this way."

On the one hand, then, there's an increasingly rigid (and almost always white) Christianism resorting more and more blatantly to political power because it's no longer confident of keeping *cultural* power. On the other hand, there's a many-voiced movement, without a center or a doctrine, that has quietly left (or refused to join) the ways and assumptions of the modern West, and is in the process of reclaiming and demonstrating the value of metaphysics—fueled by Third World immigrants who believe in what the mainstream press politely calls "spiritualism" and by disaffected Judeo-Christians looking for other paths. In between these two huge, warring factions is a thick stratum of academically trained intellectuals who can't abide either and are left behind to grouse about the history the others are making.

For it *is* history, this no-holds-barred struggle to redefine reality.

Nothing less is at stake. If the witches, ritual healers, biodynamic farmers and myth-delvers endure and continue to show results, then the consensus, the heart, of the Western view will continue to slowly shift, transform and no longer be "Western." And this will affect everything from education to how we use technology. Or—the Christianists' hold on America will tighten, and our country will live the twenty-first century as the USSR has lived the twentieth, at war with its own imagination, having to crush its spirit in order to uphold its doctrine.

May 11, 1990

Small Festivals Among Friends

The cliffs above the sea near Los Angeles. Early spring. Several women had agreed to meet there at dawn. They wanted to *do* something. One of the women is my friend, and I have never heard her refer to their action as a ritual or a ceremony; they seem content to leave it nameless. Whatever it may be called, they decided beforehand only this: that each woman would bring some kind of food for the group; each would bring some object or objects; and each would have in mind something, some action, that the gathering would perform. I know that each thought carefully about these tasks, and the offerings of each blended the festive and the subtle.

My friend didn't tell me any details of what they actually did on that hill—not that it was at all shocking or sensational; it was simply private. There was nothing witchy or cultish. Only a small festival among friends, a pooling and sharing of inner energy in the presence of, and in a kind of dance with, the sunrise, the mountain, the sea, the coming spring.

I was only told in the most general terms what happened: without a preconceived plan, they placed their objects (nothing overtly mystical—things like shells, stones, bits of colored cloth and favored jewelry) in what they discovered, as they did so, was an "altar." (My friend used that word to describe it later.) Then they performed the actions each had thought of, and the spontaneous actions that rose in turn from those—some meditative, some dancelike. Then they shared their food. The fullness of feeling they enjoyed that morning

radiated on their faces for days afterward. I have no doubt of the profound power my friend took from this gathering.

Cut to the hill country south of Austin, Texas. The same week.
Roughly the same number of women, roughly the same ages—mid-
thirties to mid-forties, and at least one in the Texas group was over
fifty. They had decided it would be a good idea to go by themselves
into the hills and . . . *do* something, perform something, something
which they too did not feel a need to name. They planned only three
things beforehand: each would bring some kind of food to share; each
would bring some object or objects; each would think of something
the gathering could do.

Again, each prepared for the event with eagerness and care. Like
the California group, first they placed their objects together. As they
did, one of the women, the artist Deborah Milosevich, said, "Women
have been making altars—forever."

The words surprised her as they came out. She said them prayer-
fully, like an invocation. Invoking what? All the generations of women
who had, alone and in gatherings, focused their—their energy? their
being? their souls?—in this gentle yet firmly purposeful way. This communion. Milosevich knew about altars, they had long been a part of
her art, but she and the other women had no intention of *making*
one. She simply recognized one when she saw it.

After assembling the altar, the Texas women proceeded exactly as
the California women had: they enacted what each had thought of
for the gathering, and what spontaneously—or perhaps organically
is a better word—grew out of those actions, and then they shared their
food. Again it wasn't witchy, cultish or even self-consciously mystical,
although, coming from a Bible Belt culture, they were perhaps more
conscious of prayer. And again, each left the gathering with a profound sense of renewal.

The only connection between the two groups is me. I know one
woman in each group very well. And those two women know each
other, some, through me. But they live far apart, come from very different backgrounds (aside from both having studied art), see each other
rarely, have one-on-one talks still more rarely, live different styles, read
different books. Neither was aware that the other's group existed.

But even to call them "groups" isn't accurate. Both were gatherings
of friends that hadn't come together quite this way before. The women

in both groups would certainly call themselves feminists if the issue came up, but it's not the first word they'd think of to define their outlook. The body of thought the Californians had in common was psychology; what the Texans had in common was Christian mysticism and the honky-tonk life. The Californians come from the middle class; the Texans are a mix of middle class and working class. I believe the Californians were college-educated and that no more than two of the Texans had been to college. No one in either group has any particular politics beyond a passionate sense of fairness. Some of the Texas women have participated in similar doings since, again with the same basic form, but with different people. The coloration of both gatherings was white.

I'm pointing all this out to emphasize the extraordinary similarity in time and, even more extraordinary, the identical form. But when I told friends of these conjunctions they weren't much surprised. A Santa Fe crafts artist told me, "Yeah, there's a lot of that going on." Same basic form. In New Orleans, a blues singer said virtually the same thing: "There's a lot of *that* going around." And an L.A. writer said she knew of "at least" three such all-female gatherings, here and in Maine, "one of Mormons, one of musicians, and one miscellaneous. I was in the 'miscellaneous.'"

I suspect this may be what the Irish rocker Sinead O'Connor means when she sings, "And there's talk in the houses/Of people dancing in rings. . . ." "Dancing in rings" was a part of ancient Celtic rituals very like what the California and Texas groups did.

The point is that the same fundamental *form* lived in all their psyches, intact, articulate, empowering, ready for use. They didn't need to teach themselves about it or have it taught them through any book or movement. Growing up in the cacophonous din of our hyper-American culture hadn't dimmed it; the very different lifestyles of the two groups hadn't filtered or altered it. It was simply there—and at a certain point of maturity, awareness and longing in these individuals, it spontaneously gave them a way to communicate with each other, and with the spirit or spirits of our planet. The form awoke in them virtually simultaneously, as though it had a will of its own.

Also—and I find this both important and beautiful—this living form is open, free. The specific foods, objects and actions of the groups were quite different in detail, but harmonious in mood, and the form allowed the kind of depth of individuality-within-unity that you find in jazz. Also: it wasn't hierarchic—neither group had a leader. Neither group even felt the need to call or think of itself as a "group," much less to announce to the world what they'd done, or to decide *not* to announce. Each person told a few friends. Who in turn told a few friends.

What is clear to to me is that if this is happening among people with little or no connection in California, Texas, New Mexico, Louisiana and Maine, then it's happening in many other places too. As though in spite of, or because of, the massive disintegration of Western culture that assaults us on all sides, something within us is being freed, waking up, reviving. Something is rising from the psyche, from our ancient heritages, to help us.

Robert Bly, in a recent interview in *The Austin Chronicle*, spoke in similar terms about parallel happenings among groups of men:

> I personally believe that no matter what happens in the outer culture, the substructure underneath the male psyche remains whole. No matter what happens on the surface of the water, the bottom is still there. The difficulty for men, as well as women, is, in a society as distracting as this one, how to get down to the ocean bottom and contact that wholeness. Of course, ritual used to help with that. . . . I think we can suffer a lot of disintegration on the upper surface of the culture without an individual's psyche being broken.

I think Bly's insight essentially true—given a minimum, if only a bare minimum, of freedom from want and violence. Being from rural Minnesota, Bly hasn't done much time on the street, hasn't seen up-close the Roto-Rooter job that poverty and brutality can do on the psyche, the *whole* psyche, whole neighborhoods of psyches, right down to the "ocean-bottom." He is witnessing fundamentally for the middle class. Still, I grew up on some of the worst streets available and can witness to extraordinary survivals of spiritual life there, too— but, in my experience, they're far more rare there; and harder, terribly harder, to live out. Yet, while the women I've spoken of are, when compared to those who live in the south Bronx, quite comfortable, it's also true that we live in an age when nobody's safe, especially women, and nobody's secure. If what I've heard of Yoruba and Santeria revivals among African and Hispanic Americans is true, it means that this inner—it's not a movement, call it an impulse—crosses color and class lines.

The media, hypnotized by the death-dance of the West, isn't interested in anything done gently, done with gentle strength, certainly not what a few non-famous women and men do at dawn in the hills—and that's probably just as well. Most people who think of themselves as the intellectual watchdogs of the culture also aren't interested, and *that's* probably just as well. Nevertheless, something independent of definitions and trends has quietly awakened. It's widespread. It nourishes. It quickens life through communion, deepens inner power. And it's expressing itself in small festivals among friends.

July 14, 1989

The Revel in Revelation

There is a "revel" in revelation. Waiting in the word is the notion that stillness and solitude are not the only ways to the sacred; that self-knowledge may sometimes have more to do with "reveling" than with the meditative lotus position or the prayerful kneel. One implication is that the sacramental has also to do with intimacy and community—and with a community intimate and daring enough to revel together.

A couple of columns back I wrote about two gatherings of women—one in Texas and one in California—women who, though unknown to each other, had felt the need for the same form of revel-atory ritual. Since that article I've received a number of not-for-publication letters about other groups, among them a couple of invitations to new gatherings and news of one striking elaboration of these rituals. Here are some of the issues that have been raised:

First, to the invitations—because they bring up perhaps the most important issue. Grateful as I was for them, my reasons for declining went beyond my chronic social shyness. The piece was called "Small Festivals Among Friends" for a reason. Rituals done at all seriously are psycho-active. Like therapy, like drugs, like making love, they affect us on profound levels—and wouldn't be worth the trouble if they didn't. But: anything important can be dangerous. Which is why nothing would seem more outlandish to Hopis or Celts than to practice such rituals among strangers.

We are dazed, stranded survivors of a massive catastrophe that calls itself "civilization," and we are groping in the dark among the shards for some connection to sacraments that we sense in our souls are crucial. We don't know what we're doing. We're moving by instinct, because we've got no other way to move—there are a few people who *know* a few things about this, but there aren't enough to go around, so we go by what we have: the images in our heads. We have to trust those images—a brave and beautiful thing, I think. But we're going to make mistakes. Most of our mistakes will just make us feel silly and ineffectual, but some will make us feel crazy. (And sometimes that's *not* a mistake; sometimes there's something in the craziness that's needed.) So in such gatherings the only safeguard is that we're among friends—people with a real stake in our well-being.

When there's true confidence in that, other experiments are possible. Someone in the Texas group I wrote of is now, with a different group (of friends), embarking on something I find extraordinary—something, frankly, I don't think I'd have the courage for, at least not this week. They're going off for four days for what they refer to as "rites of passage." Each has identified some old obstacle or hangup he/she wants to get over, blast through, face down—whatever. Each person has devised a ritual for him/herself that the group will help with; *and* the group is concocting a ritual for each person that the person won't know about in advance.

Understand that these are not a bunch of people you'd identify as very unusual. They earn their livings in normal ways and lead responsible lives. It's only that, after trying many of the available religious, social, artistic and therapeutic modes (modes that *have* been fruitful—they're not rejecting them), they are taking a step into the unknown and trying another, a revel-atory mode.

I'm not suggesting that *you* go out and do it. And it's worth repeating that *I* don't feel ready for such an experiment. But, as with the comparatively milder rituals described above, if these people are doing something this radical, then others probably are—and I'm writing to say that that is as important a piece of news as anything *Time* and *Newsweek* between them reported this week. It speaks of a surprising level of spiritual sophistication *and* need *and* daring. But my point is that these are not qualities you'd look for in a group of average Americans if all you had to go on was what Americans are willing to say about themselves and each other in their media, or at dinner parties. "The news," and the discourse, is drastically incomplete. Something else is going on out there—for what is certain is that, if a few are doing it, then many, many more are craving it. And we don't know what that craving will create, or what form, in the mass, it will take. But I'll dare a prediction: this still inarticulate craving could have an enormous influence on the 1990s.

When I spoke of this with Texas writer George Howard, he said, "They chose an unrestricted gesture that was accompanied by symbol." I love Howard's phrase "unrestricted gesture." That, certainly, is what we need more of in this increasingly restrictive, frightened culture. But he has also nailed down the nature of revelation-revels. Whether it's an object, or an activity, or a full-blown "rite of passage" ritual, these things occur to the individual as a symbol or an image. And, as psychologist James Hillman teaches, images are doorways to the infinite. There are two unavoidable qualities to any image: the image is more than you, even though you thought of it—it is itself, with an identity that transcends the personal; and it always can lead to another image—it has no end. Whether the image is a flower, or a door, or a man in a black coat, or a word written in lipstick on a mirror—all these images, any image you can have, clearly have a life of their own and, if dwelled on, inevitably lead to other images, beyond your conscious control. Which is to say, as Hillman and Jung do say, image is pure psyche, the psyche expressing itself in its purest form. (Dreams are images.) To do a ritual, to revel in the revelatory, is to enter the image.

I tried to write of this in my novel *Night Time Losing Time*. Elaine is a character who does rituals. She says of them: "That's what happens, how I do ritual. I get an *image* and *do* the image. Nobody ever taught me anything. My feel is: If you do the image pure enough, it has power."

Then the narrator, Jesse, says: "I stood, who knows how long, awaiting the image. . . . The image stirred. It rose from where it had always slept curled upon itself, breeding dreams. Not as though I'd thought of it, but as though it had simply awoken and stepped out from under Elaine's soft flesh. . . . "

Later on Jesse asks Elaine, "You're a writer. You ever write about this stuff?" She says: "And have everybody think I'm silly? No, thank you. Anyhow—wouldn't do anybody any good. You and I could tell exactly what-all we did, and somebody could do the same stuff, but they'd just be copying. I don't think it does any good to try somebody else's image. The whole thing with this stuff is that you do the image pure enough. I guess what I mean is nobody can copy the purity. You come to that, or you don't."

Later another character, a Texas alchemist called Henry, tells them: "It ain't magic, or whatever you wanna call it. It's how intense you're pointed *Out There* every hour. That's what does the work. You ain't got that, you ain't got anything. When you *do* have it, then you just do the little dance or spell or whatever to focus it, at the last minute. And if you're *really* living, you don't even need that. Just happens."

The advantage of a novel is that readers have their judgments about the characters to mitigate the impact of the characters' pronouncements. In a column, everything reads with much more surety. In fact, as I said, we are all groping. None of us really knows anything. Something *is* rising from the psyche, from our ancient heritages—to help us, is what I think. But perhaps not. Perhaps it's just compulsive and confusing. It's important to remember that this, too, is a possibility.

But that's as much qualification as you'll get from me tonight. The revels in revelation beckon us to places of the heart and spirit that are ours by right, that our very genes are hungry for, and that our ancestors (be they European, African, Asian, whatever) knew well and loved. When my Texas friend told me about the "rites of passage" the group was going to try, I said two things. First: Be careful. Second: You should begin by honoring and welcoming the spirits of your ancestors, blessing them and asking their blessing. For we all have people, way back in our blood, who knew more about these things than anybody living and—who knows?—they may be able to help us yet.

It may be that those old mothers and fathers are guiding us already.

August 25, 1989

An Unmarked Door

My first altar happened a few years ago in an apartment on Ayres Avenue near Overland and Pico. Not the sort of place you'd think of for shrine-making. An old-timey neighborhood, where you can walk to anything—laundry, groceries, movies, books, stationery, copiers, John O Groats, the Apple Pan, Junior's, Kabbalah studies, pharmacy, fax machine, barber, Captain Video, the Jung Institute. A person can go for days without driving, which makes L.A. a very different town, sunny and sweet and easy. A better and/or less haunted man might have been very happy in such a place, even without an altar.

Me, I was drinking too much, writing too hard, my erections were fewer, my dreams were scarier, and I'd begun to work seriously at losing some very dear people. You know in *Night of the Living Dead* when the little girl dies, then comes back to life and devours her mother who in turn comes back to life, and they go for the old man— something like that was going on in my psyche. The past began feeding on the present. Memories I could no longer run from were eating me alive, and in some ways I was glad they'd caught up with me. Time to get it over with. Let them eat their fill, then see what's left. Maybe that's the only way some of us ever come to know ourselves.

There wasn't anything New Agey about me and my altar. One of the problems with being a 1990 urban mystic (as though being an urban mystic wasn't enough of a problem all by itself) is that New Age pap has taken over the discourse on mysticism. But the gooey sort of wonder that seems to ooze from half the books at the Bodhi Tree—

17

good vibes and transcendence and third eyes and crystals, washed down with some bracing herb tea—hasn't got much to do with the revelations I know about. Maybe I just run with a hard crowd (New Age rough trade), but in my experience revelations are wrung from you. Epiphanies are funky. You don't get them unless you need them, i.e., unless you're in trouble. The bigger the trouble, the pithier the epiphany.

The whole business is likely to make you shudder, as they say in Texas, "like a poodle shittin' a peach pit." To be dragged kicking and screaming, not up to "another plane" but across an inner boundary to a state in which words like "psyche" and "soul" take over for words like "meaning" and "morality." And where finally all words shut up, all concepts run for cover, and you can never be quite sure of anything again except that what most people call "the world" is not all there is.

Even in a nice sunlit neighborhood like Ayres near Overland and Pico. Where, in two different places in that apartment, altars were growing, though nobody in the house knew it. In my writing room there was a narrow mantel over a rather pitiful fake fireplace, on which I'd casually placed, at various times, some shells, some rocks, a gold tooth, a railroad spike, a Day of the Dead figurine and a motel key. In the bedroom on a table beside a candle holder, other odds and ends had accumulated, along with some photographs and post cards. Each object had its nuance, its meaning. And a kind of casual care had been taken in arranging the objects beside each other. It just felt right to place this next to that, as though the memories in the objects were meant to meet and blend. So that what might have been merely knickknacks or mementos gravitated into a special relationship to become a meaningful whole. Unified sometimes by candlelight.

It can't be stressed enough that this was going on well below or beyond the level of awareness. If I'd been asked to list, at the time, what was important in my life, these altars-in-the-making would not have made the list. Though they would now.

But maybe, on such a list, I would have admitted that I had been thinking about praying. Not to implore any divinity to help me—for it seemed that help lay all around me if I could only bring myself to use it. No, I wanted to pray simply to—how can I put it?—to sit with eternity a moment. Acknowledge eternity. Greet eternity. Talk to it.

Listen to it. Perhaps touch it. This seemed enough and more than enough, for any prayer; seemed incredibly difficult, in fact; and the very effort, I was sure, would constitute help in itself—if I could get up the courage to make that effort. (My need was deep, but so was my fear. As the Harvey Keitel character says at the beginning of *Mean Streets*: "You don't fuck around with the infinite.")

I thought about it for a couple of years. Not every day, but at least every week. An old friend of mine in New Mexico makes beautifully painted jackets, vests and shirts. She'd understand about this, and I thought I'd ask her to make a prayer rug for me. *Then* I'd be able to pray. It was a good gimmick. It would take her a long time to make the rug, so I wouldn't have to face the act of prayer for months.

But starting to pray is a little like getting pregnant—you may anticipate it for a long time, but few people actually plan it. One day a person "turns up pregnant," as they say in the South. One day on Ayres I turned up praying. I don't even remember the transitional beat between doing it and not doing it. I just remember feeling inadequate to eternity and being vaguely aware of a kind of aerial shot of the neighborhood, a normal enough place where people were going about their business, people not so different from me—so who knows what's *really* going on in their heads? Hadn't about five thousand of my neighbors in that little district voted in the last election for a neo-Nazi party? And hadn't most of the rest voted for Tom Hayden? And wasn't this all I *really* knew about them, except that we all had the sense (or the fear) to let each other be? And that many of them had eyes no less haunted than mine? Anyway, in this demographically average place, on a day like any other, there I was praying, or trying to—attempting to let a little eternity into my life.

And the only place it felt comfortable to do this was in front of those objects on the mantelpiece.

It wasn't until I'd prayed there several times that I realized I had made an altar. After which I kept it a little tidier, added things to it with a little more attention—and simply paid attention to what I'd made.

And began to use it. If something in my life needed healing or purifying, I put a symbol of it there—so that it would be present when I opened the door to eternity. So that it would be bathed in that particular light-and-dark. I didn't expect to make everything better, didn't expect to make *anything* better. I just wanted more—what can I say?—touching, between the life of my body and eternity.

Months later I took a trip. Drove the roads of Arizona, New Mexico, Texas, Louisiana, looking up old friends. And found that most of them had altars very much like mine. They hadn't had them on my last trip. We hadn't spoken to each other on the phone about them, hadn't written letters. I learned that theirs had grown much as mine had, and that at some point they'd started to pray before their altars, too. There was nothing like doctrine, there wasn't even rhetoric. The sacredness was taken for granted. The importance was taken for granted. These things had grown silently and organically and separately, in each of our lives at the same time—and even *that* was taken for granted. We'd talk about it and laugh: "Of course that's the way it is! That's the way it *always* is."

Life had not gotten less chaotic for anyone. Marriages busting up. Nervous breakdowns. Friends no longer speaking to each other. Meanness. Money. Danger. Work. The usual. It was just that something at the heart of life had become more accessible. And somehow this mattered more than anyone could say, as in the poem by Juan Ramón Jiménez where he feels a change somewhere down in the depths but "nothing happens! . . . Nothing happens? Or has everything happened, and are we standing now quietly, in the new life?"

For myself, I began to feel that the altars I and my friends had separately made were like antennas, sending and receiving to each other and to what some call "the other world." And I was sure that if this was happening to us, it was happening to many others. A real change underneath the feedback-screech that this society calls "history."

Back in L.A., after that trip, I was in a story meeting for a screenplay with a very famous female star and a very sweet and desperate starlet. We were discussing the character the starlet would play, and she said, "In her apartment, my character should have an altar, you know? You know how people just kind of have altars?" And she described the same kind of altar that had grown so quietly among me and my friends.

This is the news beneath the news, something the census won't document. That in many dwellings now, there are altars. They are not Christian, or Jewish, or Moslem, or Buddhist, though the people who keep them may be. They've come quietly, from we don't know where, all on their own, and we don't know why—small, separate manifestations that have felt individual and private but, when you look around, are happening at the same time all over the place. Many people feeling the need to open a door to eternity—an unmarked door, without all the old baggage. There's no hysteria or hokum or doctrine. And nothing seems to have changed. Just a breath of eternity, wafting in, freshening the room.

April 27, 1990

The Toy from Hell

Hell moves around a lot. One weekend before Halloween I found it at the Woolworth's beside the Sears on Laurel Canyon Boulevard in North Hollywood. As good a place as any to feel that particular breakage of the heart by which you know, without doubt, that by chance or fate you just stepped into hell. Sometimes it takes you quietly: a piece of what you used to be falls off and dies. And sometimes it takes you like it took me in Woolworth's: you want to stand right there in public and weep or scream or curse or fall down, falling perhaps on your knees to pray, perhaps on your stomach to dig your face into the gritty tile floor so that you'll never have to look at anything like what you just saw ever again. (Hell, you see, saps the fight from you; if you're still angry enough to fight, it's just purgatory.)

I think the people in that Woolworth's would have understood; they did not look like people to whom hell would come as much of a sur-prise. Poor whites, blacks and browns, the "trash," the people who do the shit-work, and their children—all had a sickly pallor, skin dull, eye-whites yellowish, everyone too fleshy or too thin, and all their eyes (go see for yourself) so tired, especially when they try to smile. And they *do* try to smile, that's the miracle. Cash-register women for whom fatigue has become a way of life and whose weary humor, in the face of burdens that will never lift, is, if you'll excuse the expression, holy. Yes, those faces would understand perfectly if someone suddenly wept, screamed, cursed, fell, puked, prayed because he has just, so unex-pectedly, seen something worse than his nightmares.

22

It's a simple thing, really. I shouldn't take it so seriously, I realize that. For it was only a child, a boy of about ten, buying a toy. For Halloween. This was the toy:

A sinister white mask and quite convincing little rubber meat cleaver. Packaged together in cellophane. It's the "costume" of a maniac killer from one of the slasher movies. The boy wants to play at being a faceless, unstoppable murderer of innocent people (mostly women). At this moment, in this Woolworth's, that's this boy's idea of fun.

The boy is too thin and has rings under his eyes like an actor's or a musician's, and the paleness of his skin makes his eyes seem brighter than the sickly, malnourished bright they are. Among truly healthy children he'd stand out, but here, where the pasty look of bad food is normal, he looks fine. And he looks smarter than average. In fact, now that I think of it, he looks a little like me when I was his age. No wonder I like him.

He'll be disappointed in the psycho-killer costume. I think the mask is too big for him.

Is it selling much? I ask.

It's selling just fine, I'm told.

Understand that I didn't stand there and decide intellectually that this simple and small event is, when all is said and done, the worst thing I've seen. My body decided. My intestines, my knees, my chest. It was only later that I tried to think about it.

This boy's eagerness to "play" maniac killer is an event worse than the Bomb, worse even than Auschwitz. Reduced to its simplest terms, the Bomb is a fetish, an object of worship—like other objects of worship before it, it is used as an excuse for arranging the world in a certain fashion, allocating resources, assigning powers. It is insane, but in many ways it is an extension of familiar, even honored, insanities. As for the Nazi camps: the people being murdered knew, as they were being murdered, *that* they were being murdered; the murderers knew they were murdering; and, when the world finally knew, the camps became the measure of ultimate human evil. A crime to scar us all, and our descendants, forever.

There is nothing so clear in the Woolworth's. The boy is certainly not committing a crime. The toy's merchandisers are within their rights. To legislate against them would be to endanger most of our freedoms. The mother buying the toy is perhaps making a mistake, perhaps not.

Without knowing the boy, and knowing him well, who's to be certain it isn't better for him to engage in, rather than repress, such play? The mother did not put the desire for the toy in him. Three thousand years of Judeo-Christian culture did that. Nor has the mother the power to take that desire from him. Nobody has that power. If he can want the toy at all, then it almost doesn't matter whether the toy exists or not. Doesn't the boy's need for such play exist with or without the toy?

Nor would I be too quick to blame the boy's desire on television and slasher films. The Nazis who crewed the camps and the scientists who built the Bomb did not need television and slasher films to school them in horror. In fact, the worst atrocities from the Pharaohs to Vietnam were committed quite ably before the first slasher film was made. Keeping your child away from television may make *you* feel better, but can any child be protected from the total weight of Western history?

Let's remember that the boy is playing. And play is a very specific activity. I haven't done this sort of reading in a long time, but if I remember rightly insects and reptiles don't play. I don't even think fish play: play is the province—the invention, if you like—of mammals. (So, it seems, are dreams.) Cats, wolves, dolphins, monkeys, seals, people—all young mammals play. Something this universal and basic is probably not a whim or an entertainment; it's a need. Which means it has to do with surviving.

Watch kittens, puppies, colts, cubs, kids—all young mammals play at fighting. That's most of what their play consists of. And all young carnivores (puppies, kittens) play at hunting. In fact, the play of young mammals hones instinctive survival skills. That's apparently what it's for.

People-play is a bit more complex—but its underlying purpose seems to be the same. In other mammals, male and female play is virtually identical—both sexes fight and hunt. But people-play, whether by instinct or culture, is usually different for the different sexes: the young males play at fighting, the young females at—what can it be called? Hearthing? Not that the girls don't run wild—in pagan Europe, ancient Greece and tribal cultures girls ran very wild in specific, often ritualized forms of wildness. That feral sort of wildness is considered in our culture, stupidly, as "tomboy" behavior—but our ancestors would recognize it as quite feminine. Still, even in these times, the play of girl-people rarely took the form of fighting. That was for boys.

It's still for boys. Boys in every culture we know about try to develop some aptitude for violence. Because in almost every environment we know about, *some* aptitude for violence or force is a necessity. This is hard to explain to feminists, but nearly every generation of boys in recorded history has been called upon to risk violent death for the sake of its tribe, village, country. (Every generation of girls has been called upon to risk natural death, from childbirth. But death coming from within you and death coming from outside are very different deaths, needing very different preparations.) If you're male, you know in your bones that sometimes your society will consider the risk of violent death to be your job. An aptitude that's *called upon*, a call the boy senses and tries, with other boys, to develop. Very small boys are no better at violence than very small girls. This expectation of violence is an effort and a burden to live with, and I doubt that there is a male alive who hasn't felt that burden.

But in a world now shorn of order, stripped of traditions, molting every decade, every year, a dancing, varicolored snake of a century—pointless violence is evident everywhere, on every level. Professional soldiers are statistically safer than urban women; senseless destruction is visited on trees and on the ozone and on every species of life. No one feels safe anywhere. This has become the meaning of the twentieth century.

And in some small, gaudy, slimy way, this is why there are slasher movies—visual odes to maniacal killers. This state of affairs is what they express. Their maniacs are metaphors for the air we've come to breathe.

So I am in a Woolworth's one day, and I feel a sort of final horror as I watch a boy buy a psycho-killer toy so that he can pretend he's an unstoppable maniacal murderer. What is so horrible is that this boy is doing this instinctively, for his very survival. In order to live, in order not to go mad, this boy is acclimating himself to the idea of the killer-maniac, because killer-maniac energy is so present in his world. He's trying to inoculate himself through play, as all children have, everywhere, in every era. He thus lets a little bit of the energy into him—that's how inoculations work. Too little, and he is too afraid of the world—it's too terrifying to feel powerless amid the maniacal that's taken for granted *around* him; to feel any power at all he needs a bit of it inside him. But if he takes in too much, he could be swamped.

How horrible that he is forced to such a choice. You'd think it would be enough to stop the world in its tracks. But it's not. And so he chooses. And what can we do for him? Struggle for a different world, yes, but that won't change what's already happened to him. What can we do for that boy, except be on his side, stand by his choice, and pray for the play of his struggling soul?

November 3, 1989

The Age of Endarkenment

Part 1

"Adolescence" is a cruel word. Its cruelty hides behind its vaguely official, diagnostic air. To say someone is "adolescent," going through adolescence" or, worse, "being adolescent" is to dismiss their feelings, minimize their troubles and (if you're their parent) protect yourself from their uncompromising rage. The words "teenager" and "teen" are worse. They reek of cuteness. But we all know that being a "teen" doesn't feel cute.

People that age hardly ever use those words. They tend to call themselves "kids" when pushed, as in, "What makes you think you know so much about kids—you sure don't know much about *me*!" Or they dress up and act out and give themselves better words: "punk," "gothic," "rapper," "gang-banger," "low-rider," "freak"—words to remind us just how volatile, how dangerous, how "freaked out," "radical," "awesome," "bummed," "bitchen," "groovy," "wasted" and "bad" those years really are.

When we don't have apt words for something it's because of an unspoken collective demand to avoid thinking about it. *That's* how scary "adolescence" is. Which is also to say: that's how scary our very own unspeakable adolescence was. And when we finally are past it (which often doesn't happen till we near forty), then we turn around and see the young and pretend that they are foreign to us, that we don't know what they're going through, that we don't get their music, their fashions, their words. James Baldwin said, "One can only face

27

in others what one can face in oneself." What we cannot face when we cannot face the young is, plainly, ourselves. (And this is the song of families.) Our secrets, our compromises, our needs, our lacks, our failures and our fear that we're going to fail again—all this stirs and starts to growl somewhere deep inside when the young look hard into our grown-up eyes. It's as though, in some dark way, they are privy to our secrets, even to what we don't know or want to know about ourselves, and when they so much as glance toward those parts of us, oh, our old panics resurrect, those demons we thought we'd dealt with, grown out of, transcended, escaped—it only takes this goddamn kid, and the beasts awake. As a parent, you may measure your fears by the extent of your distance from that kid.

But perhaps, when we love them, our greatest fear is: that we cannot help them, cannot protect them, and that we have nothing real to give them. And their greatest rage is: that we cannot help, cannot protect them, and that we have nothing to give.

When something is true of virtually everyone, it's unlikely that the fault is individual, but we feel and fear this mess as individuals—kids and grown-ups both. Individually, kids can't help but judge us for this state of affairs, just as we can't help but flee their judgment. All that we share with them, then, is a scream: THIS ISN'T FAIR! We *do* have useful things to give, if they would only take them, but they can't seem to. Again, individually, their refusal to take what we try to give seems pernicious and willful, but when you look at them collectively, you see that they're obviously not in control of their refusal; they *have* *to* refuse us, no one knows why. They must, even when that refusal makes them secretly ashamed, which in turn makes them worse, which makes us worse. It seems that no matter what, the very act of raising kids will, at the onset of adolescence, throw kids and parents both into negative extremes.

It's as though kids have a fundamental craving for negatives in their dealings with their parents and with adults in general, and will stop at practically nothing to invoke that negativity. We've come (unofficially) to accept this. "How old is your kid?" "Fifteen." "*Oh my god.*" And everyone knows what that means.

Our models for dealing with these issues are psychological. Which is absurd. You can't reduce a collective phenomenon, a phenomenon that cuts across every class and culture, a phenomenon with fundamentally the same elements in Harlem and Beverly Hills, at Woodstock and Tian An Men Square, in English soccer matches and Palestinian villages—you can't reduce a phenomenon like that to individual or family causes. To do so ignores and dismisses *the* most important piece of data we have: the fact that, despite different histories, cultures, technologies and economies, the same basic thing is happening everywhere to everyone—often in waves of simultaneity.

Two writers have described "adolescence" most tellingly for me. The first is Los Angeles educator Mike Rose, in his crucial book *Lives on the Boundary* (Free Press/Macmillan, 1989): "Kids have no choice but to talk in extremes; they're being wrenched and buffeted, rabbit-punched from the inside by systemic thugs." Rose's thought gets elaborated by rock critic Michael Corcoran in *The Austin Chronicle*:

> Rap and its polar opposite but sometimes bedfellow, heavy metal, are the [present] counterpart to '50s rock & roll and '70s punk. It's rebel music, soul music, kids' music. It understands what parents and teachers don't, that puberty is not about hair or pimples or cracking voices; it's a beast, a demon. It's a beautiful rage that wants to belong and sometimes only can through dumb, simple, angry music. Rap doesn't incite violence, nor does metal. It stirs deep emotions that sometimes get out of hand. It ignites the same spirit that makes us fall in love, have children and believe in God.

We tend to think of this extremism in the young as something new, peculiar to our times, caused by pop or television or the collapse of values. The history of our race doesn't bear this out, however. Robert Bly and Michael Meade, among others, remind us that for tens of thousands of years tribal people everywhere have greeted the onset of puberty, especially in males, with elaborate and excruciating initiations—*a practice that plainly wouldn't have been necessary unless their young were as extreme as ours.* This is terribly important. It means that when conservatives talk of rock culture subverting the young, when others talk about that same culture liberating the young or when postmodern technologists talk of our electronic environment "rewiring the software" of new generations—they are all making the same mistake. They fail to understand that a psychic structure that has remained constant for one-hundred thousand years is not likely to be altered in a generation by stimuli that play upon its surfaces. What's really going on is very different: the same raw, ancient *content* is surging through youths' psyches, but adult culture over the last few centuries has forgotten how to meet, guide and be replenished by its force.

Unlike us, tribal people met the extremism of their young (and I'm using "extremism" as a catchall word for the intense psychic cacophony of adolescence) with an equal but focused extremism from adults. Tribal adults didn't run from this moment in their children as we do: they celebrated it. They would assault their adolescents with, quite literally, holy terror: rituals that had been kept secret from the young till that moment—rituals that focused upon the young all the light and darkness of their tribe's collective psyche, all its sense of mystery, all its questions, and all the stories told both to contain and answer those questions.

The crucial word here is "focus." The adults had something to teach: stories, skills, magic, dances, visions, rituals. In fact, if these things were not learned well, the tribe could not survive. But the adults did not splatter this material all over the young from the time of their birth, as we do. They focused, and were as selective as possible about, what they told and taught, and when. They waited until their children reached the intensity of adolescence, and then they used that very intensity's capacity for absorption, its hunger, its need to act out, its craving for dark things, dark knowledge, dark acts, all the qualities we fear most in our kids—the ancients used these very qualities as teaching tools.

Through what the kids craved, they were given what they needed. Kids of that age crave extremes of experience—they crave this suddenly and utterly, and are possessed by their craving. They can't be talked out of it, or conditioned out of it. It's in our genetic coding, if you like, to crave extremes at that age. (So they must certainly feel rage if, as in our culture, adults tell them that these cravings are wrong.) At the same time, these kids *need* the cosmology and skills appropriate for survival in their world. The kids can create the extremes for themselves—they're quite good at that—but not the cosmology, not the skills. And without those elements, given at the proper time through the dark-energy channels that have suddenly opened in the young and go clear down to their souls, the need for extremes is never really satisfied in its *purpose*, and hence it goes on and on (creating what we call "modern culture," which, looked at this way, is little more than a side effect). Our ancestors satisfied the craving for dark energy while meeting the need for cosmology and knowledge, and we call that "initiation." This practice was so effective that usually by the age of fifteen a tribal youth was able to take his or her place as a fully responsible adult.

Because our culture denies the craving, we can't possibly meet the need—so most of us never truly grow up or feel, in our hearts, adult. How, then, have we responded? For about forty years now, the young have generated forms—music, fashion, behaviors—that prolong the initiatory moment. In other words, we cherish and elongate adolescence (or "initiatory receptivity") as though hoping to be somehow initiated by chance somewhere along the way. For tribal people, the initiatory moment was by far the most intense period of life, lasting no more than weeks, at most about a year. For us, it now lasts decades. And it's as though the pressure to make it last decades increases its chaotic violence. This very extension of the initiatory moment is helping to drive everyone mad.

Part 2

But tribal life ended in Europe a thousand years ago, so why didn't we have "extended adolescence" until the mid-twentieth century? The answer is that before World War II we were between worlds. The prewar world, going back several hundred years, was deeply repressive and viciously exploitive—but orderly. Orderly enough, when compared with today, to enforce its spiritual and political repressions. Initiations didn't happen, hadn't happened in the West for a long time; instead, the dark craving-period in the young was utterly squashed, all the richness it demanded was denied, creating in individuals a kind of deadness, a stiffness that became "adulthood," "maturity." By the age of seventeen or so a repression from which there was virtually no release made most people rigid enough to bear the responsibilities society demanded. It was a rigidity that passed (and, in our nostalgia, still passes) for strength, a sort of lifeless life, where one did one's duty and made a virtue of stoicism. Whether or not people felt particularly alive, they got things done. Society said—and still tries to say—that was enough.

Every now and again Europe would see a burst of revolution against all this, usually expressed politically. (Politics is always an excuse to act out something deeper.) These outbursts were short-lived and things quickly returned to "normal."

The American Revolution was a special case, however. Once America had freed itself from Europe, a small population had an entire continent it could overrun, while the repressed peoples of Europe finally had a place to escape to—a nation that called for boundless energy for expansion. The dark-energy craving could be expressed collectively as this expansion. The thing we call "the Western world" was an unconscious well of dark energy that hadn't been satisfied in its purpose, hadn't been initiated—and the thing we call "America" is what that dark energy found to do.

America gave permission for this unappeased adolescent state of craving to expand and find substitute appeasement any way it could—this was called "freedom" and "free enterprise," whose spectacle got Europe as feverish as a priest who hears people screwing through a thin wall. Things heated up, and in both Europe and America the energy found a new way to expand: technology.

We hold technology responsible for lots of change, forgetting that technology is first and foremost a human *expression*. Like all human expressions, it results from needs of the soul. It's an effect before it's a cause. Technology began as a longing, a bottomless wish not to be trapped any longer in Western life. *That's* why other cultures didn't invent it. Not because they were more primitive, but because they liked their lives better.

So one or two thousand years of stymied Western energy finally found its ultimate outlet, its escape, in technology. In this sense, all the technological power surging around us is not new power, it's the impacted power of our past—squelched inner power that doesn't die when people die but stays contained, fit to bust, in the culture. Technology is made of the unused potential of our ancestors. *That* is the "ghost in the machine": the collective psyche's escape into *things*, into the computer, the car, the television—wildly breaking free.

Both World Wars were fought by means of those machines, those ghosts—that's why they were so devastating. It wasn't only people in the present fighting each other, it was also the congealed energy of generations let loose, uncontrolled. When it was over, the issue of human beings opening up and expressing their souls was over, too; the issue now was human beings scrambling to catch up to the energies that had been loosed.

The immediate personal result was that enforced repression on a family level became impossible. And not only in the West. World War II shook the whole world, and we now know that enforced familial repression no longer worked even in the most un-Western or politically repressive places. What, for instance, would have happened to Mao if he hadn't managed to harness that energy in the young for his own ends during China's so-called "Cultural Revolution"—for it is not within human capacity for one person to *create* such movement in others. Those young people were on the move, and Mao was clever enough to deflect it from himself and direct it toward his "enemies." What happened in Cambodia at almost the same time, when you strip the political lingo away, is that the kids murdered the grown-ups. While in Mexico and Chile, the grown-ups murdered the kids. And in the United States and Europe it was a stand-off.

The fact is that people born during and just after World War II hit "adolescence," the initiatory moment, with a vengeance, in virtually the same way, with negative and positive poles of the same phenomenon, almost everywhere—while adults freaked out and resisted. Please don't try to explain that with the psychology of individuals or families, or with the sociology and politics of what were then still separate societies. Far more mysterious patterns, laws of human behavior we have barely begun to intuit, were at play.

The effect of World War II on the young, then, was that the craving-period, the initiatory moment, could no longer be squashed. The war had accelerated technology to the point where adults couldn't keep up with their own changes, much less police their children's. So, left to their own devices for the first time in Western history, the young began generating forms—music, fashions, customs, an entirely new culture—*intended* to prolong the initiatory craving-period. (Just because this wasn't conscious doesn't mean it wasn't intended; instinct isn't conscious, but it has definite, specific purposes.)

This phenomenon, or complex of phenomena, multiplied wildly every year, until now the dark-tinged craving-period we choose to call "adolescence" has literally become the cultural air we breathe all over the world. And while it's true that most of these forms are now corporately controlled, they originated from the bottom up; they were spontaneously generated by young people—and the corporations that now control them are run by people of that first generation of unleashed young.

The result is that, under the guise of "entertainment" (music, movies, television), a sense of "adolescent" volatility is now enforced the way the image of "mature" rigidity once was. Where once the insulated classes of society could pretend to be "normal," allowing only a few "artists" (dark-energy stunt men) to dispense manageable and usually harmless doses of initiatory power, while the military and the poor were forced to stew in the *real* madness—now there are no more such distinctions. Chaotic "teenage" intensity, dark-tinged extreme experience, hallucinatory dislocation, is business as usual, the stuff of everyday life, everyday art. This darkness is what pop, rap, television, movies, poems and novels mostly *do*. It's what they're made of. Even billboards. You can't escape it anywhere.

The way tribal people treated this period in their young was to expose them, through precise ritual, to what the Australians call "the dreamtime"—the psyche's mysteries in their rawest form. And that is what this world cultural environment, structured by the priorities of adolescence minus the instruction of fully initiated elders, is doing: it's exposing everybody to the mysteries of the psyche in their rawest acted-out forms.

An age of endarkenment. The world is aflood with dark psychic fluid—everything's stained with it. We say we hate the stuff, but we don't act that way, we splash in it. Would we, if there weren't an irresistible collective need for endarkenment? Such a profound mass phenomenon is far beyond right or wrong, good or evil, justice or injustice—and far, far beyond any political remedy. It's going to take a while to work itself out. A century or two. How did Dylan put it twenty-five years ago? "Come on out, the dark is just beginnin'."

November 30, 1990
December 14, 1990

An Inventory of Timelessness

We've dispensed with time, so we're lost in space.

ITEM: Wells Fargo Bank has introduced a twenty-four-hour-per-day, seven-day-per-week telephone service. You can now pick up the phone at any hour, anywhere, and talk to a person, not a computer, who can answer any conceivable question about your banking needs. This stretches the term "banking needs" beyond all previous definitions of the eight-hundred-odd-year history of Western banking. Why do my bankers anticipate that I'll need them at three o'clock in the morning? Partly because there's no telling where I'll be—Tokyo, Barcelona, Moscow, desperate to know what my balance is before the market opens in Berlin or Hong Kong. But a hefty percentage of the calls are from Wells Fargo's home time zone and involve personal, not business, accounts. Which means that 'round 'bout midnight, in these United States, a number of demographically ordinary people feel the pressing need to question their banker.

Twenty-four-hour bank call-ins and automatic tellers speak of a people increasingly coaxed to live without pattern, without boundaries. Such things fuzz the boundaries between intimate time and business time, between home and work, night and day, individual and corporate, public and private, environment and psyche. Yet while, as consumers, we increasingly demand to live without pattern *in terms of services,* we bemoan the loss of pattern in our morality, our love lives, our thought.

If one individual demanded to do his/her banking at three in the morning, it would be considered pretty weird. But when a corporation provides the service, and it meets the demands of thousands . . . then despite what even the most conservative people might prefer morally or politically, their patternless consumerism disrupts the sense of time and space that contained, and gave form to, their morality.

ITEM: Life in Clarendon, Texas, a town of about fourteen hundred in the Texas Panhandle, revolves around its several fundamentalist churches. Like many towns in that part of the country, it's still "dry"—you can't buy alcohol within the city limits. But not too long ago an AM/PM convenience store opened. It never closes. And such stores flourish now in almost every small town in the country. Why do they need such a store, in such a town? Until recently, in that area, you could tune in two, sometimes three television stations, depending on the weather. These stations signed off around midnight, often earlier. Now, with satellite and cable, you can tune in dozens of stations, and they never sign off. Some show porn in the wee hours. And MTV all the time. And constant news. And movies that no one in this area would have ever heard of otherwise. (Clarendon's "picture show" went out of business years back.)

So a place that depended for its way of life upon its isolation, upon its strict regulation of what it allowed through its boundaries, upon its rooted connectedness to what it imagines to be the morality of the nineteenth century—has been penetrated by what it views as a service. It is no longer separate in space, it no longer has a farmer's sense of time.

ITEM: Utah. A place owned and run by the Mormon church, a place with no separation of church and state. With satellite and cable, late-night porn has become very, very popular in Utah. Which means: Utah is no longer Utah at three in the morning.

In America, from big city to tiny town, time and space have become tentative, arbitrary. And this in the most concrete, personal sense. There are instruments in each home eating away at the time and space of people who have become addicted to those instruments. Consciously, these are most often people who see themselves as normal, righteous and conservative, and they emphatically don't want this to change. Yet something else is operative in them, some hunger that they follow without thought or plan, in which they indulge in activities that subtly but thoroughly undermine their most cherished assumptions. Politically and socially they are demanding more and more boundaries—yet, by choice, they fill their lives with things that cause them to live less and less within those boundaries. They *want* these things, these appliances and services—so much so that they measure their success or failure by whether or not they have these things. But their very wanting is subversive to their way of life. It's fair, then, to assume that something other than consciousness, something deep within them, is doing this subversive wanting.

ITEM: The electric lightbulb. An invention barely one-hundred-years-old. In general use for roughly fifty years now. The technological beginning of the end of linear time. Before the lightbulb, darkness constricted human space. Outside cities especially, night shrank the entire landscape into the space within arm's reach. (The moon figures so greatly in our iconography because it was all that allowed one to go far out into the night—when it was bright enough, and not obscured by clouds.) But now there are few places in North America or Europe that are truly dark at night. The glow of even a small town can be seen for many miles. Light gives us all the space we want, any time we want it. Psycho-active events of monstrous proportions take place, like Hitler's Nuremburg rallies. All those tens of thousands of people in perfect formation are unthinkable without spotlights. Light creates the necessary space, pushing back the boundaries of time. Dream-time becomes a time for acting out the nightmare.

ITEM. The car is a private space that can go in any direction at any time. The motel room cinched that: anywhere you go, there will be a space for you. A fact unique to contemporary life, and alien to every previous society. But the fact that there's a room for you anywhere makes less substantial the place where you actually *are*. Thus you are a transient, without having chosen to be one. Human transience used to be defined almost solely by death. Now the fact of so much choice makes everyone a transient *all* the time—and, for most of us now, makes any single choice almost unbearably tentative. Why be where you are, who you are, when you can just as easily be somewhere else, behaving differently?

This is a question that even most demographically "average" people ask often these days. How can it not make them more and more uncertain? So, to compensate, they're craving certainty in all the wrong places. In politics, which has *always* been uncertain. In metaphysics, which by its nature is uncertain. In love and sex, where certainty breeds boredom and diminishes lovers in each other's eyes. Many of these people blame the uncertain, tentative quality of their lives on "liberalism," "humanism," "relativism," the sixties—when what is really going on is that they were once prisoners of time and space, and they will never be prisoners again, and they miss those prisons desperately.

How long will it take them to become accustomed to the new timeless, spaceless environment? This has become a crucial historical question. For until they acclimate themselves, they will continue to crave reactionary solutions that can only increase the chaos.

This all began, by the way, with Jesus. Boris Pasternak, in *Doctor Zhivago*, saw it clearly:

> In the first [Western] miracle you have a popular leader, the patriarch Moses, dividing the waters by a magic gesture, allowing a whole nation—countless numbers, hundreds of thousands—to go through. . . . In the second miracle you have a girl—an everyday figure who would have gone unnoticed in the ancient world—quietly, secretly, bringing forth a child. . . . What an enormously significant change! How did it come about that an individual human event, insignificant by ancient standards, was regarded as equal in significance to the migration of a whole people? . . . Individual human life became the very story of God, and its contents filled the past expanses of the universe.

We don't know how it came about, but we know the enormity of the result. In Judaism, God redeemed a race. In Christianity, God redeems *you*—an absolute reversal of metaphysics as it was practiced everywhere else in the world. Everywhere else, with the exception of the most highly sophisticated Buddhism, worship was *always* tribal: people propitiating existence for comparatively small favors. But now Christianism presented an unheard-of demand upon the sacred: that the *individual* is entitled to the full and undivided attention of the Universe. A staggering change in individual space and eternal time.

It took a long time—the Renaissance, the discovery of America, the elucidation of democratic principles, the technological revolution— but the Christianist sense of the individual being the center of the universe has become our daily reality.

Today, through a centuries-long process that culminated in our technological revolution, the West has what it's been praying for since the birth of Christ: every individual is being addressed directly, and constantly, by an infinite Universe. It may be a media-conveyed universe, and the voice you hear may be anyone's from Mandela to Madonna; images of sensuality and mayhem may confront us wherever we turn (though they are no more violent or sexy than the images in the Bible); we may have asked for the holy and gotten the profane (complain to the Manufacturer) -but it *is* a Universe and it *does* seem to speak to us, even dote on us, individually. In short, we asked for a paradigm and we got it.

In biblical mythology, this state of being is followed by Apocalypse.

But what is Apocalypse, exactly? In Revelation it is described as the coming of the beast. Richmond Lattimore's pristine translation from the original Greek reads:

> Then I saw a beast coming up from the sea with ten horns and seven heads, and upon his horns ten diadems, and upon his heads the names of blasphemy. The beast I saw was like a leopard, and his feet as those of a bear, and his mouth as the mouth of a lion. And the dragon gave him his power and his throne and his great authority. . . . Then the whole earth went in wonder after the beast. . . . Who is like the beast, and who can fight with him? (Revelation, 13:1–4)

From the ancients to Jung, the sea has been the great symbol of the human psyche. So Revelation's beast is the manifestation, in the waking world, of what's deepest in the psyche. And it is given its power by the dragon, the worldwide symbol of the meeting of spiritual and sexual energy. The beast is a multilayered, multiheaded image of dissonant simultaneity—a simultaneity which *in itself* is seen as great power.

"And upon his heads the names of blasphemy." The expectation is that when this psychic beast appears it will challenge all morals, all traditions, all laws.

These fearful writers of early Christianism sensed what had been started: that the new Christianist focus on the individual would sooner or later bring forth the secrets of the psyche—but in ways that would contradict their conscious morality. And they saw this, literally, as the end of the world.

Well, perhaps they were being a mite too concrete. It is the end of *a* world, certainly—the world in which waking and dreaming are rigidly separate. When this "beast" rises from its "sea," the surrealities of dreamlife become the facts of waking life.

In preceding centuries there was a pretty obvious separation between what's called the "subconscious" and the "conscious." Individual daily life was more or less ordered, however unjust or distasteful. Except for the occasional plague and cathedral gargoyle, lurid phantasms were usually left to the realm of dreams. But now we live in a technologically hallucinogenic culture that behaves with the sudden dynamics of a dream, *an environment that duplicates the conditions of dreaming.*

What I'm saying is that we in the late twentieth century live not in a city or country, not on a planet, but in a collective dream. Our everyday world is one of dreamlike instantaneous changes, unpredictable metamorphoses, random violence, archetypal sex and a threatening sense of multiple meaning. For a quarter of a million years we experienced this only in sleep, or in art, or in carefully structured religious rituals. Now, in our electronic environment, the dreamworld of sudden transformation and unpredictable imagery greets us when we open our eyes. And our response to it, against all our better judgments, is to want more, more, more—more of the VCRs, PCs, car phones and faxes that create this new surreality. For the long-suppressed psyche is as outrageous in conservatives as it is in bohemians, in capitalists as in socialists, in evangelicals as in atheists—and, through our appliances, it is finally free to feed on the outer world, and so to grow.

What distinguishes the twentieth century is that each individual life is a daily progression through a concrete but fluctuating landscape of the psyche's projections. Technology projects the subconscious into countless *things*, and thus duplicates the processes of the subconscious's greatest artifact, the dream. The surreality, simultaneity, sexuality and instantaneous change that once occurred only in our dreams now also occurs all around us.

So the condition of our subconscious is now also the condition of this physical environment we've built for ourselves.

Now we reel between dream and dream. Between the dreams of our sleep that speak to us alone, and the dreamscape of the waking world in which we make our way through millions of dream pieces colliding around us in a collective slam-dance.

It was easy, or so it seems now, to love the world as it used to be, the world of rigid boundaries. That world *was* a world, it held still long enough to *be* a world, and gave us time to learn to love it. But loving this scary state of flux? We want to love it, we have love in us to give it, but we are frightened and do not know how. Yet daily life hinges on what we are and are not able to love. So this craving not *for* love but *to* love, to be able to love what's around one—it twists itself into a mere, and futile, search for certainty.

Still—we made this world. We gobble up its instantaneousness, and we breathlessly want more. Could it be that our collective purpose is to revivify the psyche by making it deal with its labyrinthine *physical* image at every turn? Have we created this always-shifting multiculture in order to learn to live within, and use, our own immense and cacophonous psyches? Is this the collective thrust of our history, a kind of genetic demand?

As individuals, we feel that our contemporary anti-environment has been forced upon us. But I repeat—collectively, we *made* this world. And, both individually and collectively, we've eagerly welcomed each separate manifestation of this collective change. The radio, television, telephone, fax machine, VCR, computer, light bulb, airplane, car— all the building blocks of contemporary life, which manifest in reality what had only been dreams and myths—have been seized upon everywhere in the world. It is not enough to blame this on capitalism or consumerism. The very eagerness of the world's embrace of this hallucinogenic technology by the most different sorts of peoples is evidence of the deepest longing.

Perhaps it is a longing to let the beast out—for the psyche to flood forth. Or a longing, as in love, to be swept away no matter what. But it may be far deeper and more complex than that. It may be an agonized collective molting, five billion people and the planet itself on the same acid trip, creating together a living, inescapable dream (nightmare though it may seem) after which, when we wake up, we will be unimaginably different.

Nightmares, remember, are often the most telling and visionary of our dreams, the most useful for insight and change.

When I say that at the conclusion of this transformation, if we survive, we will be unimaginably different—please don't mistake that for New Age goo. The pious platitudes of the New Agers are pathetic incantations hoping to tame the untamable. Our transformation will leave humankind *different,* not necessarily better. It's just that all of us collectively have decided that it's time for the big change—though individually most of us wish it were happening to somebody else in some other space-time.

What we now know, whether or not we ever wanted to know it, is that the human psyche is one of the great forces of Nature. And what is most frightening about our new technology is that it exposes us to this force within us as nothing else ever has. We are standing in the storm of our own being. So we must face the fact that this, too, is our natural habitat. We have willy-nilly broken through all the old rigidities, all the limits we thought were Nature itself, and we can never go back. This is a new Nature. Since we, too, are a product of Nature, it can be said that this is what Nature is doing to itself hereabouts.

Dream has become reality. Dream-state metamorphoses have become waking-state conditions of everyday life. And through the fact echoes what may yet be the great axiom of our culture: "In dreams begins responsibility."

Autumn, 1987

Homage to Hugo and Antonio

My uncle, Hugo Cali, was a laborer all his life. When I was a boy he was, I think, a presser at a cleaner's. Like my father and all the Sicilian men of my childhood, Uncle Hugo wore his ability to work like a sash of honor. "Home" may have been a cauldron of turmoil and cruelty, feuds and passions, vows broken or kept (and revenge taken either way). "Home," our Sicilian homes, may have been a hell where what should have been whispered was screamed and what should have been screamed was terrorized into silence. Our cheap, humid tenements in Brooklyn and the Bronx may have been both "home" and hell by virtue of the fierce, unrelenting attention we gave each other with all our talk, talk, talk, yell, talk, scream, talk, hit, talk—endless hours of it, far into the night around the kitchen table, over cup after cup of thick perked coffee, and everybody over thirteen smoking Parliaments, Salems, Pall Malls and Camels. (How smoky those rooms were in winter when the windows were never opened.) In short, the Sicilian version of a "home" was a lot more over the edge than the pap of *Moonstruck* or the pomposity of *The Godfather*.

But balancing home was work. Work had a kind of calm about it—an intensity of skill that the men loved. They worked no matter how crazy, how old or how ill; they worked for as long as they could stand up. And whatever work they did (pressing, bricklaying, truck- and cab-driving, factory work, cooking, house painting, wallpapering, nursing, landscaping)—it was work taken seriously, done thoroughly and well. For them, it was about more than earning a living.

43

Though America has now largely forgotten such attitudes, for these men work was about the pleasure (yes, the pleasure) of having a way to be of use in the world.

When I was a boy I would watch our men work, when my mother would permit it. (She was a dedicated Communist, but she didn't want me to be "just a worker.") I loved their concentration and precision. My father, Michael, and his father, Vincenzo, would work together sometimes, all their arguments laid aside as they laid the wallpaper so smoothly, so perfectly . . . it was like a performance, fascinating to watch. They had such a touch, painting a wall or woodwork, that the paint didn't seem something added on, it seemed one with the material and created a sense of wholeness that made for a kind of glow.

I know younger people might think I'm romanticizing, because such workmanship is so rare now. I'm not. Simple pieces of craft have lasted hundreds of years because people *can* work this way. My father sent me a poem once—the only poem he's ever written. "It came to me while I was painting," he said in his letter. He was on a ladder, painting a wall with that touch of his, and found himself composing this:

> It is not necessary
> to understand
> the opening of the door
> to feel the wind.

This, then, was my Uncle Hugo's world—the brutal contrast between the boiling emotions of home and the meditative purposefulness of labor. Hugo was a quiet, canny man. When he married my father's sister Anna, he joined the talk-all-night, talk-endlessly, talk-about-anything, talk-it-to-death then talk-it-back-to-life Ventura clan—but he stood aside from it. My memory of Hugo, amid the constant kitchen clamor, is how he'd sit in his old chair in the living room watching television and occasionally send five or six piercing words into the kitchen just to prove that nothing had escaped his attention.

His eyes were kindly toward me always, he spoke with a heavy accent, he hadn't all his teeth, hardly any hair, and he was fat with that pasta fatness that is not without strength but resists exertion. I suspect that in the great world my uncle felt small and trapped—and that this may have been a source for the monstrous temper he could evoke in bursts, an anger that even the formidable Anna maneuvered to avoid. But in his own world there was something kingly about him—he was the king of a small, threadbare, all-but-forgotten country, perhaps, but a king nonetheless. What sort of father or husband he was, I have no idea; but this is how I saw him when I was a boy, and I'm telling you because Uncle Hugo took great care to teach me something, and it's time to pass it on.

It was about my grandfather, my mother's father, Antonio Scandurra. Antonio had come here from Sicily early in the century and had died a decade before I was born, when still in his forties, of alcohol and a weak heart. He was a cornet player. That was his trade. People remembered his pure, sweet tone. And how he loved to read. Until the Depression he made a good living—a classical musician by temperament, a jazz horn in vaudeville when he had to be, and a pop player in the orchestras that accompanied the silent movies in Manhattan's film palaces. His final gigs were in Work Projects Administration bands. My mother remembered that on his last jobs he was so weak he couldn't stand up to take his solos.

Something deeply broken about him is the impression I got when they spoke of him. The alcohol? Gambling? How his mother called him *nino*, "baby boy," all his life? It wasn't anything specific, just . . . the way they'd say his name. As though they pitied him. Something pure, something sweet, like his cornet tone, lived in the family's memory of my grandfather—but also this nagging pity. I disliked their attitude without even knowing I disliked it; felt a kind of unease, as though the troubled, gentle soul of Antonio Scandurra was trying to tell me something.

Hugo knew, and it was Uncle Hugo who saved Antonio for me.

As I said, Hugo didn't talk much. And he never had much to do with the children—the five Venturas, the two LoBoscos, the four Rizzos, the two Andriozzis and the two Calis (his own children) who made up our tumultuous tribe of cousins. But, perhaps because I was the oldest of them all, the first-born to the clan, Hugo always made a little time for me. And when I was little, every time I saw Uncle Hugo he said the same thing to me.

That Hugo would talk to me at all was an honor (Sicilians are taught to revere elders); but for him always to say the same thing—was odd. And annoying. I knew what he was going to say before he said it.

And it wasn't like he was doting, or absent-minded. No, it was like he wanted to be sure I *got* it. (This went on till I was nine or ten, when I suppose I'd proved to his satisfaction I'd not forget.)

Kindly and stern, in a rhythmic Sicilian accent, Hugo would say: "*Mi*-chael—come 'ere."

I'd stand before his (to me) great bulk in that chair and await what I knew was next: "I knew . . . your grahn-fahtha. Antonio—Anthony, like my son. Your grahn-fahtha . . . wahs a *saint*. If he saw a piece of bread on the sidewalk . . . he'd pick it up . . . and kiss it . . . before he put it in the garbage."

Over and over again, to see Uncle Hugo would be to see my grandfather (always, in my mind's eye, in one of those dapper Italian suits of the twenties) walking in East Harlem, where they lived, seeing pieces of bread on the concrete (what was all this bread doing on the sidewalks?), picking up the bread, kissing it, and carrying it until he passed a garbage can. The gesture grew enormous in my heart, as Hugo intended.

I don't doubt that Hugo was telling me something he saw my grandfather do—probably just once, and it impressed him deeply. Certainly the other grown-ups, always fierce in pointing out each other's mistakes, agreed with him—proving that this was in character for Antonio. Whenever Hugo told me the story, they would chime in, their pitying attitude toward my grandfather gone completely. They would say: "A saint, yes a saint."

(In our family, you never said anything once, as though if it wasn't worth repeating, it wasn't worth saying in the first place.)

How deeply Hugo's gesture touched me. How constantly it stayed with me. What a good teacher my uncle was, and how wise he was to know that nothing passed on this way to a child was wasted. Now, half a century after Antonio's death, and years after the death of Hugo, both men walk with me, and their presence, like the presence of my father, helps me live.

Kissing the bread, Antonio was kissing the earth. Kissing the bread, he was kissing the truth that human effort is precious and never to be wasted or debased; and that human need, the need for bread or anything, the need we all are so terrified of—is precious, too, and worthy of respect.

I don't know if I can take in that part even now, that *need* is worthy of respect. But I know it's true.

We cannot live by bread alone, Jesus said. But we do. And perhaps we only transcend that fact if we can bless our own bread—and isn't *that* what Jesus did, at his last meal, and may not that be what he meant? Something that Antonio knew: that we are the blessers who must keep the sacredness of each other's effort?

To Hugo Cali I say—thank you, Uncle, for tending my grandfather's memory, for caring for his truth, which was also yours, and for making certain I'd not forget.

To Antonio Scandurra I say—thank you, Grandpa, for the lesson you gave me. Thank you for telling me, through the mouth of another, this truth at the root of all sanity, all decency:

Kiss the bread.

April 13, 1990

Someone Is Stealing Your Life

Most American adults wake around six or seven in the morning. Get to work at eight or nine. Knock off around five. Home again, six-ish. Fifty weeks a year. For about forty-five years.

Most are glad to have the work, but don't really choose it. They may dream, they may study and even train for work they intensely want; but sooner or later, for most, that doesn't pan out. Then they take what they can and make do. Most have families to support, so they need their job more than their job admits to needing them. They're employees. And, as employees, most have no say whatsoever about much of anything on the job. The purpose and standards of the product or service, the short- and long-term goals of the company are considered quite literally "none of their business"—though these issues drastically influence every aspect of their lives. No matter that they've given years to the day-to-day survival of the business; employees (even when they're called "managers") mostly take orders. Or else.

It seems an odd way to structure a free society: most people have little or no authority over what they do five days a week for forty-five years. Doesn't sound much like "life, liberty and the pursuit of happiness." Sounds like a nation of drones.

It used to be that one's compensation for being an American drone was the freedom to live in one's own little house, in one's own quirky way, in a clean and safe community in which your children had the chance to be happier, richer drones than you. But working stiffs can't afford houses now, fewer communities are clean, none are safe, and

48

your kid's prospects are worse. (This condition *may* be because for five days a week, for forty-five years, you had no say—while other people have been making decisions that haven't been good for you.) I'm not sure whose happiness we've been pursuing lately, but one thing is clear: it's not the happiness of those who've done our society's work.

On the other hand—or so they say—you're free, and if you don't like your job you can pursue happiness by starting a business of your very own, by becoming an "independent" entrepreneur. But you're only as independent as your credit rating. And to compete in the business community, you'll find yourself having to treat others—*your* employees—as much like slaves as you can get away with. Pay them as little as they'll tolerate and give them no say in anything, because that's what's most efficient and profitable. Money is the absolute standard. Freedom and the dignity and well-being of one's fellow creatures simply don't figure in the basic formula.

This may seem a fairly harsh way to state the rules America now lives by. But if I sound radical, it's not from doing a lot of reading in some cozy university, then dashing off to dispense opinion as a prima donna of the alternative press. I learned about drones by droning. From ages eighteen to twenty-nine (minus a few distracted months at college when I was twenty-four) I worked the sort of jobs that I expected to have all my life: typesetter for two years, tape-transcriber for three, proofreader (a grossly incompetent one) for a few weeks, messenger for a few months, and secretary (yes, secretary) for a year and a half. Then I stopped working steady and the jobs got funkier: hospital orderly, a vacuum-cleaner salesman, Jack-in-the-Box counterperson, waiter, nail-hammerer, cement-mixer, toilet-scrubber, driver. Whether in the office or on the road, these were drone jobs, the kind of jobs that keep the rest of the economy going, though they have no status and scant rewards.

It was during the years of office work that I caught on: I got two weeks' paid vacation per year. A year has fifty-two weeks. Even a comparatively unskilled, uneducated worker like me, who couldn't (still can't) do fractions or long division—even I had enough math to figure that two goes into fifty-two . . . how many times? Twenty-six. Meaning it would take me twenty-six years on the job to accumulate one year for myself. And I could only have that year in twenty-six pieces, so it wouldn't even feel like a year; it would feel, every year, like too few days to learn how to spend time that was truly my own. In other words, no time was truly mine. My boss merely allowed me an illusion of freedom, a little space in which to catch my breath, in between the fifty weeks that I lived but *he* owned.

They say that a little knowledge is a dangerous thing. My grade-school arithmetic was just enough for me to measure my employers' power in relation to mine: twenty-six-to-one. My employer uses twenty-six years of my life for every year I get to keep. And what do I get in return for this enormous thing I am giving? What do I get in return for my *life*?

A paycheck that's as skimpy as they can get away with. If I'm lucky, some health insurance. (If I'm *really* lucky, the employer's definition of "health" will include my teeth and my eyes—maybe even my mind.) And, in a truly enlightened workplace, just enough pension or "profit-sharing" to keep me sweet but not enough to make life different. And that's it.

Compare that to what my employer gets: if the company is successful, he (it's usually a he) gets a standard of living beyond my wildest dreams, including what I would consider fantastic protection for his family, and a world of access that I can only pitifully mimic by changing the channels on my television. His standard of living wouldn't be possible without the labor of people like me—but my employer doesn't think that a very significant fact. He certainly doesn't think that that fact entitles me to any say about the business. Not to mention a significant share in ownership. Oh no. The business is his to do with as he pleases, and he owns my work. Period.

I don't mean that bosses don't work. Most work hard and have the satisfaction of knowing that what they do is *theirs*. Great. The problem is: what I do is theirs too. Yet if my companion workers and I didn't do what we do—then nothing would be anybody's. So how come what we do is hardly ours? How come he can get rich while we're lucky to break even? How come he can do anything he wants with the company without consulting us, yet we do the bulk of the work and take the brunt of the consequences?

The only answer provided is that the employer came up with the money to start the enterprise in the first place; hence, he and his money people decide everything and get all the benefits.

Excuse me, but that seems a little unbalanced. It doesn't take into account that nothing happens unless work is done. Shouldn't it follow that, work being so important, the doers of that work deserve a more just formula for measuring who gets what? There's no doubt that the people who risked or raised the money to form a company, or bail it out of trouble, deserve a fair return on their investment—but is it fair that they get *everything*? It takes more than investment and management to make a company live. It takes the labor, skill and talent of the people who do the company's work. Isn't *that* an investment? Doesn't it deserve a fair return, a voice, a share of the power?

I know this sounds awfully simplistic, but no school ever taught me anything about the ways of economics and power (perhaps because they didn't want me to know), so I had to figure it out slowly, based on what I saw around me every day. And I saw:

That it didn't matter how long I worked or what a good job I did. That I could get incremental raises, perhaps even medical benefits and a few bonuses, but I would not be allowed power over my own life— no power over the fundamental decisions my company makes, decisions on which my *life* depends. That my future is in the hands of people whose names I often don't know and whom I never meet, and I have no recourse. That their investment is the only factor taken seriously. That they feed on my work, on my life, but reserve for themselves all power, prerogative and profit.

Slowly, very slowly, I came to the conclusion that for me was fundamental: my employers are stealing my life.

They. Are. Stealing. My. Life.

If the people who do the work don't own some part of the product and don't have any power over what happens to *their* enterprise— they are being robbed. *You* are being robbed. And don't think for a minute that those who are robbing you don't know they are robbing you. They know how much they get from you and how little they give back. They are thieves. They are stealing your life.

The assembly-line worker isn't responsible for the decimation of the American auto industry, for instance. Those responsible are those who've been hurt least, executives and stockholders who, according to the *L.A. Times*, make 50 to 500 times what the assembly-line worker makes, but who've done a miserable job of managing. Yet it's the workers who suffer most. Layoffs, plant closings and such are no doubt necessary—like the bumper stickers say, "Shit happens"—but it is not necessary that workers have no power in the fundamental management decisions involved.

As a worker, I am not an "operating cost." I am how the job gets done. I *am* the job. I am the company. Without me and my companion workers, there's nothing. I'm willing to take my lumps in a world in which little is certain, but I deserve a say. Not just some cosmetic "input," but significant power in good times or bad. A place at the table where decisions are made. Nothing less is fair. So nothing less is moral.

And if you, as owners or management or government, deny me this—then you are choosing not to be moral, and you are committing a crime against me. Do you expect me not to struggle?

Do you expect us to be forever passive while you get rich by stealing our lives?

January 26, 1990

A Dance Among the Ruins

It's been many, many years since I went back to Beekman Avenue in the South Bronx, or Decatur Street in Brooklyn, and I have put myself many miles from them, but they follow me in my dreams. Even before crack, arson and kids armed with automatic weapons, these streets were places of hunger, fear and the look that parents get when they must live with the knowledge that they cannot protect their children. It was in these places that my mother taught me to read. She let me know, not through lectures but through her presence, that to read and to survive were, for me, absolutely linked. On the fire escapes and rooftops, I read to survive.

I must have been ten when I read my first novel. It was the spring of 1956. I happened on it in the children's section of the library: *Star Man's Son*, by Andre Norton, a science-fiction tale written in 1952 about the descendants of nuclear-war survivors. I've found the book since. Norton could write. Unlike most pop prose, Norton's has sonority and a sense of rhythm. The sentences are suggestive. "These broken messages only babbled of the death of a world." "Landmarks on the old maps were now gone, or else so altered by time that a man might pass a turning point and never know it." (Did I sense that I must live in that existential landscape the rest of my life?)

The story is about a young man from a tribe deep in the wilderness who sets out to find and explore the legendary ruined cities of the Old Ones. On my fire escape I knew he was coming toward me, that I was one of the Old Ones who populated the place for which he had such awe. In the novel, the city's been spared a direct nuclear hit, but radiation has killed us, our bones lie everywhere and time has left the streets ruptured, the buildings slowly crumbling. The passage that struck me most deeply, and which I have searched out after all this time to read to you, was after the hero walks up a great wide staircase into a building that's not like the rest—a place I took to be the Metropolitan Museum of Art.

> He wandered through the high-ceilinged rooms, his boots making splotchy tracks in the fine dust crisscrossed with the spoor of small animals. He brushed the dust from the tops of cases and tried to spell out the blotched and faded signs. Grotesque stone heads leered or stared blindly through the murk, and tatters of powdery canvas hung dismally from worm-eaten frames in what had once been picture galleries.

What I am about to say may seem perverse, but so be it: these words are among the most liberating I have ever read. Of course I couldn't articulate this at the time, even to myself, but I remember the sense of revelation: the city was vulnerable! Was as vulnerable, in its way, as I. This city, this enormous entity, existing all around me yet entirely beyond me, beyond my ability to influence or perhaps even survive it—this city could, would, someday fall. It too was weak; it too had something to be afraid of. For I knew in my bones, beyond question, that the city was not on my side. So if the city, too, could be afraid, that gave me a little power.

I was especially happy that the museums would not last. My mother took me to them often (the city museums were free in those days). I loved the Museum of Natural History, the dinosaurs especially; I thought of them as enormous rats, I fought them in my fantasies. But the Metropolitan Museum of Art—my mother loved it, but it made me afraid. The people there were different. Our best clothes weren't as good as their casuals. They spoke strangely, so clearly and carefully. No matter what their words said, their voices sounded flat and bored. And if they spoke to us, it was with that slight thickening of the voice that people have when they visit the sick in hospitals. We were treated with a deference that dismissed us.

But it was the art that made me most afraid. What was it about?

Who was it about?! Here and there I would recognize something as almost human, almost natural ("natural," for me, meant the street); but "almost" wasn't near enough. Every hall, every wall, had one message for me, and it was the same message I saw on television: "You don't exist."

You can see the contradiction in the sentence. In order to say, "You don't exist," there has to be a "you" to say it to. So you *do* exist: you exist just enough to be told that you don't. They will entice you into the museum, but within the museum they will obliterate you; they will seduce you with television, but on television you will either be denied or lied about. The shrinks tell us that the surest way to drive people crazy is to give them a double signal: two contradictory messages at the same time. The poor know that this theory is correct.

Even to a boy it was clear that the museum thought itself superior to the television, but both institutions wanted nothing to do with my people, the working people of the street, without whom the world does not function; so the museum seemed to me a quieter, more spacious, more dignified version of the television. Television bombards us with negative images of anyone excluded from affluence, while the museum defines "beauty" as anything accepted by affluence. To be led by the hand into what is advertised as the palace of beauty, and to see no image of one's kind or one's world, is to be told in no uncertain terms that you are not beautiful.

You're supposed to appreciate this. You're supposed to take this in as knowledge, and be grateful for it. And you try, because God knows you're hungry for beauty, and the way the painting is being used is not the painting's fault. But the institution changes the power and the inflection of its beauty.

Being a child, I did not, could not, allow myself to admit my growing rage at being told in so many ways that because I was poor I did not exist. But the rage was building within me, and it was this rage that was appeased and gratified by "tatters of powdery canvas hung dismally from worm-eaten frames." The atomic bomb frightened me; but at the same time my rage was pleased to know that, like me, the city could die in an instant.

It didn't take a bomb. Just some of what one day will be studied (or forgotten?) as American history. The city is in ruins. Not that small, comparatively tame section of Manhattan which people in L.A. refer to as "New York" and people in Brooklyn refer to as "the city"; but the rest of it, which is ruined or about to be.

In March I spent one day there, for an afternoon with my brother and to visit my mother's grave. For the first time in twenty-odd years I drove through the old neighborhoods, miles and miles of the old neighborhoods. There's no need to describe them. You've seen the same footage I have, and the footage is accurate, as far as it goes. Rubble; charred skeletons of buildings; gangs; the homeless; burnt hulks of cars. It looks much like the description in my old science-fiction novel. But there are details that the camera people tend to leave out, and, as usual, these details completely change the context of what you see: hundreds of quite functional cars parked everywhere, and thousands of people going about their daily lives amidst the ruins.

These people do not look tragic or abandoned or hopeless. They look just like people going about their business everywhere, except that they look both a little more tired and a little more alert. The point is that, in an environment that the affluent would think of as impossible and unlivable, they are living. The enormous pressures they are under show up in every sort of statistic, from health studies to crime to education; but tens of thousands of people are—just living.

You can see why this daily life is not alluded to in our various media. The fact that something like "daily life" can exist in the ruins turns American values upside down. If you can still have something like a life with so little, then who needs so much? If art and language and music can flourish as they do here, so that the whole country is imitating them, what does that mean?

I think of what the anarchist leader Buenaventura Durruti said during the Spanish Civil War some weeks before he was killed. He was being interviewed by Pierre Van Paassen of the *Toronto Daily Star.* Van Paassen was impressed by Durruti and sympathetic to the Spanish workers, but he had no illusions about the human cost of such a war, even if the workers won. He said to Durruti, "You will be sitting on top of a pile of ruins even if you are victorious."

Durruti said,

> We have always lived in slums and holes in the wall. We will know how to accommodate ourselves for a time. For you must not forget that we can also build these palaces and

cities, here in Spain and in America and everywhere. We, the workers. We can build others to take their place. And better ones. We are not in the least afraid of ruins. We are going to inherit the earth. There is not the slightest doubt about that. The bourgeoisie might blast and ruin its own world before it leaves the stage of history. We carry a new world here, in our hearts. That world is growing in this minute.

Durruti had no doubt; I do. Durruti was a violent man and believed violence could help; I'm not and I don't. But he was so right about the ruins. People who can dance in them have nothing in this society to protect. Our beauty isn't in the museums. Our sustenance isn't in the economy. There is a difference between helping this society survive and helping humanity survive. We have to learn that difference. Society is always and merely a form. We are the content. This society is dispensable. We are not.

May 3, 1991

Back to the Garden

There were these three naked men. When I think of that time, that weekend and that place, they are the first thing I think of. Yet there was nothing extraordinary about them except that they were naked. My friend and I were walking from that much peopled hillside down the dirt road toward the pond. The paths and the fields were only about as crowded as, say, Central Park on a Sunday; compared to the hillside, it didn't seem crowded at all. And walking in our midst were these three naked men.

We were older, it seemed a lot older, than most of the others. Pushing twenty-four. And we were working class, or whatever they call it in this country (they try not to call it anything, to pretend it doesn't exist), and most of these people obviously weren't. That was, and is, no small gap.

For five years I'd been a working stiff who would try to hoard a couple of hours late at night to write. Most of that time I'd supported my mother, two of my brothers and my sister in a two-, then a three-room apartment in the Bronx. As with most working people, "Turn On/Tune In/Drop Out" weren't exactly viable options for me. There was no medical insurance on my job (as on most jobs then), not even paid sick days—I couldn't afford to be ill, much less drop out, still less go to jail. To risk the job or even one paycheck—though it was only about sixty-five dollars take-home a week—was unthinkable; the consequences for my family would have been drastic and immediate.

Experimenting with drugs and/or civil disobedience were definitely *out*.

I'm telling you this not because it was true of one would-be writer but because it was, and is, true of millions. Beyond listening to FM stations and buying a few records (the "merchandising" that snooty commentators look down on, though they don't seem to mind their *comments* being merchandised), the sixties were something most of us just couldn't afford. But we did watch. Often with great excitement. Even hope.

Not political hope, however. Or at least, not much. "The Movement," as it called itself, behaved as though we working millions didn't exist. My resentment at that ran deep. SDS was, after all, *Students* for a Democratic Society. They and the other public radicals played for and with other students and intellectuals, and gave the impression that, insofar as we existed at all, the political role of us (white) working stiffs was to watch what they did on television. It was as though they didn't try to organize with us because they didn't think we were smart enough or (unlike blacks) interesting enough. It was a palpable attitude—and it doomed their movement.

Still, I and many I knew were thankful for those radicals, if only because they wouldn't let Vietnam be taken for granted and because they relished the word "revolution." Their way of going about it may often have been childish, show-offish and politically ineffectual, but there is more to revolution than politics, and they knew it. They stirred things up, and stirred and stirred, and those stirrings gave a conceptual weight to that crazy nameless something in the air, the greater stirring that the movement, too, was caught up in: good-crazy and bad-crazy both, dangerous unpredictable and alive with raw possibility; when all our light and all our darkness danced with all our hope and all our fear. (Some people call that state "love.")

A nameless but definite "something," hard to pin down, impossible to ignore. You could hear it on the radio, see it on the news, dig it at a concert, wear it, inhale it, trip with it, talk it, live it. In fact, you had no choice. You couldn't walk anywhere without it sticking to your shoes, like it or not. The privileged young could act it out, but they didn't invent it, they caught it, like everybody else.

At work we spoke of it, of one or another of its costumes, nearly

every day, into the early seventies; and late at night in the Bronx, trying to write while my family slept, I felt a part of something that the
whole world seemed trying desperately to birth. That was the ground-
note of the time.

Do you think I've rambled too far afield from the image of meeting
three naked men on a dirt road? But see, for me that whole time
somehow seems to swirl around that moment on that road. It feels
like the reason my friend and I had traveled to that hillside and (after
Joe Cocker's set, I think it was) gone looking for that pond. And there
they were.

It was twenty years ago, but it could have been twenty-thousand.
It seemed for a moment that those young, naked, laughing men were
the true representatives of the human race *as* a race, at home, even
serene for that one precious and precarious short walk through our
era; or maybe their casual, scruffy-haired nakedness had a kind of
authority about it that made my well-practiced street-kid's strut seem
awkward and artificial by comparison. But I remember vividly that
they were not being exhibitionists, there was no self-consciousness
about them, none of the unmistakable air of people who want to be
noticed; they really were just walking and talking, laughing among
themselves, just going from one place to another. What made them
stand out was the very fact that, though there were hundreds of clothed
people around, those three naked men *didn't* stand out. Nobody else
in sight was naked, yet people passing them on the road paid them
no special attention. And it was the very fact that they didn't stand
out, a fact immune to the callow rhetoric of that day or the resentful
revisions of this, that makes them so important.

Why? Because these were not half a million "freaks" or "hippies"
assembled that weekend on Max Yasgur's farm—those are words that
warp the context and avoid ideas. (Which is why the media still invoke them.) Far from being freaks, these were half a million normal
people—the ensuing twenty years have proved just *how* normal most
of them really were. Yet some fleeting congruence of the music, the
mood, the historical moment, the astrological line-up, sunspots,
whatever—inspired them one weekend to casually jettison at least a
thousand years of heritage, habit and training. And *that* is what was
so enticing to some and so threatening to others.

For when naked people can walk the road among strangers without disruption; when half a million disoriented, surprised individuals who don't know where their next meal is coming from can stay crowded together without tension or violence—in fact, in a spirit of camaraderie; when sexual strictures reinforced by every power of state, religion and family seem suddenly to evaporate; when you consider that most of those people were *not* on drugs (drugs were scarcer than food that weekend); when something as ephemeral as music was able to sustain all this; and when you remember that virtually all these people were fairly average specimens of their world, of a society that (in practice) has always been antagonistic, even viciously hostile, to the values that that weekend stood for . . .

Then it's hard to avoid realizing how tentative *any* human arrangement is, even the "real world" which the few who manipulate its powers would like us to be "realistic" about. The present dominant version of "how to be a world"—is only one version of human possibility, and if the elements are right it can be swept away in a weekend.

The so-called real world may come roaring back the next weekend, it has tremendous force of inertia behind it—but it's only inertia, not "human nature." Human nature is just like other sorts of nature, capable of staggering varieties of organization and expression. A quarter million years of humanity has evidenced myriad ways to live, and, as that weekend showed, there are more to come, each with its own graces and nightmares. The yearnings of a few in one century can become the motivating ideal of millions in another. (That's not fanciful; it happens regularly.) A new gadget like a compass or computer chip can turn the course of generations. A new music can be the seed, the laboratory, of half a dozen world-challenging movements. While things that seem imperishable perish all the time. And new ways, at least new for us, can manifest even here, at any moment, spontaneously, from the most unexpected source (a shipyard in Gdansk or a shabby recording studio in Memphis), beyond anyone's capacity to predict or control.

That's the truth people are running from when they poo-poo that weekend, those people, that era. For it was an era when this truth was celebrated by many. Just because it's not being celebrated now in America doesn't make it any less true.

Farther down the path was the pond where nearly everyone was naked. Not me, though. (A Sicilian upbringing is apparently harder to discard, at least in the open, than a WASP one.) I sat near the water, feeling a little silly and quite happy, full of admiration for the people around me. Sad, too. On the street, judging the toughness of others is a precise and necessary skill. If you don't have it, it is hard to stay alive and impossible to keep your manhood. So I knew that, however lovely these people were, they just weren't tough enough. It would take more than loveliness, more than goodness, to sustain these changes. It would take the will to gain the knowledge to go the distance. And it would take not being afraid of the dark. There wasn't near enough of any of that in this movement. So, thinking of the three naked men, I wrote this note:

"We know now that our dreams are not going to come true. Are never going to come true. We have learned that our dreams are important not because they come true, but because they take you places you would never have otherwise gone, and teach you what you never guessed was there to learn."

August 11, 1989

That Kitty Kat of the Mind

In a joint called the Kitty Kat in South Bend, Indiana, a naked young woman moved her body to loud music. Men watched her. If it was like most such joints, the drinks were pricey, the air smoky, the look shadowy, and it was hard to see anything clearly except that naked woman, which was fine because the men hadn't come to look at each other anyway. As for the naked women, they always seem to be looking at Mars unless you tip them well, and then they look through you with a smile that says, "You and I both know you don't exist." (Their eyes add, "Join the club, I don't exist either.")

Beneath the thudding music this kind of place is awfully quiet, really. People don't come to talk. Even when several men walk in together, their banter pales before the nakedness they've come to . . . inhale, in a way. It's as though something is satisfied by simply being exposed to someone else's nakedness. No, "satisfied" is not the right word, not nearly; something's answered, called to, beckoned, lied to, cursed, derided, laughed at, cried to, depending on who you are and what you bring to it.

Are you a regular? Do you need this often? Are you so far from your own nakedness that this is the only way you can meet the nakedness of others? Still, you haven't been reduced just to staring at magazines or videos—you leave your place, go out into the night, where something just might happen. Does your imagination feed on the "just might" while your cowardice relaxes in the anonymity of the situation? Is it a sudden impulse, every few years, or just once that you need to be exposed to women who apparently can go farther than any woman in your life? Or are you a businessman traveling, and it's easier to be alone here, with this queer mix of intimacy and coldness, than in a hotel room?

Whoever you are, you're probably going to masturbate later—and, unless you are far more spiritually developed than most of us who end up at joints like the Kitty Kat every now and again, you're going to feel a little soiled at touching yourself. Every masturbator's genitals are second-best: they'd rather there'd been someone else to touch. For men, that's always all too clear during the awkwardness of having to clean up.

Or—and this, I think, is the worst—are you going to go home and think of that naked dancer while you hold the woman you live with? Don't imagine for a minute that your lover doesn't know. Not in her mind, where she doesn't want to know, but in her flesh, where she can't help but know. "Any human touch can change you" is the frightening truth articulated by James Baldwin, and somewhere in us we know when we're being changed, though the results may not become evident for months or years (when we will pretend to be surprised—pretend to ourselves more than others, so we won't have to take the full weight of our fate).

Make no mistake: when you watch those women your body does what it's supposed to—erectile tissue erects itself; sometimes you can feel the dancer's moves in your knees or in your mouth. Are you filling yourself with desire artificially, as it were? Getting a kind of transfusion of desire from watching these young women, because on your own your desire has shrunk and dried more than you know, because it doesn't rise in you as forcefully anymore because it's been attacked and defiled too long by forces you haven't tried to understand? Or do you just love the blank slate of their flesh, on which you can draw any reality you choose for as long as they can dance?

And then there are the women within those lovely bodies—achingly lovely, sometimes. A loveliness utterly out of context: there's nothing lovely about the mood, the dancing is just a kind of sexual calisthenics, rarely beautiful in and of itself . . . but there's still that body, lovely in spite of all. A strange discordance, meaning whatever one wants it to mean. I take it to mean that some beauty defies cheapening, though that defiance may be futile, and in any case nothing stays lovely very long in joints like the Kitty Kat.

But there I started to speak about the women *within* the bodies and got sidetracked by their loveliness. As usual. So: What of the women?

"I dreamed that I myself was the concept of the limit of E to the X," a Texas dancer-hooker told me once. Then she tried to explain the math, but I was way out of my depth. She didn't fit into any pigeonhole I've ever heard of. Women come to this dance from all sorts of places and backgrounds. They arrive at a nakedness that is not really theirs—for on that stage, or platform, or bar, they too are consumed by an image, an archetype, that neither they nor the men who watch them are responsible for. The Naked Dancer, female or male, is ancient, as old as humankind, there's no way to make one or another ideology or system responsible for that image. No matter how any given system or mindset distorts the Naked Dancer, the Naked Dancer dances on through time, through all human society, like it or not.

In our society the figure has largely been reduced to joints like the Kitty Kat, because we choose to drive such images underground, or onto screens, in an attempt to degrade them and keep them out of daily life. Still it's the same Naked Dancer. And it is no mean sensation to step into Her or Him for a time, even on the lowest level of the incarnation, at least until the seaminess of the scene gets to you. These dancers are doing something that, in our world, is both strange and socially suspect at best, an act of transgression (a fact important to many of them). But it's also ancient, even holy. That's quite a thing to put your psyche through: the sad, crass scene mixing with an ancient, sacred echo of what you may sense only as a kind of fleeting thrill.

Think I'm mystifying it? Go dance naked in front of strangers and see whether it's a small act.

All of which is to say, there was nothing simple about the Kitty Kat Lounge, nor anything especially harmful—it's less harmful, surely, than what, according to statistics, goes on in the American home in terms of violence, sexual abuse, accidents and psychological stress. (Americans are paying billions for therapy because of what happened to them at home, not in bars.) No, the Kitty Kat and its ilk are just modest, shabby places where people need the shadowy decor because they're being more transparent than they'd ever admit.

You'd hardly think as august an institution as the Supreme Court of the United States would be interested in the joint.

But in a five–four decision written by Chief Justice William H. Rehnquist, the court decided that the public's "moral disapproval" was sufficient to stop naked dancing in a private establishment, namely, the Kitty Kat Lounge. The government was "protecting societal order and morality." Rehnquist goes on: "Public indecency statutes such as the one before us reflect moral disapproval of people appearing in the nude among strangers in public places."

Whose moral disapproval, exactly? That of the court, of course, and of the St. Joseph County prosecutors who handled the case, and of whoever made the complaint—and, oh yes, of that woman I saw on CNN, part of some very proper organization involved with the complaint. She was identified as a housewife, and her smile was really something. Somebody should have told her that smugness doesn't photograph well. She was talking about how bad it was for husbands to stop into places like the Kitty Kat on their way home from work. That was the "crime" she felt so righteous about quelling.

Which raises the question: What *is* moral disapproval? I'd say there are two kinds. First, we morally disapprove of actions that directly harm us. That's reasonable. But the court went out of its way to say not only that the Kitty Kat's dancers weren't harming anybody, but that in the strict legal sense they weren't even obscene. Nude dancing, Rehnquist admitted, is "expressive conduct within the outer perimeters of the First Amendment."

The second kind of moral disapproval, the court's kind, gets a little murky: we morally disapprove of actions that we disagree with to the extent that they make us uncomfortable, *really* uncomfortable, make us squirm with resentment that people who *do* such things even exist—though these actions have never directly touched us, and even if they did (even if that lady's husband indulged at the Kitty Kat), the harm would be hard to prove.

Didn't this used to be America, where you're free to live as you please, no matter what anyone else thinks, as long as you don't impinge on anybody else's freedom? Not according to Justice Antonin Scalia, who in his concurring opinion opined that the court hadn't gone far enough.

He contended that America has never adopted "the Thoreauvian 'You may do as you like, so long as it does not injure someone else' beau ideal." That's too much freedom for us. "Moral opposition to nudity supplies a rational basis for its prohibition." (Using the same reasoning, Scalia said, "Homosexual behavior is not a fundamental right," citing a decision last year to uphold a Georgia law "prohibiting private homosexual intercourse.")

So the court's "moral opposition," which is now sufficient cause to abridge our First Amendment, on examination is nothing more than somebody's prissy resentment over any act that disturbs their peace of mind—as long as this "somebody" is, or seems to be, more in the numerical majority.

The real question becomes: Why does it disturb their peace of mind? More specifically: What is the process by which their minds are disturbed?

Would their minds be disturbed by naked dancing if the act didn't loom so large in their imaginations? Look how large it looms in Scalia's. This is the image he came up with: "The purpose of Indiana's law would be violated, I think, if 60,000 fully consenting adults crowded into Hoosier Dome to display their genitals to one another, even if there were not an offended innocent in the crowd." Nobody prodded him to that image. His imagination produced it all on its own. Sixty-thousand naked souls wagging their privates at one another in an arena—*that's what's going on in Scalia's mind.* (Very Roman of you, Tony.)

That's why he has to make these harsh judgments. Because when somebody mentions a few naked girls in a dingy joint in South Bend, that's not what Tony Scalia sees. His psyche is suddenly plunged in the midst of 60,000 naked bodies, and he can't stand it.

So it's not what's going on in the Kitty Kat Lounge that's being quelled; it's what's going on in the minds of these people. Nude dancing in Indiana, gay screwing in Georgia (what Caligulian imagery did that inspire, Tony?). If, in fact, their imaginations weren't feeding on the act, dwelling on the act, coming back to the act again and again like a tongue favoring a sore tooth, then their peace of mind would not be disturbed. Like most people, they wouldn't really care what goes on in South Bend. But they care very deeply, because they can't stop thinking about it.

How do they give themselves permission to think about it? They oppose it. That way they can concentrate very very hard on all this nasty stuff—with a clean conscience. Jesse Helms can't get the (vastly overrated) photographs of Robert Mapplethorpe out of his mind, *and he doesn't want to.* So he'll oppose them and all they stand for till he dies, because his opposition to homosexuality gives him permission to concentrate on gay acts. That's why these people are so implacable. They *need* to think of this stuff, their imaginations are hungry for what they see as dangerous sexuality—but they can't give themselves permission to concentrate on these images unless they can tell themselves that they're out to destroy evil.

Rehnquist used that word, by the way. "Public nudity is the evil the State seeks to prevent." His WASP reserve doesn't go in for Scalia's exuberant fantasies. It's sufficient for Rehnquist to call a few naked girls dancing on a stage "evil." But since there's no record of those girls hurting anybody, that evil can only be occurring in one place: Rehnquist's mind.

Forgotten in all this, as America has chosen to forget them almost since the day they were written, are the Ninth and Tenth Amendments to the Constitution, which conclude what we call "the Bill of Rights."

> Article IX: The enumeration in the Constitution of certain rights shall not be construed to deny or disparage others retained by the people. Article X: The powers not delegated to the United States by the Constitution, nor prohibited by it to the states, are reserved to the states respectively, or to the people.

Read these again, carefully, if only to learn how you've been lied to. They say clearly, they say twice, that the Constitution promises Americans certain specific rights, but that it "shall not be construed to deny or disparage [other rights] retained by the people." Just because a right isn't stated in the Constitution doesn't mean you don't have it. Like the right to decide who you make love to. Or where you take off your clothes. Or whether you keep the baby in your body.

The Kitty Kat Lounge doesn't appear to be a bastion of liberty. Not heroic like the Alamo, nor dignified like Faneuil Hall. It's just a place of nakedness and sadness where people came together in their own way, for their own reasons, did what they did and went home, I'd imagine, more tired than excited or liberated. Just a dive. But some of those dancers thought they lived in America, and when the city tried to stop them they fought back all the way to the top, to the Supreme Court. Where they were told, "No, you're mistaken. You do not live in America any longer."

July 26, 1991

Part Two

A Hard Beauty to Love

Las Vegas

The Odds on Anything

Part I: Up and Atom

One of the first responses I had coming to Nevada was whether this was really part of the United States.

Joe Yablonsky, Former FBI Chief

Where else but Las Vegas would they make the atom bomb a picnic? An honest-to-god picnic. From 1951, when the bright mushroom first bloomed in the desert north of town, to 1962, when some killjoy treaty drove the testing underground, the casinos sponsored picnic lunches to view the A-blasts. Maybe the women would wear "The Atomic Hairdo," designed by a hairdresser at the Flamingo: the hair was pulled up over a mushroom-shaped wire form and sprinkled with silver glitter. And maybe they'd drink the popular "Atomic Cocktail": equal parts vodka, brandy and champagne, with a dash of sherry. Thus coiffed and oiled, folks would perch on the hillsides as near as was allowed (which was pretty near), and make a party of it.

Even if you didn't get *that* close, you could see the explosion pretty good from anywhere in town. One joint called itself the Atomic View Motel, advertising an unobstructed sight line to the bomb blast from the comfort of one's lounge chair.

At that time our president was a bald, competent and (some historians now claim) impotent general named Dwight D. Eisenhower, and he decided that Americans didn't need to know about the dangers of fallout. His successor, John F. Kennedy (not as competent, but notoriously potent), let that decision stand. People downwind as far as Nebraska were contaminated by the blasts. Small farm towns became gardens of leukemia. And our Vegas picnickers, and the unobstructed guests of the Atomic View Motel, thrilled by the bomb's concussion-wind mussing their hair—judging by the effects of the tests on people so much farther away, a lot of those picnickers probably died young.

But who can deny they saw something worth seeing? Wouldn't *you* have gone on a Bomb picnic? Be honest, now. I know I would have.

I can see myself as I was when I first discovered Vegas. In my early thirties, the new money of success hot in my pockets, not caring *too* much that my first film, *Roadie*, was a lousy one, nor that a master of the Hollywood hustle had tricked me out of more money than the government would soon take—in other words, too dumb to know that I was actually broke. (A terrific state of mind for Vegas.) My often-suspect sense of romance drew me, in those days, to three general sorts of women: honky-tonk angels, non-separatist lesbians (who were prepared to sleep with me parenthetically, as it were), and the otherwise-married. Vegas was an especially delicious place to rendez-vous with the otherwise-married.

So I can see myself, at the Flamingo maybe, shelling out money that I didn't know I didn't have, tipping big, blowing a couple of hundred a clip at roulette, squandering with a vengeance—the way only a poor kid can—and doing this with an equally vengeful Otherwise-Married Woman. Nobody we knew was likely to run into us in Vegas—we were liberals, *leftists* for heavens sake, and New Agey to boot. Our crowd never made this scene. So I could make like I was Steve McQueen in *The Cincinnati Kid*, and she could wear something that, if her kids saw her in it, they'd have to spend five years in therapy someday to get over it. And she could pick up this gorgeously cheap outfit in one of those casino sleaze shops because I'd buy it, I'd buy her anything, what did I know? (We'd leave it in the room for the maid when we checked out.) We loved Vegas because we knew the house rules, which are as follows: as long as you don't bother the other customers, you can do *anything*.

That's the promise of Vegas: Anything.

Not that most people have the stuff for Anything—but being in Anything's general vicinity is heady and, in Vegas, not too threatening. (You can always go home, where you think Anything can't happen, and where you're wrong.) Being around Anything in a guaranteed controlled situation—guaranteed by the Mafia, no less—is a neat way to do a vacation.

So that's what Vegas is for—to be safe in the presence of Anything. Vegas as we know it was the brainchild of a talented murderer named Bugsy Siegel who opened the Flamingo, in 1946, on a piece of land that was then five miles away from a small desert pit stop. Siegel financed it with money from a veritable genius of a murderer, Meyer Lansky. The other American institution these two started is now known as Murder, Inc. It took a couple of killers to understand Anything. To dig that everybody's just enough of a killer to harbor a kind of envy for the real killers, and that if everybody's a bit of a killer, then everybody's a bit of everything—and that includes Anything. And that if, in Puritan America, you dedicate a city to the pursuit of Anything, and you put that city far enough away from everywhere—then Puritans will find a way across one of the most dangerous deserts in the world just to rub shoulders with Anything without ruining their safe lives. The gambling is just an excuse, a way to participate in the Anything.

And you can't get any deeper into Anything than the Theory of Relativity harnessed in the service of inchoate rage. So I can just see me and this Otherwise-Married Woman who's looking pretty good in her see-through chintz of Flamingo neon-pink—and if it had been, say, '59, and if the casino had offered an all-you-can-drink picnic on a hill overlooking the *atom bomb*? Oh, yes.

I mean, it isn't every day that you're invited to a rehearsal for the Apocalypse. And imagine *sharing* that with someone. Doesn't it get you just a little horny: arms around each other's waists, hip to hip, thigh to thigh, a little high, and the ground trembles under foot, and a hot gust smacks your face as the cloud rises up and up, shimmering with rainbow tints of radiation, and you feel a waft of how it felt to write the Book of Revelation? Yes, the neon of the Strip and the glow of the Bomb go well together. They're both about Anything.

Part II: The Geology of Anything

But anything is nothing new in the Nevada desert. If you have a big stake in the idea of permanence, then you probably should avoid the Nevada State Museum in Lorenzi Park in Las Vegas, and you should definitely not look at its relief map of Nevada circa thirty thousand years ago. Now thirty-thousand sounds like a lot, but it's a tiny span geologically, and not even a terribly long time in the history of our species. Our molecules have been doing the people-dance for about a million years. And thirty-thousand is only one-thirty-third of that. Folks like you and me, with the same brain load, were around for what I'm about to tell you.

You can see it on the Nevada relief map: thirty-thousand years ago Nevada was all lakes! Hundreds of square miles of huge lakes covered about 20 percent of Nevada's surface. A 200-foot-wide river flowed through the Las Vegas Valley. Mammoths and camels roamed here. Nearby Death Valley was an *enormous* lake. The entire place was an environmentalist's wet dream.

Until, only twenty-thousand years ago (while "civilization" was already well under way in several parts of the world), Lake Las Vegas and the other great Nevada lakes "drained suddenly."

Drained suddenly?! What the fuck are they talking about? Dozens of big lakes, enough moisture to support lots of large mammals and all the plants that they ate, and it all just . . . drained? Suddenly?

I don't know about you, but I find that fact incredibly threatening. I'd be happier if there were a bad guy. Like, didn't the developers do it? Wasn't pollution responsible, or the defense budget, or Styrofoam cups? But no. The planet just decided: "To hell with those lakes, those mammoths, that river, those camels. I'm bored with all that. I'm draining all that suddenly."

By ten-thousand years ago the place looks like it does today. There isn't a camel for fifteen-thousand miles, and there ain't no mammoths nowhere.

This gets weirder when you realize that this happened about twenty-thousand years *after* the last Ice Age glacier receded from what we now know as the United States. In other words, while Nevada was drastically changing, most of America (New England, for instance) looked pretty much the way it does now. In other words, the Wild West was wild before we ever set foot in it.

So the people who became the Paiute Indians made the best of things, got used to their new desert, got to love it. Then came *their* Apocalypse. First, just a few Franciscan monks in 1776 (portentous year, that). Then, in 1855, Mormons. In fact, the first building on what is now Las Vegas Boulevard (also known as the Strip) was the Mormon fort. There's still a piece of it left.

Of all the people who've tried to use America as a staging ground for Paradise on Earth, the Mormons have been the most determined and, by any measure, the most successful. And Mormons don't think Paradise is worth a prayer unless you and your whole family can be there pretty much as you are here. You *can* take it with you—a Vegas thought if there ever was one.

As it happened, these particular Mormons bickered among themselves, and Brigham Young called them back to Utah. Lucky for Bugsy Siegel. Or unlucky, maybe. Without disparaging those Mormons at all, it's fair to say that Bugsy, the man credited with starting *Vegas*, had more than a little in common with them: he was a devout but bickering member of a highly organized, effective and rigid institution (the Mafia is an outfit with superb business acumen, dispensing valuable benefits to its members in return for strict obedience; an organization dedicated to building its own version of Paradise on Earth). Except that when Brigham Young recalls you, you start fresh somewhere else; when Meyer Lansky and Lucky Luciano recall you, you get shot in the eye.

While recognizing that Mormonism is a profound spiritual movement, while the Mafia is just profoundly evil—still, structurally (and only structurally), there are strong similarities. Odd, isn't it, that such similar social structures were drawn to the same place in the same immense desert, and that each built its first abode on what is, in effect, the same street. Another way to say this is that what Mormon pioneers, the Mafia *and* the atomic military have in common is a keen, highly developed sense of Anything—a sense of Anything that felt a kinship to the place itself, as though this desert were calling to them.

Connect the dots: atom bombs, "drained suddenly," the Neon Anything. Religious fanatics, Jewish and / or Sicilian gangsters, atomic maniacs. Mammoth Apocalypse, Paiute Apocalypse, rehearsals for *the* Apocalypse. Spiritual Paradise on Earth, carnal Paradise on Earth. Lakes drain suddenly, the United States builds a couple of dams, and some lakes *un*-drain suddenly. Shit sure happens in that part of the Mojave.

It's a scene, see. It didn't start with Vegas. Rather, the concept that culminated in "Vegas" got drawn toward a place where some very strange and not dissimilar stuff has been happening for a very long time. The stuff that is "Vegas" is coming up out of the ground out here. I'm very serious. In other words, Las Vegas as it is presently constituted may *not* be a gross ecological travesty; as an expression of what Lawrence Durrell calls "the spirit of place," Vegas may be what the place *wants*. This is, as they say in Vegas, the "juice," the "action," that this environment itself likes. It's been drawing strangeness to itself for thousands of millennia.

Call it coincidence, or a flight of fancy, or a flash of insight into the human-planet interface, or tabloid non-sense—either way, the pattern shimmers.

And stir in this little grace-note of a fact: in 1864, President Abraham Lincoln declared Nevada a state—on Halloween. Now, Halloween is not just a children's holiday. Halloween is what survives from the most important celebration of our Pagan European ancestors, the night they celebrated their new year with rituals in which psychic and spiritual forces were unleashed. The Pagan New Year's Eve. And it's Nevada's birthday. (Happens to be mine, too. Hmmmm.) Not that Lincoln was aware of these nuances. It's just that, as I say, the place seems to draw this stuff.

This is how strong I think that draw really is: four-hundred years before Vegas happened, Spanish Conquistadors kept trying to find it. They were *sure* that somewhere to the north and west, across the great deserts, would be a city of gold and light, incredible riches, eternal youth, exquisite pleasures—an intoxicating city of riches and dreams. Expedition after expedition failed to find it, yet still they were sure. They just *felt* it out there. Many of them staked everything on their certainty that a city very like Las Vegas already existed. And they would never know how right they were—right that there was such a city, right that it lay in the great western desert. They were just wrong about when.

The place itself was generating Vegas-vibe, and they felt it and were called by it; but the place would need four-hundred more years to generate an actual Las Vegas.

Halloween. Unleashed forces. "Drained suddenly." Mormons. Liberace. Boxing. The Bomb. Sinatra. The Strip. Quickie divorce. Legal whores. Instant marriage. The Mafia. Wayne Newton. Un-drained Suddenly. Howard Hughes. The Mecca of Anything.

But in the middle of nowhere? Because let's not forget, we're talking about *nowhere*. The Mojave. One-hundred ten in the shade—except there is no shade. Where even a healthy young person can dehydrate so fast that a brisk walk can be fatal.

This place, this utterly hostile environment, is the fifth fastest growing city in the United States—and if you count from 1930, when there were only about five-thousand Vegans, to now, when there are more than seven-hundred-thousand, it may be the fastest growing city in the Western world. And more than *seventeen million* people visit Vegas every year now—with a marvelous faith in the ability of electricity and piped-in water to keep them alive, no matter what, in an environment otherwise capable of killing them in a matter of hours.

Do I sound a little hysterical? It's just that the level of weirdness we've come to take for granted (about everything, not just Vegas) astonishes me. Not the weirdness itself—I like that—but how we take it for granted. That's the weirdest thing about the weirdness.

As for Vegas—it couldn't be much weirder if this town were on the moon. The place just seems to pulse with whatever it is that makes weirdness weird. The place feeds on it. Likes it. And the weirdest thing is—it always has.

Part III: One Step Beyond

Mars ain't no place to raise the kids.
Elton John

Not everyone takes the weirdness for granted. Nevada in general, and Las Vegas in particular, "ranks highest" (according to *The New York Times*) in teenage suicides. And for every kid who commits suicide, there are a lot more who come close.

They don't seem to care that Vegas is the best city in America for faces. Etched, walking-photograph faces everywhere, the kind of faces you see in carnivals and prisons and on ranches. The kids don't sit in off-the-Strip restaurants like Capazzoli's wondering about the lives of the waitresses, bitterly etched tallish women in their fifties and sixties with great bone-structure and coiffed dyed hair who look like they once were chorus-line dancers, beauties from the days of the bomb blasts, wisecrackers with hard, tired eyes and smiles that happen by reflex for the customers—but you're dying to ask their stories, you know each one has a story, and that it's something, these days, to be a story, to have a story. More and more people don't. The kids don't.

The kids don't care about the gambling cabbie ("Do you gamble?" "Oh yes, you gotta gamble") who moved here from Chicago because one day he told his wife, "When I retire I'll move to Vegas," and she said, "Why wait?" They don't care about his inside information: that the best tippers are from the house builders and the heavy-construction conventions, the worst from the doctors' conventions. The kids don't think it's funny about doctors being the worst tippers. They don't think anything having to do with Anything is very amusing.

The kids who are dealing with the highest teen suicide rate in America aren't impressed that at the Horseshoe casino downtown there's a million dollars on display, one hundred $10,000 bills in a glass case. And whose picture is on the bill? Some guy named Chase. One of the people I was with on my last Vegas run shares my passion for American history; neither one of us had ever heard of the guy. Later I looked it up. It's Salmon Portland Chase (1808–1873), an Ohio senator, secretary of the treasury, and chief justice of the Supreme Court who presided over Andrew Johnson's impeachment hearings and founded the national banking system. So now me and my friend know. And we like knowing. But the kids don't want to know. Because it doesn't help them any. And they're right.

Likewise, the kids aren't impressed that Las Vegas has to be the most racially integrated resort in the world. The casinos are one of the few institutions I can think of in the United States where blacks, whites and Asians mingle without noticeable tension. But you don't see Latinos. This last trip I don't think I saw any. Not among the guests, I mean. Just among the maids. Like the one who looked at me with such exhausted eyes when I opened the door and told her, "Come back in an hour, we'll be checked out by then," and she came back, but we weren't near ready—we'd ordered something from room service— and I said, "I think it'll be another hour," and for a moment the veils lifted and her eyes said, "You rich fuck."

The kids growing up in the ever-present glow of casinos where only money counts—they'd understand that pretty good. And they also wouldn't buy that stuff about "racially integrated resort," because they'd know about where the local blacks actually live, in acres of dismal one-story government housing, featureless, lifeless, and so quiet in the heat.

If I could get them served without hassle I'd like to take them to the Tropicana's bar at about 1:30 in the morning, where the women of the chorus of the Folies Bergere unwind before they go home. Most of the suckers are either asleep by then or drunk at the tables, and almost every seat at the bar is occupied by a leggy woman in jeans, late twenties, early thirties, heavy lines under the eyes, savvy mouth. The Tropicana's where you dance near-naked when you're too old for the chorus at the high-roller casinos but you're still a looker and you can still kick high. (One day you may be a waitress at Capazzoli's, but not yet.) The women banter with the bartenders and talk their back-stage shoptalk. Some of them have great nicknames—"The Alabama Slammer," that's my favorite. She looks like Lainie Kazan; the bartender named her after her favorite drink, and it seems to have stuck, at least for this gig. The scene goes on for about forty minutes, then within five everybody leaves. You get the impression that it's the best time of their day. I'd like to take the kids there just to show them some down-home, human exchange under all this heartless glitz—but they'd say it's not enough, it doesn't help, and they'd be right again.

But for me, the scene that stands for the worst of Anything (worse than the Bomb, in a way—the Bomb is at least *thrilling*), the scene that goes hand-in-hand with the teenage suicide rate, hangs on just one thing one man said at Whoopi Goldberg's show at the Golden Nugget a few days before New Year's.

The Golden Nugget features an enormous chunk of gold in a heavily guarded case on the casino floor. It's where the *real* high-rollers go, the gamblers who bet thousands. And, with Caesar's and Bally's, it's where the stars play. Lots of tough glitz in that crowd, lots of jewels, furs, thousand-dollar suits. The sick grin of Anything was like static in the air.

Whoopi came on, and she was Something. She started easy, getting a big laugh and applause about Jim Bakker being sentenced to forty-five years. Jim Bakker had gotten his, and the crowd was glad. Until they got theirs: "1989 was a bad year for pussy. You couldn't get elected if you fucked *anybody*. That's how George got in. Look at Barbara Bush—you know she don't swallow."

They laughed at that, a laugh of surprise, not fun. You didn't have to look far or hard to see that this was an audience that hadn't experienced much swallowing. Whoopi kept it up, Lenny Bruce-style, making them laugh at what they hated to admit—pussy jokes, the-government's-selling-crack jokes, and edgy jokes about race. Some people stopped laughing. This one guy, his wife was laughing hysterically while he just stared from her to Whoopi and back with a face of stone-cold hate. He would never forget nor forgive either woman for this laughter.

Then Whoopi wisecracked about the reunification of Germany.

"WHY ARE YOU WORRIED? GOT A LITTLE JEW BLOOD IN YOU?"

It was a silver-haired, beautifully groomed man, perhaps sixty, in a perfectly cut suit. His voice was strong and cruel.

There certainly must have been Jews in the audience. They said nothing. I said nothing. Whoopi, obviously thrown, danced away from the sentence with some lame patter, but all the life had gone out of her performance—"drained suddenly" would be an accurate description. She was off the stage in five minutes.

Anything had snickered. Anything had caught us off guard. Anything had reminded us that an atom bomb, or a Holocaust, is not a spectacle, not a magazine cover, not a weird thing to read about on the toilet. It's an atom bomb. It's a Holocaust. And it wants the death of everything. Anything had spoken up, lest we forget that a gangster is not a movie star, Al Capone is not Robert De Niro—a gangster is a reptilian force utterly lacking the quality of mercy. Reptiles, of course, are very much at home in the desert.

"GOT A LITTLE JEW BLOOD?" The voice of the lizard. And, as is said to happen when a reptile stares at you, everyone froze.

As the kids are frozen. And for the same reason. Anything is hissing at them all the time. Especially in Vegas, where they "rank highest" in suicides. And *most* especially in Vegas, where it's more out in the open than most places. And I like that. I have a passion for Anything and would love to write a piece saying the more Anything the better, because it's what I feel in my bones. But the statistics on teen suicide say that my bones may be bad wrong.

They're building Vegas up so fast! It's not just the new gargantuan casinos. (The Mirage alone cost $630 million.) At the rate things are going, the entire Las Vegas Valley will be residential within a few years. It'll still be just a spot in an enormous desert, but it'll be a major spot. Walled-in single-family developments are going up all over, with ludicrous names like "Mountain Springs" and "Rainbow Meadows." Newly paved streets stop suddenly, and beyond them stretches the patient desert, the Mojave that waits to come back and knows it will.

There's not much graffiti in Las Vegas, hardly any by comparison to most places, but on the wall of one of those streets one of those statistically threatened kids had written: *One Step Beyond.*

I could see myself as one of those kids, sixteen, say, out on a hillside, smoking cigarettes and dope, staring at the pulsating neon in the valley down below. It's probably inevitable that I'd have known a few of the local teen suicides. Maybe I'd even thought about doing it myself. Maybe I've got a good friend; maybe we're wrecked together. We keep looking at what, from our hillside, seems a tiny neon city, a perfect plastic model city, with it's lights pinprickly clear in the desert air. We stare at it as though we're asking it a question. Its light pulsates back as though it's answering. We've lived in the capital of Anything every day of our lives, we understand the answer, even if we can't articulate it.

But . . . it doesn't apply to us. There's nothing in it about how to grow up or what to do. Anything is about the wildness at the heart of the universe. It's about Kierkegaard saying, "With God all things are possible. God *is* all things possible. All things are possible *is* God."

Which is a statement utterly beyond good and evil, as terrifying as it is hopeful. But if you're a kid it's hard to hope. You just get the terror of the Anything. And growing up becomes a matter of enduring terror. And some people just don't make it.

Part IV: The Card So High and Wild

> Like any dealer he was watching for the card that is so high and wild he'll never need to deal another.
>
> *Leonard Cohen*

Next time you're in a gambling town, stand by a roulette game a while and take in the wheel. Make sure it's a good casino—because a cheaply made roulette wheel is a sin against creation. The good ones are beautiful—shining inlaid woods, silver or gold or bone numbers. And then the wheel spins, and the colors of the wood grains blend into a smooth, shimmering, rippling circle as the numbers flash their light, and the black or silver or red ball rattles from one groove to the other till a tiny piece of fate, maybe yours, is decided. *Decided.* No argument, no appeal. The wheel is spun, the ball finds a number, and whether you bet one buck or a hundred, something is different afterward—a little different or very different, depending on the bet. And there's no going back. It's a lovely game.

Almost a ritual. Which, in fact, is how wheel, dice and card games all began (for they are many thousands of years old). Shamans invented dice, cards, and the wheel for divination and to draw powers into and out of their rituals. And the people got such a hit from those rituals that (greedy for the kick but eager to avoid the meaning, like the rest of us) they copied the shaman's tools and secularized the rituals, substituting money for spirit.

Those must have been some hellacious rituals, because thousands of years down the road, even our bastardized wheels, dice and cards often radiate of themselves and draw down the powers. I've seen it.

I was walking out of my apartment, bag packed for Vegas, an otherwise-married woman already in the air heading from another city in the United States of Anything—and the phone rings. It's a Texas friend subject to psychic flashes. "Three." "That's all you got for me?" "Three."

That night at the roulette table at . . . I think it was the Sands, I went down $180-odd bucks playing the three, playing it slowly, two or three bucks at a time. There are several ways to bet, but the most interesting are the numbers and "the corners." The odds on winning on a single number are thirty-five-to-one. Or you can put your chip on a corner where if one of four numbers wins, you win, the house paying eight-to-one. I was playing the corner of 2-3-5-6 and, simultaneously, the three.

Now, whether you're betting numbers or corners, the odds at roulette stink. ("Smart gamblers" never touch the game; they play cards or dice—much better odds.) But I fell in love with roulette the first time I sat down to it, and if I had the money and the drinking capacity I'd probably live at a roulette table and let my life go to hell.

Because of the wheel. The kick of cards is strategy—great card players are strategists, and the raw power of the cards is tempered by their knowledge of the game, their sense of when to push and when to fold and the struggle of one strategist pitting savvy and luck against another. The kick of dice is the feel of the "bones" in your hand, the static between your body and the dice—and more than that. There are so many ways to bet craps, and the pros have such a stunning, computerlike grasp of *all* the ways, that dice-feel becomes secondary to how you scope the table. And it all happens so fast, and it's a group game with shouting and groaning. But roulette—baby, it's just the wheel.

The kick of roulette is the very fact that no strategy or computation is possible. The game simply exposes you to the wheel. That's what it's there for. If you bet the corners your odds are better, but that can hardly be called a strategy. Nothing comes between you and the wheel. In roulette, all you can do is pick your numbers—and await the wheel. It's the thrill of giving yourself up to the wheel that makes a roulette player.

Okay, that's my game, and I'm playing the three. Losing $180-odd is losing 30 more dollars than I ever made in a week before the age of thirty two. It's losing the equivalent of almost five months' rent on our slum tenement in Brooklyn when I was a kid. Fuck it. Let's lose a *year* of that rent. Let's lose a *month* of those salaries. The wheel is making me crazy. Or rather, I'm relishing how my Anything rises in me as the wheel spins. That's why I'm there.

The number three hasn't come up in what seems like three-thousand years, a period with the slow-motion intensity of a car crash. Am I willing to lose my hotel money? My gas money?

Then three hits! Well, it was bound to hit once. But it keeps on hitting. It's like I've finally broken through to the wheel—finally, this once, had what every roulette player sits there for, a hotline to the wheel. The wheel has heard. The wheel, at which over the course of ten years I will lose a total of several thousand dollars. But because of this one night I won't resent a dime of the money I've lost, because tonight the ancient wheel and I are *together*, together in the cave, together in the temple, together in the energy of Anything. An unforgettable sensation, and worth the cost exacted.

So three keeps hitting with fantastic improbability. I go way over a thousand, maybe two—I wasn't counting—then three disappears for a while, I'm down to $500, and then, to show me I haven't been dreaming, the wheel starts giving me the three again. I walk away with nearly $900. But by now, I don't care any more about winning the money than I do about losing it. The money was just my way to the wheel.

In roulette you can put your bets down as long as the wheel is still spinning. Twice, around crowded tables—once at the Marina and once at the Tropicana—I've seen this: a man (not the same man twice) who's walking quickly past the table stops short; looks sharply at the table, the way you turn around when somebody unexpectedly calls out your name; and, without hesitating an instant, reaches out his arm and slams down some chips on a number. And the number wins.

What I saw at those roulette games were two Masters of Anything tuned to a pitch of trancelike awareness wherein they could hear the wheel. What a thing that must be for them, to go in and out of. Because the likelihood is that they are not very conscious individuals—it's very hard on your consciousness when the dominant (and not very merciful) culture has no room for your talents and tendencies. In the first place, you tend to accept the culture's definitions—"sick," "crazy," "compulsive," what all—you learned them so young you can't help it. In the second place, what you have a talent for goes on in a shadow world, an underworld where sensitivity and vulnerability are not exactly rewarded.

So you don't know what your powers are for. You think they're for gambling, for money, and they fade in and out, and drive you mad and broke. You don't know that if you had lived a few thousand years ago you might have been a shaman and the wheel and the dice and the cards would have spoken very differently to your spirit.

Part V: The Family Slot

Las Vegas—The American Way to Play!
Santa Monica Freeway billboard

Until recently the ancient ways of the wheel, the dice and the cards were how Vegas made its money. Slots weren't considered a draw and weren't advertised. As one casino owner quaintly put it, the slots were there "for the wives." (To my eye, the male–female ratio for roulette and blackjack is about even, but poker and craps are overwhelmingly male.) But now that the emphasis is on "family casinos," the slots are the big draw.

Wait a minute, hit the pause button—*"family* casino"? Isn't that a contradiction in terms? Real average American families, with working mothers, overextended credit, where the television's on six to ten hours a day, where the kids score abysmally on tracking tests, where fathers spend less than ten minutes daily talking to their kids, and where there's a 50-percent chance of the whole shebang ending in divorce? *Those* families? What are they doing here?

Mostly the grown-ups (who plan the vacations, after all) are playing the slots.

An interesting thing about old-timey gambling is that (unless you bet on bridge, which isn't a Vegas game) you bet alone—but the game itself creates a brief community. You play cards *with* people. Craps is pointless without several bettors. As for roulette, there are few things more desolate than being the only one at the table. And couples can play roulette standing beside each other (though I prefer the woman to be across the table where I can see *her* better). Same with craps. And you can have fun, cheer each other on, give each other good or bad luck, get jealous, feel neglected, feel close. You've bet the same number and it wins and you've both won a hundred bucks and are juiced enough to take it for a sign that the wheel approves your love. In short, human contact. Real life. Anything can happen.

But slots and video poker—these are not Anything games. You don't get excited; you get dazed. Watch these people. Even when they win their expressions don't change. The masturbatory slow-motion pulling of the lever lulls you into a timeless nether-mood. You're not surrendering to even a bastardized technique of divination; you're giving yourself up to a computer into which you have no input but coins. And unlike the wheel or dice, that computer is not governed by the Goddess's sense of humor. (The ancient games go back to the time of the Goddess religions.) The fix is in, it's been programmed, there are X many times it's going to lose—something that was decided long before you said, "Honey, let's go to Vegas."

And where *is* honey, by the way? Working a machine on another aisle, usually. Slots are the loneliest way to bet.

No community. No contact. Little to cheer about. Nothing to fight about. Interesting that the family crowd seems to prefer the games you play alone. Most people don't magically transform on a vacation (at least not without a good dose of Anything), so playing-games-alone is probably the way they are at home, too.

And yes, there's a lot more for families to do than slots—there's the Gold Coast Casino, for instance, with its seventy-two bowling lanes, two first-run movie houses, and day care for the kids till midnight. There's Circus Circus, with a different circus act every hour. And lots of places have golf, tennis, swimming, shows, rodeos, an aquatic park for the kids—and all of that not-wildly-profitable stuff is supplied for one very profitable reason: the slots.

The Gold Coast has all those nice family things—and 2,000 video poker and slot machines. Because that's what people mostly do. Dazed. Alone. The way they secretly feel inside their own homes.

And why come to Vegas for it? Maybe it has something to do with

Heaven. For to do nothing special in Paradise, to have all your needs tended while you stare and twiddle your thumbs (or pull levers) in the general vicinity of Anything—is pretty much the image most people have of Heaven.

Bugsy's idea of Paradise has mingled with the Mormon family idea of Paradise to attract Christians who've given up all hope of Paradise.

For now that America has gotten so dangerous, now that it can offer no safety, no security, no sense that the future will be worth waiting for—Vegas seems more and more safe. In a U.S. of A. that now stands for the United States of Anything, the way Vegas does Anything is comparatively well ordered. Not like the Anything at home, unadmitted and repressed and ricocheting off the headlines, from the television, out of your kids' eyes, and out of the way you hate your job but have to say you love your life or you're not a good American. No, now you can come to Vegas to get away from all that. Here the sex and danger and stealing and phoniness and chintz are completely up front, not repressed at all. You don't have to wonder about them or be afraid they'll ambush you. You can pick and choose among them. Vegas is the shopping mall of Anything. The American Way to Play.

These folks are just hanging out at the mall. And they queue up for the bargain buffets, stand in line for an hour to save the five bucks they'll blow in the next hour on the nickel slots. Anyway, room service would make them too nervous, it's not nickel by nickel; you *know* you're spending money with room service. They want to spend without knowing. (They elect people to run their country that way, too.) Nickels. Quarters at the most. More than a billion bucks' worth per year.

Family casinos. Talk about Anything. Who would ever have imagined family casinos? What fat Rand Corporation futurist would have predicted that someday such a town would draw the average American family to the tune of 17.5 million people a year? And now there are Vegas-style casinos in Atlantic City and Canada. Soon there'll be more in South Dakota, Indiana, Iowa, Kansas and Ohio. While the country *pretends* that it's more and more conservative. Votes for faceless rich people as a way to lie to itself, as a way to convince itself that it *really* still believes in values vaguely associated with the nineteenth century or the Bible or sitcoms or something. While it sinks deeper and deeper into Anything.

These folks don't play the wheel, but that doesn't matter. The wheel spins. The inlaid woods shine. The numbers flash. There's nothing between you and the wheel. There never was. There never will be. The rest is a lot of rhetoric and bustle. It doesn't matter whether any particular wheel is played or not, the wheel's on fire anyway, the cold fire of Anything, and whether or not you play the wheel, the wheel plays you. Which is, finally, what Vegas has to teach. Not a lesson but a question: Are you playing the game, or is the game playing you?

The desert won't tell and the wheel won't stop.

February 2, 1990

Grand Illusion

Eve Babitz said it in one of the best (and surely the gentlest) books about our town, *Slow Days, Fast Company* (1977): "In Los Angeles it's hard to tell if you're dealing with the real true illusion or the false one." This confusion, not between reality and illusion but between illusion and illusion, goes back a long way in these parts. In the sixteenth century our state was named after a fifteenth-century Spanish novel portraying a miragelike paradise called "California." (The woman who wrote the novel made up the word like a song, for its sound.) See, even California's first westerners were smitten with this land's air of mirage.

They named its first legendary city (somewhere to the north of us) after an infinitely kind man who spoke to birds, furniture and fire because he believed they could understand him; who ministered to lepers; and who, according to witnesses, sometimes floated several feet above the ground. The city of San Francisco has tried to live up to Francis of Assisi, and on occasion (festively during the Summer of Love and seriously in its response to AIDS) has succeeded.

But while San Francisco was named after a real person, our town was named after beings (angels) who, according to science, do not exist. Science has been wrong before, and if you choose to believe in angels your belief will be tolerated in literate society provided you keep it to yourself. If, however, you *insist* angels exist you're apt to be shunned or even put away. So Los Angeles was named after beings who don't exist but can get you arrested.

91

And then there's Hollywood, the most famous name associated with Los Angeles. Do you know there isn't any such plant as a "hollywood"? At the turn of the century a real-estate promoter supposedly heard the word "hollywood" on a train and coined the name "Hollywood-land" because he thought it would sell back East; *he* built the sign, before the movie people ever got here. Later they took off the "land" part. At present the word "hollywood," intended to describe a hillside, means "American movies," "ultimate glamour," "bottomless deceit," and all that's associated with how we film fantasies in the town named after the beings who don't exist in the state named after the paradise that doesn't exist.

By the way—most movies in this town were never made in Hollywood. Even in the early days, when the name stuck, there was more filmmaking in Silver Lake, Glendale, Burbank, Echo Park, Los Feliz and Culver City.

All of which is to say that around here identity problems seem literally to come with the territory. I mean, it's not that way back East or in the various Wests (Mid-, North- and South-). New York was named after the Duke of York, Harlem was named after a Dutch farmer. Virginia was the queen's nickname, Washington was the name of Washington. Or they'd steal Indian names. Or the place-names would be descriptive: Tombstone, Muleshoe, Wounded Knee, Twin Peaks (which *is* what people in those parts call those mountains). No way around it, most of the country's names have some basis in reality. While with California, Los Angeles, Hollywood and Echo Park (think about *that* name for a while), the basis is precisely the opposite: unreality. Surreality. *Our* reality.

Can you sniff the whiff of destiny? From the start, this place was drawn irresistibly into the No Person's Land between "the real true illusion and the false one." But Eve Babitz goes one better in *L.A. Woman* (1982). She suggests that, even though everyone complains about this ethereality of ours, it is in fact why we come and why we stay. (Which is a good spot to ask if you've noticed that many move from New York to L.A., but almost no one moves from L.A. to New York.) We come and we stay because conceptually Los Angeles is an unmarked town. No boundaries. You can reinvent yourself to your own private specifications. In New York you ultimately have to assume the trappings of a New Yorker if you want to be taken seriously. In the South you have to learn what they consider their manners. But in L.A. you're judged only by the integrity and effectiveness of your self-creation.

Which, like everything else, has its down side, articulated best by Steve Erickson in a 1986 interview:

> Los Angeles is a blank slate on which you can write basically what you want to . . . [and that's] why so many people who come here wind up so lost. Because if you live in New York you may not know who you are but you know you're a New Yorker. You don't have that here. If you come here expecting the city is going to give you some kind of identity, you're going to wind up one of those crazy people walking Hollywood Boulevard. It's a great town for self-invention, but the problem with self-invention is you've got to know what you're inventing. You've got to come here with some sense of self.

Yet maybe those who babble on Hollywood Boulevard are the lucky ones. Madness is *some* identity. But what of all those people from Texas, Minnesota and Massachusetts who come here before they've understood how much their personal-*ity* was really just a present from home? A Southern Belle's charming drawl, a New Englander's manly reticence, a Midwesterner's agreeableness, a New Yorker's skepticism . . . are often accidents of place that have little to do with one's deepest nature. In fact, the qualities grafted upon us by the style of our locales serve usually to hide our true natures from ourselves.

Which catches new residents of Los Angeles in a paradox. If they've depended more than they realized on former environments for their identity, that identity gradually will thin and dissipate the longer they stay. They'll feel less and less like themselves, and the only newness they'll feel is a kind of confused diminishment. At parties you'll hear them blame that on L.A., when the real problem is they never knew themselves in the first place. Or, worse, the jellylike vagueness that soaks this town will frighten them into a hasty or flashy reinvention of their personas from all the wrong parts. You see such people all the time around here, sad walking collages of misconceptions and fear, wearing whatever mask it was easiest to make, whether it's West L.A. yuppie, showbiz wiz or arts-crowd snide-mouth—living lives that have nothing to do with their eyes.

These conditions are all the more dangerous for being so subtle. Sensing this, people look upon the bright sunlight of the place with a kind of squinting foreboding.

The sense that this town is, as Joan Didion called it, "the intersection of nothing," a mirage, a vampire of identity, was noticed fifty years ago by Nathanael West in what is still the finest novel written about L.A., *The Day of the Locust* (1939). He saw that everybody was in costume, all the time:

> As he walked along, he examined the evening crowd. A great many of the people wore sports clothes which were not really sports clothes. Their sweaters, slacks, blue flannel jackets with brass buttons were fancy dress. The fat lady in the yachting cap was going shopping, not boating; the man in the Norfolk jacket and Tyrolean hat was returning, not from a mountain, but an insurance office; and the girl in slacks and sneaks with a bandana around her head had just left a switchboard, not a tennis court.

That's true of everywhere now (denims were the workwear of farmers, remember), but in those days it was only true of L.A. Which is to say, it started here. Or to put it in a more accurate way: the slippage of Western identity and culture manifested first in this newest and least Western of the developed world's great cities; the city that came to fame by producing images that these older, sterner places could not help but gobble up and imitate. They've never forgiven us for feeding and hence exposing their secretly weak self-worth and its accompanying hunger for shameless fantasy—lacks they'd hidden well until they were unable to resist Hollywood's imagery.

Raymond Chandler said in *The Long Goodbye* (1953): "In Hollywood anything can happen, anything at all." (As opposed to places like Mississippi or Boston, where only Mississippian or Bostonian things tend to happen.) Chandler meant that sentence in the most sinister sense possible. Eve Babitz put it gentler yet scarier: "There was no point in owning anything in Hollywood." Nathanael West thought all the "glories" of Western history would end as useless, discarded props in a junk heap on a studio backlot. And Steve Erickson has seen, with the eye of his prose, desert sands blow in while the seas slowly rise on a people with so little sense of self left that they pretend not to notice.

A city named after sacred but imaginary beings, in a state named after a paradise that was the figment of a woman's dream; a city that came to fame by filming such figments; a city existing now on sufferance from the ever-hotter desert and the ever-rising sea, and that feels every day, to so many of us, like a mirage as it waits for its great quake. Its suffering is real enough, God knows. But its beauty is the beauty of letting go: letting go of where you came from; letting go of old lessons; letting go of what you want for what you are, or what you are for what you want; letting go of so much—and that is a hard beauty to love.

September 21, 1990

The Great Bay Area Quake

Disaster Area: 17 October 1989

Maybe I'm drawn to earthquakes. Three of my seven have been on trips far from L.A.—one in Mexico, one in the desert, and this time in Oakland. So far I've been on fairly good terms with my earthquake-self. There's this odd, sudden, happy feeling he gets—he sort of *likes* earthquakes. And he's much faster than I usually am, and he thinks with far more directness and clarity. In Oakland, he would have been out the back door in two seconds, but my friend Dave's earthquake-self yelled, "The kids!"

My earthquake-self doesn't have kids. So I had to step in and restrain my quake-self from running swiftly outside, had to make him wait while Dave dashed up the swaying stairs to get eight-year-old Gareth and twelve-year-old Becky. But it was my quake-self who was clear enough to think, "Don't go with him, you're the back-up. If a falling wall or a collapsing staircase gets you both, the kids have no back-up." I wasn't quick enough to think this on my own, but my quake-self knew, so I stood in a strategic spot in the kitchen doorjamb waiting, watching, listening, till Dave was back—it seemed to take so long, but I think they were down before the shaking stopped, so it was within fifteen seconds—and the kids were ahead of us out of the house.

Standing in Dave's back yard, I was fairly happy with my quake-self, because when the quake had hit I had just poured a mug of Dave's home-brew, and it was still in my hand, still full. My quake-self has to be reminded to think of anybody but me, but he moves fast, doesn't flake out and doesn't waste beer, at least not Dave's beer, which is the best beer I've ever had. Dave's quake-self had had other things on his mind, so Dave had to go back in the house for his beer, after-shock or no aftershock.

Some of our fear of disaster isn't a fear of the event, it is the fear of ourselves: of which self among all the selves we contain will sud-denly leap out and *be* Michael or Dave or you, getting us through with or without grace. That's why people are trained so strenuously for combat or to fight fires—so that that particular action-self can be met and developed before the event. Disasters don't give us that chance. The world is out of control, and we are out of control—some stranger in the psyche is acting on our part, for good or for ill, and it's not till the action's over that the part we call "I" is back and has to remember, reconcile and live with those incredibly quick, decisive moments when our usual "I" was barely present.

So for Dave, the kids and me, the shake itself wasn't that bad. It was the next few moments that shocked us more. Standing on the steep, tiered land behind Dave's house and looking out at Oakland, we could see that for other people this had been bad, really bad, and it could get worse, for them and for us.

Dave lives in a neighborhood of steep hills and winding streets. Somewhere beyond the next hill a thick black plume of smoke rose into the sky. A big fire. Had the water pipes burst under the streets? Because if they had, there wouldn't be any water pressure, and without water pressure a fire department is useless. It was a shock to realize that even the most modern of cities could burn to the ground if only a few of the major pipes cracked.

As it turned out, some pipes had cracked, but most hadn't. Still, it was my first realization that all the talk of "preparation" doesn't mean very much. If "The Big One" is thirty-three times worse than this, as they say it will be, a lot of pipes are going to crack. In North Hollywood, I live near a fire station. The sirens wail six, eight, ten times a day. Sometimes more. Fire happens a lot on the most normal of days. What happens if there's no water pressure for even one day?

"Dave, you all right?" an old man's voice called from over the fence. Dave called back and asked if the man needed any help checking the gas. Dave is the sort of man you want in your life raft or in your disaster—he knows how things are made and how they work and what to do with them when they don't. He knows how to check for gas leaks, how to find your gas main, how to shut it off. I didn't. Some of the neighbors didn't either. One old woman wasn't strong enough. I realized that if this had happened at home I'd be relying on a neighbor to know what Dave knows. But what if that neighbor's relying on me?

The kids, still jittery, went with us to the front of the house. Neighbors had gathered, talking, huddling. No smell of gas anywhere on the street. The power was out. It would probably be okay to light candles. I lit a cigar. We were hearing sirens now. The smoke over the hill was blacker and thicker. Nobody was ready to go back into their houses yet.

Anne came home—she had seen a hospital wave in the air like a bamboo pole, and the structure she was in (an adjacent hospital) had cracked in at least one place. Most of the things that cracked were made of brick—in Oakland, this included government buildings that were supposedly up to code. I see lots of brick in L.A. It's hard to believe that a quake thirty-three times worse than the Bay Area quake is going to leave much brick standing, no matter how "reinforced."

And then it got dark. Which is when the term "disaster area" began to reveal its meaning. So far, on this street, nothing terrible had happened to anyone. The children had been frightened, but now they were bored. Or so they said, while storing their fears for future reference and bickering about who did what to whom. The grownups had done what grownups are supposed to do. And everyone had enough water, food, candles, flashlights, batteries—for a night, but not more. And this was the situation for the great majority of Bay Area people. Then Dave found an old transistor radio—and that's when we found out how cut off we were.

Maybe the rest of the world knew what was going on, watching it on television through World Series hookups—but, in this so-called "information age," we learned that what stops first in a disaster is information. Information is, it turns out, a very vulnerable commodity. It is not an exaggeration to say that *nobody* in the Bay Area, nobody from Santa Cruz north to Oakland, knew much of anything. Except what was right in front of their eyes. That, and the sound of sirens.

Televisions were useless. Even the few people who had power had trouble with reception unless they had satellite dishes—the local transmitters and cable sources apparently were out. Which left battery-powered radios—if you had one.

But at the radio stations, power was out too. They were operating on minimal auxillary power. Their computers were down. Their wire services were down. Their television hookups to the outside world were down. *Their* only way of getting information was by phone—and phone service was at first problematic, and then next to impossible. Someone, somewhere was always managing to get through, and the station would broadcast the call, but there was little information, and certainly no comfort. Nothing but fragmentary impressions like ours that couldn't convey the extent or depth of the emergency.

One radio station suddenly went off the air—when you're sitting in the dark and that sound is your only connection (however inadequate) to the rest of the world, the sudden silence is in some ways scarier than the quake. These radio announcers also indulged liberally in the ridiculous. Highway splits that were plenty big enough to wreck cars were called "road discrepancies."

The radio stations did manage two-way radio hookups to helicopters, but the connections were bad—often every third word of a broadcast was lost. They broadcast it anyway because it was all they had.

And even if the connections had been good, how much can a chopper see of a blacked-out city? The choppers could spot the fires and crisis-points like the Nimitz and the Bay Bridge that were lit by headlights and flashlights, but the little information they had often turned out to be false. All the choppers could do accurately was tell how traffic was moving in the blacked-out city—something at least useful to people in their cars. But assessing damage to roads and bridges was pure guesswork. In fact, some bridge damage—to the San Mateo, on which traffic had moved almost the whole time—wasn't discovered till two days after the quake.

At first, the phones were working. I managed to get through to L.A. twice in the first half hour or so. But then they weren't. For what seemed a long time you couldn't get through to anywhere. What happens if there's a bad aftershock? Or a fire spreads? Or there's looting? Now, even if we had to call the fire department or the police, we could not. We were on our own.

Take that in for a minute. All in all, Oakland and San Francisco weren't that badly damaged. Except for the Nimitz and the Marina district, damage, injury and fatality were comparatively minor. But the city was helpless. Communications were down. Nobody knew what was going on. Officials took hours to find any way to *be* official, and then they weren't much use. The only really functioning units seemed to be the fire departments, and they could only go where they were called *and* where there was water pressure. Even though there were few fires, compared to what might have been, they were taxed to their limit.

If the Bay Area's 7.1 quake is any clue, there isn't any "preparation" I've heard of that's remotely capable of coping with an 8.0 "big one." Without communications you can't get help where it's needed, and without water pressure fires will burn out of control. If streets are blocked by downed power-lines, phone poles and rubble, there won't even be mobility for a long time, no way for help to get to you, no way to leave where you are, especially if you're injured or are caring for the injured. Helicopters can come in and bring out the injured— but how do they know where to go if you can't call them, how do they fly in a sky blackened by many fires, and how many helicopters do you think it would take to service an area of roughly thirteen million people? That's about the number of people who live between the San Andreas Fault and the ocean in Southern California. In a disaster of this magnitude, every last one of us is on our own.

Becky, thinking better than the grownups, thought to fill all the available containers with water, in case an aftershock broke the pipes; but none of us thought to put some of those containers outside, in case an aftershock broke the house. It didn't look like anybody else on the block thought of it either. Our useful quake-action selves had gone back to wherever they go when they're not standing in door-jambs or rescuing kids, and we were a bunch of dazed people wanting information, huddled around a few transistor radios—and the broadcasters had nothing to tell us except that there'd been a big earthquake. Something we sort of knew.

The officials aren't going to say it outright, partly because they are officials and partly because people don't want to believe that such things happen, but the Big One is going to go something like this:

A lot of structures are going to fall down, including buildings and bridges and roads that you've been promised won't fall down. (The Nimitz had been repeatedly inspected and reported to be sound.) Power, phones, communications of every sort—won't exist. The only thing you'll know for sure is what you can see in front of you. There will be little, if any, water pressure. There will be many fires. Fallen power-lines, poles, and buildings will make much of the area impassable. All you can depend on for two days at least, and quite possibly for ten (it's two days after the quake as I write, and Santa Cruz is still without power and water), is how you and your neighbors have prepared—food, water, skills, medical supplies. And your relation-ship with your neighbors may well become the most important thing in your life—your life, in fact, may depend on them.

It might be a good idea, before the Big One, to learn your neighbors' names.

October 27, 1989

You, in Particular, Are Going to Die—No Matter What You Eat, How You Exercise, or How Much Money You Have

The Health of the Country

The Statistics are overwhelming: we're sick.

It's not just that we have the most overweight population in the West, nor that we have the highest infant mortality rate of any industrialized country in the world. It's not that heart disease is the worst epidemic since the Plague, not that *one in three* Americans will get cancer, not that it's been documented beyond quibbling that most of this pain could be prevented by more naturally grown food, fewer chemicals in the environment, less rat-racing and more exercise. It's not even that our young people, in addition to being the most ignorant, are also the fattest, the wheeziest, the least physically active and the most neglected (thirteen million latchkey children under the age of fourteen) of any developed country on Earth. No, the sickest thing about us is:

That we hear these facts over and over again (the data are undeniable and have been broadcast for years), yet, as a people, we do nothing. And we tolerate elected representatives who do worse than nothing, who collaborate in causing these conditions. Their re-election coffers bulge with dollars contributed by the same corporations that, in effect, sell ill health in pretty packages.

So we're not just sick—we're crazy. Because it's crazy to have had the information for years and to have done next to nothing.

We're so dazed we can't seem to take in two congruent facts. One: the United States is the least healthy major industrialized nation. Two: the United States is the only major industrialized nation without nationalized health care. The American people, their government, insurance companies and the American Medical Association act as though these two facts have nothing to do with each other. Which is to say, the politicians are killing us because they don't want to make waves; the insurance lobbies are killing us because nationalized health care would gut their power base; the doctors are killing us because they want to die rich; and we're killing ourselves by letting these bastards get away with killing us.

We can't seem to see what's in front of our eyes. When asked, as a people, to describe ourselves, we give dysfunctional answers, answers that are contradictory and/or don't correspond to reality. On the first day of the 1990s, the *Los Angeles Times* published the results of a nationwide poll in which it reported that "only 5 percent of Americans consider themselves to be in poor health"—despite massive data to the contrary; 89 percent claim to be "satisfied" with "the way your life is going," although 25 percent "feel unsafe walking alone at night in their own neighborhoods," while half of us keep a gun in our homes, and "one in 10 reported that they or a member of their household has been the victim of a serious crime *in the past year*" (my italics). One in ten Americans has considered suicide; 47 percent claim to be satisfied with the "national situation," yet 65 percent are dissatisfied with the nation's "moral values"; 87 percent are satisfied with their communities, although it's practically impossible for a middle-income American child to go to a first-rate high school, and although these same pollees overwhelmingly "regard crime as 'the single most urgent problem facing this country today.'" And if 87 percent are satisfied with their communities, why do so many of us feel we need a gun?

During the eighties, as reported in *USA Today*, handguns alone killed more than 75,000 Americans. That's half again as many as died in Vietnam. Dig it: in ten years of a shooting war, fewer Americans got shot dead than during ten years of "peace" in their own country. Yet 89 percent claim to be satisfied.

This poll describes, albeit unintentionally, a dysfunctional population—a population incapable of connecting the dots. People who can't describe themselves can't change. (At least not consciously.) All of which may be connected to the scariest statistic of all, parroted proudly by Walter Cronkite on a recent special celebrating the fiftieth year of television: "In this country we do more TV watching a day than anything else except sleep."

Take that in. As a people, we watch television more than we work, more than we play, more than we talk, more than we fuck, more than we walk, more than we do *anything* except sleep. Watching television and sleeping constitute the bulk of our collective life.

What is such a people loyal to? What can such a people believe in? What can such a people contribute? Is it so surprising that these are the unhealthiest people in the developed world? And the dumbest? (Last October, reported the *L.A. Times*, 55 percent of college seniors miserably flunked a test on "basics" designed for seventeen-year-olds.) Will history one day describe us as a culture that lulled itself, technologically, into a state of trance—a trance so deep that the culture could no longer make sense of the information crucial to maintain itself?

This is where you have to start when you talk about health in America: that, when compared to much of the world, we have become a physically weak people, in a plagued environment, suffering from a self-induced state of severe dysfunction.

Specter No. 1: Drugs

Fact: Dr. Ronald K. Siegel, author of *Intoxication*, has been quoted as saying that tobacco kills 1,000 Americans per day (*L.A. Times*, 14 August 1989). The *Times* did not challenge the figure, and new information suggests that it may be low. Current research on the lethal effects of "indoor pollution," primarily tobacco smoke, may drive the statistics much higher.

Yet tobacco, though medically addictive, is a legal drug. Advertised.

Sold freely. Still accepted in most places as a social institution. The movement against smoking grows stronger every year, but cigarette sales are still brisk. Another little-known fact is that, again according to the *Times*, 125,000 Americans die every year from prescription-drug "problems." Doctor prescribes a drug, patient takes the drug, and zap. Either one of these figures (365,000 tobacco casualties, 125,000 prescription-drug mistakes), much less the two figures combined, describes many, many more than the total number of people killed by heroin, crack, coke, PCP, handguns *and* AIDS yearly. (In fact, the total number of Americans with AIDS from January 1984 to June 1989 was estimated by the Centers for Disease Control at 115,158).

Many studies suggest that it's the very illegality of drugs that causes the trouble. If drugs weren't illegal, the crime rate would dip way, way down. Prescription drugs are more fatal, alcohol is as degenerative, and tobacco is far more fatal *and* degenerative. Why, then, the terrible fear of the illegal, mind-altering drugs? Plainly the society, at least as expressed by its government, doesn't want minds to alter. *That's* the crime as the society sees it; and thus far it's been willing to tolerate the worst levels of violence and imprisonment in Western social history in order to insist that mind-altering is criminal.

Is this, or is this not, collectively dysfunctional: creating conditions of massive violence in order to eradicate a non-violent practice? Is American society so uncertain of its own concept of "mind" that it's literally driven crazy by any other state of mind? And must all of our lives be disrupted by this institutionalized insecurity?

Remember that massive drug use is strictly an American problem. In Europe, and in most of the rest of the world, a tiny percentage of the society uses drugs, and the crime rate is minuscule in comparison to that of the United States. America is *the* drug market. Americans use the drugs partly to get into other states of mind, and partly as a desperate reaction against the general dysfunction of their society; and their society responds—through its institutions, dysfunctionally— against all the studies, against all the data, i.e., against reality, and creates a situation ultimately much more dangerous to its people and its institutions than the use of mind-altering drugs could ever be.

This is madness. This is a society putting itself at risk—for no goddamned reason. Who can speak of "health" in a society like this?

Specter No. 2: AIDS

Statistically, it's unlikely that AIDS will ever equal heart disease as a killer. Yet the causes of heart disease are comparatively easy to tend. So why did it take the heart-disease activists the better part of a century to create the level of awareness that the AIDS activists have created in less than a decade? Because when you think "heart disease," you don't think "sex."

Remember that tobacco kills a thousand Americans per day.

If AIDS were killing a thousand Americans per *day* (in 1988 the figure averaged about eighty per day), the country would be in a state of total hysteria. Every newscaster would knell the previous day's death figure—a little higher or lower than a thousand. Everywhere people would be horrified into sexual paralysis by "the Plague." Billions would be spent on research. The culture, from its heights to its depths, would be in a state of alternately panicked and stupefied shock.

I suspect that, as has happened during many of history's plagues, people would need a scapegoat, and that gays, artists and bohemians in general would be mobbed and murdered everywhere—would, in fact, feel lucky if they were only penned up by a government that had suspended all civil rights for the duration of the emergency. For few would question that the random and premature deaths of a thousand people a day constitute an emergency.

I don't mean to minimize the horrors of AIDS. Especially if you've done some walking on the wild side, you can't have a persistent cold without feeling some real fear. And I won't pretend to comprehend how it must feel to be part of a community that's been decimated, and for whom friends' deaths have become part of the fabric of life. But I think AIDS strikes the imagination as viciously as it does the body, not because it's a difficult death (rare is the death that is pretty or easy); nor because it tends to fell people who are still comparatively young (so do cancer and heart disease, now, and with far greater frequency); and certainly not because of the numbers of dead. No, AIDS has become mythic among us for three reasons: there's as yet no reprieve; it doesn't hit you alone, but threatens your most precious intimates; and conceptually and physically, AIDS combines three things that stir up Americans like nothing else—sex, death and homophobia.

If AIDS were caused, say, environmentally, or genetically, would it have become mythic? A reasonably cautious heterosexual's chance of contracting AIDS is far, far less than one in three, which is his/her chance of getting cancer. I am *not* suggesting reckless behavior, but I am saying that, for people who are not high-risk, what's behind the panic over AIDS is that it's a convenient way to mask and act out fears that have deeply infected them all their lives—sex, death and homophobia. Not to mention the almost equally potent fear of freedom: fear of AIDS serves the many people who want to run back to the culture's old strictures because they're frightened of their own psyches.

In this way, AIDS (to paraphrase Susan Sontag) is disease-as-metaphor as much as disease-as-virus. And, as a metaphor, as a channel of our worst fears, it infects people. So, among those who aren't high-risk, the *perception* of AIDS is dysfunctional. Statistically, they're in far more jeopardy from prescription drugs, tobacco and fatty foods—but they feel a good deal more threatened by sex. Not to mention being threatened by having to admit that no matter how much exercise you get, no matter how well you eat, no matter how much money you have, you are very certainly going to die. You're going to fucking *die*. And it's probably going to hurt. A lot. And you're probably not going to be able to pick the time or place, and you might have to go it alone.

Other cultures have found paths toward dignity in the face of these inevitable facts. I don't know whether their practices made dying any easier, but they seem to have made living more meaningful. In American culture, we find the facts sort of shameful. As we get older we feel not that our bodies are doing what they're naturally supposed to do, looking like they're supposed to look—we feel our bodies have betrayed us somehow. We walk around as though we've been made some sort of promise that we can defy the laws of life and death—if we believe the right things, or eat the right things, or do the right things, or make enough money.

AIDS charges at our psyches like a dragon and gobbles those illusions and vomits them all over our insides as we sleep. Most of us aren't going to get AIDS, but all of us are terrified at what it makes us think about: the diseased thing in us that fucks when we do and sometimes turns the meaning of the act into something nearly unbearable; the fag and/or dyke within who sometimes gives us desires we think will destroy us; and death, death, death, which is coming, coming, coming, for me, you, everyone.

That's a lot to fear, and aren't we lucky we can cloak all that fear in one word: AIDS. But to do that, to cloak such core issues in fears that are not statistically very rational—is, uh, dysfunctional. Makes you crazy. Makes me crazy.

And, as I've said, we're crazy enough. How much crazier can we get? What can be the meaning of "health" in a world where so much craziness overlaps?

Health in L.A.

Health in L.A.? Don't make me laugh. I was in the Bay Area quake, remember?

To live between Blythe on the east and the Pacific Palisades on the west, between San Diego on the south and roughly Santa Barbara on the north—is to live in the path of a locomotive, of ten thousand locomotives, of a quake big enough to collapse thousands of structures, kill (at its worst) tens of thousands of people, and threaten millions of others with injury, illness, radiation (from the atomic reactors to the north and south of us), chaos and more assorted kinds of trouble than any one human being should have to imagine, much less live through.

And there are at present thirteen million of us who are in for this experience, maybe tomorrow, maybe twenty years from now, maybe fifty—the scientists don't know. All they know is that it's on its way. The pressure has already built up on the various faults. It's *got* to go— maybe before you finish reading this article.

So everybody in L.A. is playing a kind of roulette with their survival. Hoping it won't happen while they're in town, or while they're alive; hoping that it will be worse toward Indio or San Diego, and we'll just get the ends of it; or hoping even if their roof falls in they'll survive, and that all their loved ones will survive. Everybody knows the facts and ignores them at the same time. Again, a kind of dysfunction. Go to the gym, eat health foods, don't allow anyone to smoke in your presence—and wait for the Big One.

Yet L.A. is the best place in the world to get sick—if you have money. For people with money, L.A. is the capital of health and can claim the widest variety of straight and alternative healers—M.D.'s, chiropractors, acupuncturists, kinesiologists, herbalists, psychic healers, masseurs and every conceivable form of therapy. (For people without money, L.A.'s just a lot of electricity at the far end of the desert.)

I suspect that these two facts—the Capital of Health and the Big One—are related. I suspect that L.A. in particular, and California in general, is the most health-conscious place in the Western world because on some level everybody here lives with the Big One. What we ignore collectively one way, we compensate for collectively in another. And it's not a bad way of being crazy, as crazy goes, and it makes for a higher concentration of beautiful bodies than anywhere else in the country.

L.A. demands a certain standard of beauty—and if you're not beautiful, the least it demands of you is style. Whatever the style of your social circle is—Rodeo Drive or post-punk, the Polo Lounge or the Palomino—L.A. equates health with beauty and style with knowledge. Questionable equations at best (what many do for beauty strains health, and style comes far easier than knowledge), but it makes for a certain panache. It was Hemingway who gave us the idea that L.A., and places like L.A., lives on: that in a morally bereft world, style can function as a kind of ethic, and beauty can pass for grace. For L.A. more than anywhere treats health as something primarily *aesthetic*. This is a weirdly attractive dysfunction, but it's unlikely that treating health as fashion is ultimately good for one's grasp of reality. And how can you be truly healthy without a reasonable grasp of reality?

Meanwhile, far beneath our feet, the earth slowly shifts. One day it will snap. Tonight. Fifty years from now. And everybody in L.A. knows it. And they stay anyway. They *move* here. In droves. (The population increased by more than 10 percent in the eighties.) Why do they come? Why do they stay? Money? Bravado? Denial? A combination of all three?

Either way, it doesn't sound terribly healthy, does it? And when you see "health" in that frame—and frame it further by the general, and often lethal, dysfunctions of America, which are more prevalent in

L.A. than in most places—then you see that the health movement in Los Angeles is essentially a cosmetic. People hide in their health the way they hide in their money or their beauty or in any other of the fragile belief structures that shield them, temporarily, from the general dysfunction.

The Health of the Planet

There is no way around the fact that we are involved with each other. It is still one of the greatest expressions of our language, a truth the rest of the world is remembering though we seem to have forgotten it in our shared trance, namely, John Donne's "No man is an island . . . any man's death diminishes me, because I am involved in mankind. Therefore send not to know for whom the bell tolls. It tolls for thee."

It would be lovely to stop there—because that would put the entire problem in our hands, and, as shaky as our hands may be, it would be like a Frank Capra film to think that we could change things if only we could learn to care.

Except that we've infected the planet itself. It has a fever. Its fever is called "the greenhouse effect." I've read enough to be more convinced than my president that it exists, and that it's going to change everything. (The six warmest years on record are 1988, 1987, 1983, 1981, 1980, and 1986.) It's such a huge thing that it might not matter at all whether or not Bush is convinced. If the negative feedback effect has cut in, it's already too big to do anything about. In that case, in twenty years L.A. will probably be a ghost town. There won't be enough water within a thousand miles to sustain it. On top of which the sea will have risen, and the place will look like a Steve Erickson cityscape of blowing sand and submerged streets. All that real estate you thought would sustain you in your old age? You may spend your old age begging for food in a refugee camp in Canada. And the homeless whose eyes you've avoided will be cackling at you from up there in Homeless Heaven.

Do you know what even a *mild* greenhouse effect is going to do to your country, your beauty, your health, your life? The World Watch Institute reported that in 1988, for the first time, "America ate more food than it grew." Can you make time to comprehend what that means when combined with the greenhouse effect?

The planet probably doesn't mind. To the planet it may be less a fever than a ripple of hyperactivity, a flush, a blush, a hard-on. (It's Father Earth as well as Mother Earth, I'm sure.) Perhaps the planet could care less. It may even be enjoying itself. We have no idea and no way of knowing. (Anyway, we're made of the planet, we're just the planet on two legs, so who knows what the planet's doing? It may be as crazy as we are.)

Still, and despite our ignorance in such matters, the point is that your health cannot be disengaged from the society's, and the society's health cannot be disengaged from the planet's. And until we accept these facts—nobody can say truly that they are healthy. Not without cutting themselves off in a very unhealthy manner from level upon level of reality. To be physically astute and psychologically tended, yet morally insulated and conceptually blind—is to be crazy, not healthy. To the point where our very concept of "health" becomes just feedback screech in the generally dysfunctional cacophony.

January 12, 1990

Addendum

L.A. Times, 16 June 1993: "AIDS has surpassed cancer, heart disease and accidents to become the leading cause of death among men ages 25 to 44 in California, accounting for 24% of all such deaths in 1990, according to the first systematic study of its kind by the U.S. Centers for Disease Control and Prevention. . . . The researchers cautioned that deaths among young adults accounted for only 7% of all deaths. . . ."

My belief in this piece that AIDS would not surpass heart disease as a cause of death was dead wrong, though it has yet to out-do tobacco in general as a killer.

The Wind's Dominion

There was a geology book when I was a kid that had maps of the North American continent as it had been through all the ages of the Earth. One eon there was a Florida, another eon there wasn't. At one time, according to that book, the Pacific came all the way in from Baja, cut around the Rockies and didn't stop till the Texas Panhandle. (On the mesas of Arizona you can still find seashells.) Sometimes there was a California, and sometimes there wasn't. If you flipped the pages, you could watch the continent change just like a cloud in the wind.

I think of that book when I drive through the West, where the sky and the earth seem so close sometimes that they trade places, play tricks with your eyes, and it can be hard to know whether you're driving up or down an incline. Sometimes it unsettles me—and sometimes I get a kick out of it—that as far as God is concerned, I'm driving through a cloud. Like in the Paiute Indian woman's song that Robert Bly translated: "Sometimes I go about pitying myself/and all the time/I am being carried by great winds across the sky."

In that state of mind, headed north on Interstate 5, bucking a light Santa Ana, climbing the Tejon Pass at a steady seventy, it wasn't too surprising to see a sign read: "The Umbrella Viewing Area Next 18 Miles." And then to see the big golden-yellow umbrellas up and down the hillsides, rippling in the wind—there's always a wind in this pass, and the material covering the umbrella frame was designed to ripple gently, giving those big, stolid shapes an illusion of lightness. As a friend said, they looked as though they'd floated down—sent by some extraterrestrial agency—and alighted randomly.

The late twentieth century is a time when one such umbrella might make for a classy hot-dog stand, but several hundred on some hillside are capital-A Art. Well, it was at least capital-D Design and seemed harmless enough. The offramps and access roads were crammed with people toting cameras and camcorders, doing the classic American gawk. It doesn't matter what it is, Christo's umbrellas or the Grand Canyon, it elicits the same behavior: you work yourself silly to earn a weekend or a vacation, then go someplace you know only from photos or television, ignorant of its past as well as its present— someplace, in other words, that you're titillated by without being *really* interested in. When you get there, you experience this place by taking your own photo or making your own video, as though this duplication of what got you there in the first place somehow verifies and legitimizes the fact that you're there; then, as soon as the duplication is accomplished, you leave. And this sad, mechanical little dance, this substitute for any real exchange between the observer and the observed, is seen as solid, normal fun, when it's no more than one of the less harmful behavioral tics of a passive and bewildered people.

Three-hundred-odd miles north of the Tejon, on a refrigerator door in Oakland, I saw a card quoting Anne Herbert: "Practice random kindness and senseless acts of beauty." For a moment it made me think my judgments of Christo too harsh—but that was after my ride up the Altamont Pass, another place of strong wind, five hours up the road from Christo's umbrellas. There, instead, the hillsides are lined with rows of giant propellers. It's a wind-farm that goes on for several miles. If you called these propellers art and put a famous name on them, the same people would be doing the same thing on *these* off-ramps and access roads.

As the hissing laughter of Andy Warhol came in on the wind from his small settee in Eternity, I pulled off at Livermore just down the road, near the labs where they haven't stopped designing weapons that can destroy the entire planet. I ate at a McDonald's, assured by the place mat on the tray that no McDonald's anywhere in the world uses beef raised on decimated rain forests. The people at several of the tables were all traveling together; they looked Indian and Hispanic, and they talked excitedly about how they were looking forward to Billy Graham's broadcast that evening, and isn't it wonderful that the end days are here?

The end days. That's what it looked like by the same time next day—at least on that block in Oakland where my friends Dave and Anne have lived for so long. We had walked that morning in the Oakland Hills, surprised by the strong, L.A.-style Santa Ana wind. And as we drove back down to their house we saw the first smoke. By nightfall the neighborhoods we had driven through were gone.

I have indulged my appetite for apocalypse before in Dave's back yard, built in tiers up the steep hill behind his house, with the top tier commanding a good view to the west and north. Two years ago, almost to the day, we'd stood there after the Bay Area quake had shaken us out of the house. We'd watched plumes of smoke from the quake fires and listened to sirens converge on what we would learn was the collapsed Nimitz Freeway, not two miles away. Now we stood in the same place, watching the mileslong wall of smoke get closer by the hour.

The light was strange. Apocalypse-light. Smoke overhead, smoke for miles, and through the smoke a dull-red circle glowed: the sun. Everything smelled of burning. (The next day, hundreds of miles away, my jeans would still smell of it.) Dave and Anne, their kids and their neighbors kept looking at me funny. How come I always show up for their disasters? ("I don't know, the wind just kind of pushed me this way" is how Robbie Robertson answered a similar question in a song.) But I think what *really* aggravated them was that they sensed, however I tried to hide it, that I was enjoying myself. I liked the light. I liked the smell. I liked the spectacle of the billowing smoke covering the sky for miles. And more than anything I liked it that on days like this everybody must admit what is true every day: that no one knows what's going to happen next.

I wasn't the only one enjoying myself. A young mother next door was packing to leave. With an infant in her arms, she spoke to us across the fence about what she was taking and how strange and terrible it all was, and the whole time she talked she seemed unaware of her great wide grin and of how her eyes sparkled. That woman was actually quite happy. Such reactions are now labeled "hysterical," and now we have "trauma teams" who fly in and "debrief" the "victims." Part of this debriefing is to help people forget how glad they were at the possibility that they would no longer be able to live as they had been living. And "victims"? I remember my geology book, the continents shifting like clouds after flood, fire, earthquake and wind—the normal behavior of the planet. We try to give it human gender, insisting it's our "mother," and then we're shocked when it doesn't behave like a mother (or at least like a "normal" mother). "The Earth is an abusive parent! *Now* what are we gonna do?!" You wonder if we'll ever progress far enough to judge the planet in terms of its own behavior, and not in terms of what we want from it.

Meanwhile, the radio spoke of trees *exploding* with the intensity of the heat and flames, and fire jumping four blocks at a time on a gust of wind. The reporters described the most awful things with the most unmistakable relish: "We still hear explosions, loud explosions, as the fire continues to rage across the hillside! It's coming our way and there's nothing stopping it!" The scary thing was that nobody could say exactly *what* the fire was doing or where it was going at any given minute, though all the resources of the authorities and the media were fixed upon it. You could see how much people have come to depend on the authorities by watching their fear over how quickly these authorities had reached the limits of their knowledge and power.

Funny thing, though: neither on Dave's block, nor in any footage of the crowds, did I see people taking photographs. No, there was one—a guy on a rooftop across the way from Dave's. But he was the only photographer I saw, and I was looking for them. Most people didn't need a camera to create a relationship with that fire. It *demanded* a relationship, and that relationship involved us totally all day and into the night.

World War II-vintage bombers converted to firefighters flew in and out of the smoke cloud as it descended the hill. Helicopters carrying water buckets flew a flight path that early in the afternoon was about two miles away, but finally they were coming in right over the house, the fire was getting that close. Their buckets trailed a spray of water as they passed. After dark the whole horizon glowed, and as we watched the glow got brighter, coming toward us. Then, about three-quarters of a mile away, it wasn't a glow anymore; it was flames, two huge tongues of flames shooting up from behind a ridge, backlighting a house and some trees. We figured we had an hour, maybe two, before it would reach us. But just as we were doing our figuring, the wind died.

Not a breeze. Nothing stirred.

The fire quieted, the flames on the ridge went down—they never reached that house or ours.

Two days later I drove over the dam at Lake Powell, on the Utah-Arizona line, where humans have filled a canyon with water as, eons ago, the sea once did. Just across the dam on the Arizona side is the town of Page, and at a little diner, Bubba's Texas-Style Barbeque, people were talking about the Oakland fire. A small, chubby guy with sun-bleached hair and bruised workingman's hands spoke with real sorrow, saying he knew every place they'd mentioned in the news broadcasts because he's been there, played there as a musician in the sixties. I told him and the others my fire stories. He kept going back to how sad it was, how great that place used to be. I asked when he'd been there last, and he said not since the sixties, "when the music was happening." What did he play? Drums. Anything I'd know? His voice got a little softer, he looked not at me but directly across the counter as though it was hard to say it, and said, "The Bobby Fuller Four—'I Fought the Law (and the Law Won).' That's my drumming on that record. But I haven't been in the business for twenty years. I got a boat-repair place here now."

A different sort of wind had brought him from Berkeley to Page. We never did exchange names.

Nearly a thousand miles farther down the road I heard that an unexpectedly strong and sudden wind had toppled one of Christo's umbrellas and killed a woman, so Christo was taking his umbrellas down. They were talking about it in an Austin bakery.

Boris Pasternak said that all art is really a meditation on death and would have thought that any art that turns and runs at the first death is no art at all. But when you have only to call something art for it to be art, then you can't expect it to stand up against so much as a Santa Ana wind in the Tejon Pass.

And now, in Austin, the wind has brought the cold winter rains early here, with a tornado to the south and floods to the east. There's a flash-flood watch in five counties tonight. If the wind turns a little it could flood here, too. The air is sweet and tense with it. People are talking about it. It's starting to rain.

November 8, 1991

A Riot Every Day

Yesterday was Judgment Day—
Ho 'dja do? How 'dja do?
Were you sleeping
When your nightmares and your visions all came true?
Butch Hancock and Jimmy Dale Gilmore

A few doors down the hall of this motel in Austin, Texas, a man is screaming into a telephone. What an image of impotence: raging into a plastic receiver. From my room it's just a wordless din, but when I step out to the ice machine I can hear him clearly: "Gina, tell that bastard to come to the phone. TELL HIM! Do you want me to come over there? Then you tell him. MAKE HIM!" When I return with my ice, my message light is on and I call down to the desk, where a young woman informs me that Lillie Kretchfield has some information and I'm to call tonight. But I've never heard of a Lillie Kretchfield. "It's for Room 327, that's your room," the desk clerk says. So it is. Ms. Kretchfield didn't mention a name, only a number; she has left her message for the wrong room. It's a normal night in America: one man screaming to someone who won't listen; one woman leaving her message in the wrong place; and on the television, L.A. is burning.

Isn't someplace *always* burning on the television? Isn't that what we take for granted now? Isn't *that* our century? One by one, country by country, each city and each generation discovers what it's like to

118

be in the midst of a given day's flash point. Beirut, Baghdad, Sarajevo, Kabul, Belfast, Miami, Moscow, Peking, San Salvador, Johannesburg, Philadelphia, Berlin, New Delhi, Jerusalem . . . L.A. Speaking as one whose old neighborhoods in Brooklyn and the Bronx have been destroyed in similar riots, and who has both made and received the inevitable calls to and from New York, South Florida, Oakland and now L.A.—riot-time seems to have become part of our shared education. No, strike the word "education"; we learn from history that little *is* learned. It's just "shared experience"—though it's fair to say that until the prolonged riot that is the twentieth century materializes in your presence, you are not yet truly a citizen of this age; you do not yet know in your bones the *seriousness* of the energies afoot.

Now and then the television cuts away from the fires in L.A. to feature a mayor, a governor, a police chief, a fire chief, a president, a candidate, a leader, a film director—all of whom, whether their names are Gates or Bush or Brown or Jackson or Singleton, say precisely what you knew they were going to say, and what each of them knew the other was going to say, and all of it is uncannily identical to what other fire chiefs, presidents, leaders and mayors have said in other decades, other cities.

There are also interviews with people on the streets, people of all colors and ages. Consistent through their various viewpoints and levels of intelligence is the demand that *their* riot be viewed more seriously than they themselves viewed the riots in, say, Miami or London. Not bloody likely. Though there have been sympathetic flash points as far off as Seattle and Tampa, other people will, for the most part, treat our riot as we've treated theirs, as a form of entertainment, fast food for thought.

We share something else with those who have made statements at every flash point, riot, flood, earthquake and war: the poignant and fierce hope, voiced by citizens and officials alike, that this event will be a "judgment day," a "defining moment," a day we can frame and point to and say, "Here something ended, and here something new began." We need to think this, we *must* think this, for it gives us the personal power to act. It's even true on a personal level: during such events individuals experience moments that change them forever. It's even sort of true on a slightly larger, citywide scale: shifts in social forces and changes in the terrain compel our behavior to shift and change with them—though often that sort of change doesn't go very deep.

In a still larger sense, however, there are no "defining moments" in history, not really. History behaves more like a great wave, rising and falling in vast interconnected patterns, than like a train proceeding from point to point. History behaves like a storm—wind, humidity, air pressure, terrain, solar phases, tides, a million variables, ultimately uncountable, forming a system that keeps its wholeness, its coherence, for just a short while before it changes into something else, some other pattern, some other weather. In history, one pattern of "weather" can last centuries or decades or just a few days, and the element that seems to change the pattern can be as dramatic as an assassination or as silent as the drying of a water table—but neither the drama nor the silence holds the key, for the drying of the water table could have influenced the conditions that led to the assassination, or the assassination could have changed how people perceived the *meaning* of the drought, which in turn changed how they did such and such . . . and on and on, in the wild growth that is life rather than history.

In this longing for a defining moment, in this clamor for solutions and proposals lies the assumption that here, at the close of the twentieth century, there's something *abnormal* about a riot, though it's clear that the whole world is rioting in one form or another all the time, that it's all one vast riot bursting out in one flash point after another, with webs of interlocking causes and ripples of overlapping effects.

For instance, all the street actions in Peking, Moscow, Berlin and L.A. over the last several years have at least one cause in common: the vast amount of money spent on armaments has drastically deprived people everywhere of resources and opportunities. Yet this newspaper, as part of its solution to L.A.'s and America's problems, will probably suggest that you support the same Democratic Party that just overwhelmingly approved President Bush's defense budget without so much as a trim. What does this mean? That hidden in most of our "solutions," no matter how well intentioned, are future riots, here and everywhere. We can't seem to get around that.

What *can* we do? To say that there's nothing one can really do is to be hopeless, and we don't want to be *that*. Yet any program, as soon as it's proposed, is revealed as limited and ineffectual. This is because the worldwide riot is happening on the same scale and plane of activity (the political and historical plane) on which the proposal is proposed. The behavior of our legislators has been, in effect, a kind of riot—a quiet riot, a pervasive and hysterical panic that has them going round and round in circles. Because any new legislator immediately becomes part of that riot, what we can *do* politically is limited. What is far less limited (and the riots themselves prove this) is how we can behave.

The television, for instance, is at this moment displaying some strange behavior: black, white and brown people are helping each other destroy some property. They seem to be having a lot of fun, and they display no fear or anger toward each other whatsoever. The announcer is saying that this behavior is apparently not uncommon this evening. It's a strange way to conduct what's being labeled a "race riot." It means that within this tumultuous event, where elsewhere people are dying, a few unexpected decisions, and behaviors, are being enacted. Everybody expected the instantly famous image of the truck driver being beaten; everybody expected that somebody—in this case Koreans—would be targeted; *nobody* expected this image of interracial rioting. If you can distance yourself from your fear of property damage, there's something *new* about this riot. These people are *doing* something, choosing something, enacting their own program, and there's something in their behavior to watch and respect. *Their* solution, tonight, is their behavior. They've decided to fight their environment without fighting each other. They've demonstrated how original and generous behavior can be, even in a riot.

For myself, that's where I look for hope. Perhaps this strikes so deep in me because four days ago I stood outdoors in a crowd of more than 10,000 listening to Al Green in New Orleans. This was at the Jazz and Heritage Festival. At least half, perhaps two-thirds, of Al Green's crowd was black. In this huge mixed crowd there was no forced friendliness, but neither was there fear. As usual at the New Orleans festival, there was a sense of *allowing*—of people gathered for the same purpose and without any other agenda. There was a minimal police presence, at the outskirts of the festival—I barely noticed them. And, standing listening to Al Green give his heart to this crowd as we gave ours to him, I realized that this was the first time in twenty-five years that I'd been in a huge interracial crowd without tension. Without drawing any grand conclusions, it was just so refreshing to be reminded that it's possible.

Notice that both at the Al Green concert, and in the case of those kids happily destroying property together, the society as it's been given to us by our government and our economics was ignored, abolished, discarded—for a brief time. The lesson I draw? My suspicion is that we must be more and more ready to find our lives at the limits of this society's conceptions. Our solutions won't come from the center and won't be condoned by the center, because the center (government, business, even what passes for culture) is in a state of perpetual riot called "history," a set of preconceptions about what "order" and "prosperity" mean that seem to be systematically destroying the well-being of all of us. The change may be in what we most fear. Metaphorically, if you like, it's not about how you stop the riot, it's about how you *join* the riot. Because we're all already in an enormous riot, one that, for the present, seems unstoppable.

Once more I try to call a loved one in L.A. Once more the circuit's busy. Once more my gut contracts in fear. On the screen, the city I love is burning, and I find I've been listening to the circuit signal on the phone for several minutes while I *think* my way to a face in L.A. and try to send some soul there. Yes. It's all a question of how to get through, and can your heart reach out where the system can't?

May 8, 1992

Part Three

War Is the Health of the State

The Ghost of Randolph Bourne

Randolph Bourne is hard to find. It's hard even to find anyone who's heard of him. The man who wrote "the object of an education is to know a revolution when you see one" isn't on many curriculums. And it's been fourteen years since Bourne was in print, since *The Radical Will: Randolph Bourne—Selected Writings 1911–1918* was published by Urizen Books in hardback only, and good luck finding it. (I had to go to the Freedom Bookstore in London.) Still, Randolph Bourne is a good man to know before a war.

If, for instance, I had opened with the following words, would you have been able to tell that they were written in 1917?

> We are learning that war doesn't need enthusiasm, doesn't need conviction, doesn't need hope, to sustain it. Once maneuvered, it takes care of itself. . . . Our resources in men and materials are vast enough to organize the war-technique without enlisting more than a fraction of the people's conscious energy. . . . This is why the technical organization of this American war goes on so much more rapidly than any corresponding popular sentiment for its aims and purposes. Our war is teaching us that patriotism is really a superfluous quality. . . . The government of a modern organized plutocracy does not have to ask whether the people want to fight or understand what they are fighting for, but only whether

they will tolerate fighting. America does not cooperate with the President's designs. She rather feebly acquiesces. But that feeble acquiescence is the all-important factor. . . .

Responsibility lies always on the shoulders of those who failed to prevent. Here it lies upon the cowardly middle classes who failed to curb militarism.

Many of us have bought the media-dispensed view that *because* of media, we are living in a brand spanking new world, with new realities and new rules. If you think video, fax machines, the rise of rock & roll and the fall of socialism have changed everything, here is Randolph Bourne writing in 1917, the third year of the First World War:

They told us that war was becoming economically impossible. . . . in these days of international economic dependence, of inextricably interlacing communications, and financial obligations . . . [They told us] that the more the world became one vast market and the more each nation's economic interests became definitely implicated in those of the others, just so much the more unready would be any government [to make war]. . . . They told us that war was becoming physically impossible. The very magnitude of the armaments was making their employment hazardous. It seemed incredible that any modern government would take the initiative of letting loose those incalculable engines of destruction. The more formidable and complicated the armaments became, the safer were we in reality from their use. . . . The nations, armed to the teeth, disclaimed nevertheless any offensive intentions. . . . [They told us] the "international mind" was becoming more and more universal. . . . They said, and we almost believed, that a new international morality was arising. . . . This new morality had only to be codified to become the constitution of a veritable Federation of the World . . . We came to believe almost that it was true, as the nations said, that these vast armaments were mainly preventive, a costly form of insurance. . . .

Sound familiar? Couldn't that have been written this morning? Do you feel, as I do, a little embarrassed, even ashamed, that it's all happening again, with the same hustle, the same excuse? So much the same that the words of a forgotten man, a man who died in 1918, describe our contemporary moment *precisely*? It means we've been had yet again, in the same way, by the same kind, from whom we've taken the same shit.

I am ashamed, too, that our country has let this writer become so forgotten that I could have signed his words as my own and who would have known? Well, we may not be able to stop this war, but we can honor Randolph Bourne a little. His words are still strong enough to help.

How did I find him? By chance, a long time ago, reading the John Dos Passos novel *Nineteen Nineteen*, wherein Bourne appears suddenly for about a page and a half: "This little sparrowlike man, tiny twisted bit of flesh in a black cape, always in pain and ailing. . . ." The day I read that happened to be one of the few this century when a Bourne collection was in paperback (*The World of Randolph Bourne*, 1965), and I happened to walk into a bookstore where it lay face up on the counter.

Thus was I introduced to a dwarf, hunchbacked, with a misshappen head (twisted by forceps in what Bourne referred to as his "terribly messy birth"), who was born in New Jersey in 1886. He worked his way through Columbia as a proofreader, secretary and piano player. He attended the Second Communist International in Vienna. His first essay, "The Handicapped—By One of Them," was published in *The Atlantic Monthly* in 1911 when he was twenty-five. Then he wrote steadily for *The New Republic* until he got too dangerous; they fired him toward the end of 1917 for his stand against World War I.

A brave little rag called *Seven Arts* took him then, but Bourne's war views lost them their financing and they folded. By now "friends didn't like to be seen with Bourne," Dos Passos tells us, and "his father wrote him begging him not to disgrace the family name. . . . He was cartooned, shadowed by the espionage service and the counterespionage service; taking a walk with two girl friends at Wood's Hole he was arrested, a trunk full of manuscript and letters stolen from him. . . ." At this point many writers would have quit, but Bourne wrote some of his best stuff in the next year, the last of his life, when he was ill and he knew there was no outlet for his work. (It was published posthumously.) He died in 1918 at the age of thirty-two.

Dos Passos cautions against feeling sorry for Bourne:

> Weak health and being poor and twisted in body and on bad terms with his people hadn't spoiled the world for Randolph Bourne; he was a happy man, loved *Die Meistersinger* and playing Bach with his long hands that stretched so easily over the keys and pretty girls and good food and evenings of talk. When he was dying of pneumonia a friend brought him an eggnog. Look at the yellow, it's beautiful, he kept saying as his life ebbed into delirium and fever. He was a happy man.

Randolph Bourne's thoughts were more intricate, subtler, than can be suggested in this space, but let's try. Most of what follows is from his greatest piece, "War Is the Health of the State," unfinished at the time of his death.

> [W]e have the misfortune of being born not only into a country but into a State, and as we grow up we learn to mingle the two . . . into a hopeless confusion. . . . The history of America as a country is quite different from that of America as a State. . . . War is the health of the State, and it is during war that one best understands the nature of that institution.

> With the shock of war . . . the State comes into its own. . . . The government, with no mandate from the people, without consultation of the people, conducts all the negotiations. . . .

> There is no case known in modern times of the people being consulted in the initiation of a war. The present demand for "democratic control" of foreign policy indicates how completely, even in the most democratic of modern nations, foreign policy has been the secret private possession of the executive branch of the Government. . . . When the declaration of war is finally demanded by the Executive, the congress could not refuse it. . . . To repudiate an Executive at

the time would be to publish to the entire world the evidence that the country had been grossly deceived by its own government, that the country with an almost criminal carelessness had allowed its Government to commit it to gigantic national enterprises in which it had no heart. . . . War can scarcely be avoided unless this poisonous underground system of secret diplomacy is destroyed.

For the benefit of proud and haughty citizens, [the State] is fortified with a list of the intolerable insults which have been hurled toward us by the other nations; for the benefit of the liberal and beneficent, it has a convincing set of moral purposes which our going to war will achieve; for the ambitious and aggressive classes, it can gently whisper of a bigger role in the destiny of the world. . . .

[But] it cannot be too firmly realized that war is a function of States and not of [countries or] nations, indeed that [war] is the chief function of States. War is a very artificial thing. It is not the naive spontaneous outburst of herd pugnacity; it is no more primary than is formal religion. War cannot exist without a military establishment, and a military establishment cannot exist without a State organization . . . they are inseparably and functionally joined. We cannot crusade against war without crusading implicitly against the State. And we cannot expect, or take measures to insure, that this war is a war to end war, unless at the same time we take measures to end the State in its traditional form.

The State is not the nation, and the State can be modified and even abolished in its present form, without harming the nation. On the contrary, with the passing of the dominance of the State, the genuine life-enhancing forces of the nation will be liberated. If the State's chief function is war, then the State must suck out of the nation a large part of its energy for its purely sterile purposes of defense and aggression. . . . It devotes to waste or to actual destruction as much as it can of the vitality of the nation.

This situation is very difficult to fight, Bourne argues, precisely because it is not rational. It seems he thought that the Marxist explanations for war were wrong precisely because they were logical. "It is logic that life mocks and contradicts at every turn," he wrote in 1913. "Too much rationality puts the soul at odds with life." He added in 1916: "Intellectual radicalism should not mean repeating state dogmas of Marxism. It should not mean 'the study of socialism.' It had better mean a restless, controversial criticism of current ideas." Bourne came to a frightening conclusion about why war is always with us:

> A nation at war . . . is engaged in liberating certain of its impulses. . . . It is getting certain satisfactions, and the actual conduct of the war or the condition of the country are really incidental to the enjoyment of new forms of virtue and power and aggressiveness. . . . For war is a complicated way in which a nation acts, and it acts so out of a spiritual compulsion which pushes it on, perhaps against all its interests, all its real desires, and all its real sense of values.

Bourne didn't give up hope for a political solution, though he didn't live long enough to propose anything concrete. But his contribution was, in part, the hint that a political solution would have to take account of the "spiritual compulsion." And he knew that anything with what he called a spiritual source was, for good or evil, elusive. He had written in 1911, in an essay called "The Experimental Life":

> The spiritual world is ever-creative; the same experiments may turn out differently for different experimenters and yet they may both be right. . . . We can be certain of a physical law that as it has worked in the past, so it will work in the future. But of a spiritual law we have no such guarantee. This it is that gives the zest of perpetual adventure to the moral life.

Randolph Bourne liked that word, "adventure." He wanted life to be about "the effort of reason, and the adventure of beauty." For this, one needed friends: "A friend becomes . . . the indispensable means of discovering one's own personality." And one needed faith. In "Mystic

Turned Radical" Bourne wrote, in 1912, "Society so habitually thinks on a plane lower than is reasonable that it behooves us to think and to hope on an even higher plane than seems to be reasonable. This is the overpoweringly urgent philosophy of radicalism."

And one needed to cleave to that faith with "a radical will." In 1917 he wrote one of his strongest thoughts, a thought I'm keeping close by as we tilt toward war again: "One keeps healthy in wartime not by a series of religious and political consolations that something good is coming out of it all, but by a vigorous assertion of values in which war has no part."

And he asked a question that still pierces: "Now, while everything that is respectable in America seems to be putting its effort, with a sort of joyful perversity, into the technique of destruction, are there no desperate spiritual outlaws with a lust to create?"

Randolph Bourne was our ancestor and our mentor, and his words have proved strong enough to find us even now, all on their own. I like the last glimpse John Dos Passos gives of him: "If any man has a ghost Bourne has a ghost, a tiny twisted unscared ghost in a black cloak hopping along the grimy old brick and brownstone streets . . . crying out in a shrill soundless giggle: *War is the health of the state.*"

January 11, 1991

Addendum

Since this article was written, *The Radical Will: Randolph Bourne— Selected Writings 1911–1918* has reappeared in paperback, published by the University of California Press.

Possessed by War

That was my editor on the phone, asking me whether I wanted to go to Saudi Arabia if there's a war. "If?" I said. For we all know, even as I write a week before January 15: there will be a war. The coffee tastes of war, the sky looks like war, the service station smells of war. A musty foul tinge stains life now: this presence of war. Not just any war (somewhere there's been a war every day I've been alive), but a war with an unusually virulent capacity to infect the future.

Go to Saudi Arabia? Be a "war correspondent"? I suppose I should have expected that call, yet as I hung up the receiver I felt a strangeness, a sense that this request was more than it seemed. Sitting up into the night I thought:

"So—through my friend and boss, this war is calling to me, as it is calling many others. I wonder if Kit knows that tonight he is a kind of mouthpiece for the war. That the war has overtaken, perhaps even overwhelmed, his function of newspaper editor, and made him turn to a friend and ask what otherwise he would ask only in the most extreme personal emergency: that this friend put himself in danger. So that's not Kit on the phone: that's the war itself calling. *That* is the power of war: that in its name, and by its sanction, you do what you never would otherwise consider. And the fact that his request seems perfectly reasonable to both of us, however much we like to think of ourselves as independent men, testifies to the authority with which war speaks to and through us."

I've got to sort this out and decide whether or not to go. For you need a reason to go on such an adventure, and it had better be your very own reason. The stakes are too high to submit to any other. I don't know why I didn't think about dying or about the loved ones I'd leave, except that I never think enough of my health or my loved ones. I was thinking only of my life as a writer. So why would a writer go to this war?

For the experience, some would say. Which may be forgivable in someone twenty years younger than I am, hungry for great formative events and imagining that the world (rather than one's heart) provides them. Others feel not quite here as they go through their daily rounds, and nurse an unconfessed hope that the extremes of the world will shock them into life. But isn't it obscene to approach the ghastly suffering of war as a kind of theme park for spiritual tourists hoping finally to grow up?

What about going for the deeper reason of experiencing war in order to understand this phenomenon that, in effect, *is* history? Understanding is surely a transcendent motive.

Well, maybe not always. The assumption is that to "see action," to look upon the dead in the desert sun, to experience what this war will be, is a justifiable means to an end. Just because the end is "understanding" rather than "oil" doesn't alter the fact that war has become, for you, a means. And a means to an end is *always* war's rationale. Thus, like the politicians who set the thing off, you accept the war for your purposes just as those politicians accept it for theirs. Your beliefs may be against it but not your behavior. To go is to participate. *Any* acceptance of war feeds the war fever. Justifies the process. *Is* the war. The seeker-after-truth is as culpable as the soldier or the president. For all of them, war is not only a theme park but a career move.

What about going to the Middle East simply as a journalist reporting the war? To bear witness. Isn't that a legitimate, even perhaps exalted function? The military will lie and we will tell the truth. Especially we of the "alternative" press. We'll give you a vision of this war that you can't get anywhere else.

In the Vietnam War this view had some validity. It is strange to remember that in those days Americans assumed their government did not lie. Now they know. The polls show that few believe we're liberating Kuwait; everybody knows it's about oil. The polls also show (as if Vietnam wasn't proof enough) that most Americans don't care how many civilians we bomb, or what we bomb them with, so long as we win and get out fast. The people know the drill: the president and the Pentagon will lie; they will justify their lies as essential to national security; some journalists will uncover some of the lies. But the people already know they're being lied to. The Pentagon knows they know. We have reached a point, on a national level, where the specific lie doesn't matter much. The phenomenon of the *acceptance* of lying matters enormously, but the lies themselves are judged for their entertainment value. Tune in to *Nightline*, watch C-Span and CNN, talk about it with your friends. There's a bit of scandal, somebody's disgraced, but what changes? In such an ambiance, is bearing witness a useful act? Or is it just a liberal's way of feeling included in history while in truth remaining as powerless as ever? A way of participating in the war while appearing to protest?

How many times must the story of war's horror be told? I believe Mathew Brady's photographs. I believe *All Quiet on the Western Front* and *Dispatches*. I believe *War and Peace* and *The Naked and the Dead*. I believe *Guernica* and *Apocalypse Now*. At what point does the repetition of the story become a way of ignoring its truth? A way of not hearing? Art about the horrors of war has become part of the expected ritual of war. Anticipated. Accepted. Ignored. Ignored because it is experienced by most as just another way to participate. As writer and reader, how long until we understand this? When do we say, "Enough, I'm convinced, I believe, I will act on that belief." Because if we believe these depictions of war, then how can we, directly or indirectly, ever participate again?

Finally, there is this:

The American men and women in the desert are no more or less real to me than the Iraqi civilians and soldiers. All seem equally caught in a terrible moment, equally duped by leaders without conscience. Powerless, they await whatever the tumult brings. In my heart I can take no sides. But if I go there, even as a writer, my stake changes. If I'm with a combat outfit on the ground in Saudi Arabia, I want them very much to win. I suddenly have an enormous stake in the success of the policies of George Bush. If he can save me and these soldiers by bombing Iraq senseless, I'm not going to have mixed feelings about that, at least not right then. But . . . 45 percent of the population of Iraq is under fourteen.

Is Saddam Hussein really so important that we are willing to massacre a nation that's half children rather than wait another six months, another year, for economic sanctions to work? Is our prestige that important? Is our prosperity, such as it is, that important? There's no way around it: if I am on the ground with the allied forces in the Middle East, I have a stake in the deaths of those children. Allowing oneself to be in that position, no matter who you are or what your function may be, is either tragically stupid or deeply immoral, depending on whether or not you knew what you were getting into. It is a forgetting of one's soul. And that's further than I'm willing to go for my country or my profession.

That's my decision, then. The motives of getting experience, gaining understanding, and bearing witness, like the motives of freeing Kuwait and crushing the tyrant and just incidentally controlling the oil—are in the end excuses for succumbing to the magnetism of war.

Any so-called reason to play one's part in war invites possession—a kind of demonic possession, possession by the war energy. It works this way: the war finds some personal emptiness in you (inexperience, ambition, illusion) and rushes in to fill it. Suddenly you are not yourself. You are yourself plus the war. You are more and you are less. Less *because* you are more: because the "more" that you feel is not really a part of you. It's imposed by something alien: the war. You are living in its name and by its energy. So when it's over, when it leaves, you are drained and diminished.

This helps explain the confusion of the veterans of the Second World War who, after doing such amazing things, became mere suburbanites. It was baffling to them, that what they felt during their war could simply disappear. They didn't know those feelings weren't really their own. Vietnam veterans fought a more crazed, surreal conflict. Many are still in deep shock and shame at having, through no graver fault than being young, opened themselves up to war possession. The war demon used them viciously, then viciously cast them off. Many, when they speak of it, have a presence like that of women who've been raped.

Entire populations sometimes feel this way. It's a feeling not confined to people who participate directly in a war, or people who are "for" a war. Many who are "against" a war can also be possessed by the war energy. It can be very exciting, having a war to protest. Your small personal life takes on cosmic historical significance. It *feels* like you're gaining stature, but actually you're at risk of losing your identity. As a protester you, like the soldier, are not quite yourself. You are yourself plus the war. If you lean too heavily on that role of protestor, when your movement has no more war to protest, you too will feel diminished, lost, less. War is dangerous to *everyone*, on all sides of the issues. Being against a war doesn't insulate you from its demonic properties.

I don't in any way mean to discourage protest against our Middle East war. It is a gruesomely stupid venture for the worst of motives; its consequences will be horrible; we need to stand against it. I am only saying: Take good care. The quality of war is that it seeps into everything. Into you.

That is why two friends, otherwise not unintelligent, an editor and a writer, could have a conversation that in effect went: "Saddam Hussein and George Bush are about to commit mass murder, and to coerce many others to do likewise, so shouldn't you participate?" "It seems like I should, doesn't it? Isn't that my job?" This conversation didn't take place between two people; it took place between where the war had lodged in one and where it had lodged in the other.

Don't let this war speak through your mouth.

January 18, 1991

Demonstrate It

Americans were frightened of getting into this conflict, but it's clear now that what they feared wasn't war but failure. As I write on the fifth day of fighting, our pricy weapons seem to be working beyond expectations and Iraqi resistance has been pitiful. Experts say that American casualties thus far are what they'd expect from a military *exercise* with this many ships, planes, and people. Saddam's missiles have done minimal damage to Israel. And now that it appears we are not going to fail, America doesn't much mind this war.

Crunch this: polls show 76 percent of American women, and 87 percent of American men, agree with Bush's decision to go to war—over 80 percent of the country as a whole. More than 60 percent believe there should be no protesting while our troops are fighting. ("Wait till *after* the war to protest it" seems to be their thinking.) Democrats of the lower middle class and poor support this war by three to one. Blacks were "overwhelmingly" against it a week before we attacked; they're split 50–50 now.

All of which could change tomorrow. The numbers will tilt wildly on the latest news break. But what the numbers say on any specific day doesn't matter much. What matters deeply is what these polls prove: that for the majority of Americans the war itself is not the issue; the issue is whether we're good at it. If, as in Vietnam, we're not, then the public might be coaxed into wondering whether we should be there; but if, as in the Gulf so far, we excel, then clearly their feeling is "Go for it."

The Bush administration has been smart enough to understand this. Smart enough to see that the debate was less about the morality of this war than about the hassle. Even "No Blood for Oil," a pretty good slogan, plays less on conscience than on the fear of pain. As individuals, most Americans feel horror and grief at war; as part of the collective, we feel fear that it might further disrupt our society. But these are very different feelings, with different motives, from different parts of the psyche. And Bush (like Reagan) understands that the emotions through which people connect with the collective, and not what they feel individually, are the heart of politics.

So while the left appeals to our individual consciences, Bush plays on our collective shame. While lefties make speeches trying to shame America into behaving, Bush understands that the majority can't bear any more national shame. The national psyche is bursting with shame at failure, shame at shoddiness, shame at collapse. For not only did we lose Vietnam, we lost Detroit and New York. The Vietnamese fought harder, the Japanese make better cars, the Germans do money better, while all over Europe and the Pacific Rim others are healthier, give their kids a better education, and enjoy safer streets. As if this weren't enough, in Vietnam we lost more than a war, we lost our reputation. We will never again be seen as clean. Not by others, not by ourselves. Success in the Gulf, then, is a tonic. If we can't be happy or good, perhaps we can be, in the street sense, "bad." This is not a feeling to be underestimated in a people hooked on violent entertainment, arrogant music, and the conflict of sports. It is easily tapped.

The left always goofs when it comes to America's collective identity. Tragically, the right has a much better feel for such things. It has usually understood that people act one way in privacy, another in matters of livelihood, and still another when they're thinking of themselves as part of a large group. The psychologist R. D. Laing analyzed this:

> Consider the metamorphoses that one man may go through in one day as he moves from one mode of sociality to another—family man, speck of crowd dust, functionary at an organization, friend. These are not simply different roles: each is a whole past and present and future, offering different options and constraints, different kinds of closeness and dis-

tance, different sets of rights and obligations, different
pledges and promises.

The catch is that often your different selves or centers don't consult
each other, aren't even aware of each other, yet they all speak with
the same mouth and sign the same signature.

Thus many of us don't connect our heart's ideals to what we do
for financial security. Or our sensual and intellectual centers will have
conflicting agendas. Or we'll judge our private and collective behaviors
by entirely different standards. And we'll hardly know it. Otherwise
sane people will marry someone whom all their friends can see is nearly
psychotic. Whites who "believe" (with one part of their psyche) in in-
tegration and citizenship will send their children to a private school
to avoid both. Artists passionately critical of the government will live
off NEA grants. And people desperate for peace in their own lives support a war in the Gulf.

(Much of this will be defended by calling the heart's ideals "im-
practical" and the public life "real." But that's only a way of labeling,
and assigning values to, one's fragments. Naming is a way of choosing. What would happen if we called our ideals "real"?)

The irony is that the right pretends not to understand psychology,
while the left thinks it knows it all. Perhaps it's that the right *doesn't*
understand, but finds collective thinking easier and so appeals naturally
to wide numbers of people. While the left, believing that it understands,
keeps trying to appeal to the wrong part of the psyche. For if you
appeal to the individual part of the psyche for a collective purpose,
you're on dangerous ground.

First, you tend to attract a kind of subcollective of people who
(rightly or wrongly) think of themselves as individuals—bohemians
like me, who look crazy on television. The inner split I spoke of happens in bohemians this way: we're very proud of looking and behaving differently from those of the middle class and we love to criticize
them; at the same time we want their money, demand to be included
in their deliberations, and get piqued when they don't take our ad-
vice. Understandably, they're not very impressed with us and don't
trust us. They have the idea that we're asking more from them than
we're willing to give in return, and they're right.

Second, what unifies a movement? After we go home from the demonstration, *are* we still a movement? Only if we're grounded in a shared vision. "Give Peace a Chance" is not a vision, it's a sentiment. Having a vision means we have some fundamental idea of how we want the world to be. In the pro-choice movement, the freedom of women to control their own bodies is a concrete step toward a very different world; that's a vision. But end the war and what? Go back to where we were a month ago? Six months ago? That's only a protest, not a movement. There's a difference. Protests will mean very little if the war proceeds successfully; a movement articulates something for the future, and that is always important.

What, then, should the left appeal to?

We could take our cues from Gandhi and Martin Luther King, Jr., and the people at Tian An Men Square and in Eastern Europe. King was a minister, Gandhi was a lawyer, they had deep respect for their communities, and wanted to give regular people good reason for getting out in the streets. They *assumed* individual conscience, but appealed beyond it to the most common causes in their respective peoples, causes that could be felt collectively and positively. Which is to say historically. They could make people feel not that they were resisting somebody else's history but that they, themselves, were history.

With Gandhi, King, Tian An Men and Eastern Europe, the core of the argument was a non-violent critique of their entire society. They saw the power of the state as resting purely on its capacity for violence, and they opposed that power bravely with a non-violent vision of an entirely different kind of state. They presented this vision not by shaming society but by *demonstrating* something better. That's what a "demonstration" means—it's certainly what it meant to Martin Luther King. You are there to demonstrate your belief, to show how it works. So King's and Gandhi's civil disobediences weren't hectic or frenzied or showoffish; they presented the world they wanted, they were dignified, courageous, peaceful. They articulated a great collective dream. When you see film of their actions, you know what they stand for by the way they behave.

King, Gandhi and the Eastern Europeans achieved structural change. The behavior of the white American left has not. That speaks for itself.

A war that's being won is impossible to stop. A victorious government with 80-percent approval doesn't care about your protest. But the *country* (which is different from the government) can be made to care about your *demonstration*. It's not enough to express our individualities. It's certainly not enough to accuse America of being rotten—not if we expect to change it. You must ask the questions that King and Gandhi asked: What kind of a world do you want for everybody? And how can that world be demonstrated?

January 25, 1991

What Is War?

We all know what war does, but is that the same as knowing what war is? In the Gulf War, do we even know who and what we're fighting? Each side sees the other as alien. Yet the alphabet you are reading originated in Iraq, along with the very concept of writing as we know it. Algebra and geometry, the foundations of our engineering and science, started there. The Iraqis began the concept of governing by written law and were the first to live in cities, irrigate systematically and use vehicles with wheels. Thus ancient Iraq, which we call Mesopotamia, was the first Western culture, the civilization out of which the West grew. We are fighting our cultural ancestors, which is to say: we are fighting ourselves.

Abraham, the Jewish patriarch with whom Yahweh made a covenant, was born in a town in ancient Iraq. He was an Iraqi. Abraham, Moses and Jesus are revered in Islam. It's not surprising that conflict among Moslems, Jews and Christians has the rabid feel of a family feud. We share so much that we really know how to hate each other. But, as in families, to hate each other is ultimately to doubt ourselves.

In the Gulf there seems no end to us fighting ourselves. Iraq's biochemical technology was purchased from the United States, West Germany and Italy; nuclear know-how from West Germany and France; missiles from France, the Soviet Union and Italy; planes and tanks from France and the Soviet Union; land mines, by the hundreds of thousands, from the United States. Our people are threatened by our own stuff.

What are the Iraqis battling? We are a people they've spent years and fortunes trying to imitate. It's said that the Iraqis tolerated Saddam because he modernized (read, Americanized) their lives. Iraqis are fighting the very objects of their desire.

What about the righteousness we march in the name of? Saddam isn't doing anything now that he wasn't doing when we treated him as a privileged client. In fact, he's done little that we haven't. It's a matter of record that through the CIA (which Bush headed) we've financed and trained torturers. Saddam's chemical weapons might not exist if the United States hadn't vetoed U.N. proposals to abolish that technology. As for his annexation of Kuwait and his treatment of the Kurds, it's not much different from our annexation of half of Mexico (now called Texas, New Mexico, Arizona and California) and our treatment of Indians. The domain of the United States was achieved with tactics identical to Saddam's lies, broken treaties, surprise attacks, atrocities and the mass dislocation of former residents. I'm not saying this makes Saddam Hussein right, it just makes him usual. I'm not even saying our past makes us especially wrong. All nations grabbing power (England, Israel and the Aztecs, to name a few) have done the same, with the hearty approval of their peoples. I'm just pointing out that there's a sense in which we Americans are fighting a personification of all that we can't bear in our own history.

Then there's the question of fighting for oil. We're spending half a billion dollars a day in the Gulf. How much research do you think we could buy for half a billion dollars a day? What if, at the invasion of Kuwait, the West had said, "Oil is too much trouble, it's all going to run out in the next century anyhow, this is a good excuse to spend the money on research and retooling for alternative fuels. Meantime, no more arms for anybody in the Middle East." But nothing like that ever seems to happen.

So we have descendants fighting ancestors, suppliers fighting customers, imitators fighting their models, and people of the same religious family ripping each other apart, all indignant about each other's crimes (which closely resemble their own) and battling over oil they don't need to need.

Americans gloss over all this by saying we are fighting Saddam Hussein. But what, in practice, do the words "Saddam Hussein" mean? Thousands of bombs have been dropped, but not on Saddam. Our weapons aim at many, all over Iraq. It's an illusion to call the many "Saddam." Likewise, the words "George Bush" are an Iraqi abstraction. George Bush is oceans away. Iraqis and Americans have massed against each other to fight *each other*, not Saddam or Bush.

We tend to think of troops as drones. We assume that the likes of Saddam and Bush use their people for their own ends. But what if Bush and Saddam are in turn being used by their peoples to rationalize and excuse behavior that would otherwise be irrational, inexcusable? The troops participate directly, the rest vicariously but avidly, in the intensities of war. In psychological terms, these leaders and masses are *enabling* each other. The leader may be serving the darker urges of his people just as much as the people serve their leader's ambition. As Tolstoy observed in *War and Peace* (1869): "The activity of the millions who migrate, burn houses, abandon agriculture and slaughter one another, is never expressed in the account of the activity of some dozen men who did not burn houses, abandon their fields and slaughter one another." Strip such activity of the rhetoric that always surrounds and justifies it, and you are left with a frightening picture: a silent-movie long-shot as directed by Abel Gance or D. W. Griffith, masses of humanity in wild motion, stampeding for no coherent reason toward a future none can guess.

Tomes have been written about the causes of such activity, blaming war on the struggle for markets and resources, class conflict, patriarchy, fundamentalism, power-lust, nationalism. Yet there were wars long before there were nations, classes and markets; people of the same religion and politics have often battled; to blame the mass behavior on only half the population (male) is to ignore the totality of war. The quality of war is that it permeates everything; in fact, war can't be successfully conducted *unless* it permeates. In every war I know about, women have ranted as gung-ho as the men once the action started, and for as long as their side won. This war, with so many female soldiers, makes hash of simplistic notions of gender.

When so many causes create the same phenomenon, does it still make sense to speak of them as causes? Can it be that the phenomenon causes the cause? War releases a tremendous collective emotional flood: Can it be that the release of war is such a strong collective need that practically any cause will suffice as a channel for it?

If so, then the answer to "What is war?" goes: war is something collectives seek when their interior pressures become too much to bear. Those pressures may be economic, racial or religious; the family structures of a culture may not function anymore; most people may be doing meaningless work to support dead-end lives—anything that can create in individuals a terrible hunger for significance equaled by resentment that demands expression. Pressure builds on all levels of society, and as it builds more and more resources are directed to the military: the elites allocate money, the middle classes approve, the poor join up—a mass instinct that conflict is the easiest way to release the commonly felt but individually unbearable pressures. Sooner or later the irrational excuse comes and there is war: the release everyone has been longing for. The crisis doesn't end until the need for release has been pretty much played out. Only then do cultures voluntarily change their structure.

War, then, is what collectives do when desperate for change. It's not that there are no rational solutions to their problems; it's that, no matter what the form of government, collectives have never acted rationally—not for so long as the lifetime of one generation.

These thoughts frighten me, because how can you protest such a phenomenon, much less check it? Protest assumes rationality—assumes that a government and a people can be convinced of your point. But if war has nothing to do with rationality; if war, in effect, causes itself, in that any issue may serve as an excuse for the collective burst . . . then where can I stand? If, as often happened in the sixties, protestors demonstrate an irrationality that mirrors the war, then they're just the war in another form. If protests are rational, calling for the problems to be addressed, they seem dull to a people that has conspired to give itself permission to be irrational.

What, then? I am part of the collective, its momentum affects me, that can't be helped. How do I demonstrate my feeling, privately or publicly, in ways that won't add to the madness? If I try to ignore how the collective touches me, just go about my business, my feelings will express themselves in some other way that will probably be hurtful. What part of myself can I trust?

I choose the part that grieves. To return my anger to the hurt it comes from and transform it. To express in some way my inconsolable and unanswerable grief that we are made as we are made and have built what we have built. To sing my grief, walk my grief, sit my grief.

The madness swirls around and through me, and a part comes from me. My grief allows me to cleanse and purify some bit of it. Cleansed, I can act. My anger can be turned against me, can be manipulated and used, but not my grief. Grief hurts no one, yet it softens the air about one, and increases possibility. In that softening, love moves—a little.

February 22, 1991

Burner of Eden

A Last Letter to the War

Santa Barbara

Since we defend the Constitution every time we speak freely, let me be honest: I am sick of yellow ribbons. Sick of billboards with big yellow bows on Highway 101. Sick of every shop, restaurant and home that needed a war to show the flag. Sick of decals. Isn't there something perverse about displaying support for the war on the very vehicles that have, indirectly, caused the war? (We support our troops but we're willing to let them die for our right to fill a gas tank inexpensively.) I curdle inside every time George Bush asks me to pray. If he had the grace, as Lincoln did, to pray for *everyone* in the war; if he was enough of a Christian to do as Jesus taught and pray for his enemies—I'd admire him and join his prayer. Instead he makes a conscript of God. I find this so profoundly blasphemous I don't know what to say, but I know there is a price to be paid for everything, and I wonder what will be the price of this.

The Pacific glints on the drive to Santa Barbara. I visit my kid there. We play Risk, a game of global war. As it happens our strategies center on the Middle East. My forces take it. Then his. Mine counterattack. He wins. We share the irony of our little game, but we don't joke about the war. Later I read that war games are selling like crazy all across the country, and I have the image of all these people sitting around all these boards with the intense concentration of play, moving their armies this way and that toward victory and defeat, bloodless, brainless, little nodes of madness. But they're fun, these games. And they look amazingly like the charts General Schwarzkopf and his briefers use to teach us about their war. We who have played such games know that the generals are having fun.

Patton had the depth to admit he loved war. Schwarzkopf pretends to hate it, but no one becomes so superbly skilled at, or devotes such a long and passionate life to, something he hates. I don't know how many other lies Schwarzkopf is telling us, and it's conceivable that he's not telling many—but we know he's telling one, and it saps any trust I might otherwise have in the man. Clearly he relishes what he's doing, his entire life has been directed toward these weeks. We are watching a man in the process of fulfilling his deepest wish: to command a great army in an important war. This sense of profound fulfillment is the source of the presence he exudes—for no one who has seen him in these weeks will forget him or, no matter how much one disagrees, will fail to be impressed. And yet there is this one evasion, this one fundamental corruption, which makes him more politician than warrior: he cannot, will not, now or ever, admit how thankful he is for this war, how profound and total is his fun.

Driving back to L.A., there seem to be even more flags and ribbons. Would a people who really believed in the rightness of their cause need such shrill display? I wonder if the very act of tying the ribbon and raising the flag is a way to silence a gnawing private doubt in ourselves, and the doubt we fear in others. Norman Schwarzkopf will be president one day, I say to myself. He projects less doubt than any man who has ever been on television.

The Mojave Desert

We near the twenty-first century, Eden is the memory of a memory. We remember a passage by the writers of the Old Testament, who in turn remembered an already-old tale that they doctored to sell their new religion. Yet can't you almost see, and don't you half believe, the image of a garden beyond description that was once your birthright?

Driving through the Mojave on Interstate 10, there is so little to impede one's imagination that it's easy to see Eden. Some contend that Eden was in Africa, others that it was a lush expanse of Iraq, Kuwait and Saudi Arabia. The theory or fancy that Eden was in the Persian Gulf casts an odd meaning on the region's oil. If oil is composed of ancient life, if it's a coagulation of lush vegetation and extinct animals, then all that Arab oil may be the residue of Eden.

So in my '69 Chevy, with all its body work finally done, its paint shining, its buffed wax so strangely skinlike to the touch, its V-8 hardly audible—when I hit the gas I'm a burner of Eden, a true-blue fool of an American. In my Chevy I know that I'm a sinner, but I love my sin, love hitting the road in this car, and to the extent that I won't give up my love for some more-ecological vehicle I, too, am *for* the Gulf War—no matter what I say or do. My thoughts don't want their oil but my behavior does.

Kierkegaard once said that thought without paradox is as foolish as love without passion. And so I'm propelled forward by the burning of Eden. This war makes me sick at heart, but I have no nostalgia for the Garden to which both the left and right want to return. Let Iraq be spared, but let the Garden burn, and with it the image of perfection in our hearts—our naive desire to live without contradiction, refusing to see how every day opposites evoke each other before our eyes, demanding purity like that petulant god Yahweh who drove our mythological ancestors out of the Garden in guilt. Would that Adam had turned around and torched the place, ridding us of the thought that anything can be all one way or another.

Kingman, Arizona

During the Second World War a woman I know was, as an infant, given over by her mother to be used in satanic-like rituals out in the desert not far from this town. I mention it only to say that things were never *not* strange, here or anywhere, ever.

The Arizona–New Mexico State Line

It's been dark for hours. I've been playing this song over and over, thinking not about America and Iraq but about love.

> Tears of rage, tears of grief
> Why do I always feel a thief?

And suddenly a quick white thing runs into my lights and I feel it break beneath the wheels. Its bones make a clanging sound when struck by my oil pan. It's shocking how strong a small animal really is; this is a 3,000-pound car, but I feel the shudder all the way through.

Far away in another desert, near where God is said to live, there are bodies wracked with the same appalled surprise of sudden death, but we will never see them.

Gallup, New Mexico

A motel room in the wee hours. CNN. Will we have a land war today? Tomorrow? Has it already begun? Will Gorbachev's initiative save something or someone?

The television screen's so clean it should come wrapped with a sanitary band like the toilet. All these clean images, hardy generals, erudite experts, charts, graphics, soldiers waving, pretty flashes of cannon-fire from a distance. But war looks like the creature I crushed twenty miles back. Why aren't they letting us see it?

They say that in this age of instant communication the enemy will get information from our broadcasts. In the same breath they say the enemy can't even get information from himself: his communications are ruined, Baghdad can't see the battlefront, combat commanders can't call each other. It takes Iraq's ambassador to the U.N. two days to get an ungarbled message. Anyway, our generals tell us that no Iraqi ground forces can make a move without getting plastered by our planes;

the allies have little to fear from the Iraqis. So if there were to be a decent waiting period for airing of news—say three days, roughly as long as it took footage from Vietnam to be shot, edited and cleared for anything classified—what possible military justification could there be for censoring our press? Nobody in Baghdad or the trenches can watch their television anymore anyway.

The people that the military are really afraid of are you and me, here at home. For us the war is all yellow ribbons and flags and charts, and they want it to stay that way; we got a little sick the one day we saw the real war, the twisted bodies from the Baghdad shelter. But it isn't only the White House and the Pentagon that want this censorship—polls show that the American people think the press isn't censored enough. The government doesn't want people to see the real war, *and the people are demanding not to know.*

This is the beginning of the death of the republic. When the people clamor to be shielded from reality, when they praise their government for keeping things from them, when they choose to conduct their lives within the limits of whatever fantasy the government supplies, then they are no longer consenting to be governed, they are begging to be ruled.

The elements of totalitarianism are in place. Totalitarianism is not something imposed from above. It takes the "totality" to implement totalitarianism: a collaboration between citizens who no longer want to exercise choice and rulers who don't want to let them choose. A dictatorship (such as Saddam Hussein's) is the rule of one man or party imposed by force; in totalitarianism whole segments of society—the bureaucracy of the Soviet Union or the middle class of Nazi Germany —collude with the military for the sake of order. Order, clarity and efficiency, whether illusory or not, become the prevailing ideals; liberty, individual conscience and complexity become contemptible. What we are seeing in the United States now is the exhilaration, shared by the masses and the elite, that comes when a totalitarian system is in the first states of jelling.

That doesn't mean it's inevitable, or that it will take on predictable forms. The United States is more vast than Germany, and its trade and culture require a more fluid technology and social system than the Soviet Union or China. But if it comes, it will be an extension of this war: an exuberance for might and order, an impatience with liberty that will turn mean, and a fiercely insisted-upon distinction between the included and the excluded.

When you see masses of Americans with raised fists yelling "U!S!A! U!S!A!" you are looking at something new in American imagery: a shameless lust for individual strength through state power. Odd how, in country after country, the totalitarian impulse always takes the form of a raised arm menacing the air.

Gallup—The Next Morning

Waking up to the Iraqi acceptance of the Soviet peace proposal. The U.S. isn't having any. In the next booth at the McDonald's, a middle-age Navajo couple, intelligent faces, are reading the paper. Almost everyone in the place—almost everyone in this part of the state—is Native American, mostly Navajo and Hopi.

I drive slowly through Gallup on its main drag, the road that once was Route 66. Pawnshops, cafés, bars, Indian crafts. Something's off, and I can't put my finger on it. Then I realize: from one end of town to the other I haven't seen one flag, yellow ribbon or Desert Storm decal. No, there's a car antenna with a yellow ribbon, and that's it. I guess there's no reason that one more victory for WASP technology should generate any enthusiasm among the Navajo and Hopi.

Several hours to the northwest are the great mesas where the Hopi have lived for more than a thousand years. On what the maps call First Mesa is the oldest continuously inhabited town in the Western Hemisphere. When you stand at that place, you cannot distinguish between heaven and earth. In certain lights the far-off mesas seem like clouds, the clouds like stones, the earth itself like light, while the sky has the sheen of something that might be walked on. The seen blends with the unseen. There is nowhere to go, nothing to do, no way to be, but to stand between the seen and the unseen and live one's life.

Somewhere in the distance, a country is changing. It calls itself America but no longer knows its real name. Both the seen and the unseen press upon it. If you are a citizen of that place, you are a citizen not of a country but of a change. There will be nothing easy about what comes next.

New Mexico

On a drive of more than 3,200 miles, from West Hollywood to the New England village of Thompson in northeastern Connecticut, getting off the interstate to cruise the towns and look around, I see only one blatant statement against our government's policy: "STOP THE BOMBING," printed on cardboard and hung in the window of a bookstore in Albuquerque.

Years ago, the Club Cafe in Santa Rosa was the most famous diner on Route 66. It's a dead certainty that John Steinbeck, Woody Guthrie and Cisco Houston ate here in the thirties and forties. Buddy Holly and Roy Orbison, driving from Odessa and Lubbock to gigs in Albuquerque and Santa Fe, would have stopped here in the late fifties. Anybody with reason to cruise these roads regularly, then or now, ends up at the Club Cafe sooner or later. It's right up the main street (which, as in Gallup and Albuquerque, used to be Route 66) from the bridge over the Pecos River.

A large hand-lettered sign on the door reads: "We Support Our Troops." Underneath are thirty-one names from the town and county, all of them in the military, most of them in the Gulf. An enormous number of people for a place so small. Most of the names are Hispanic. In this part of the country that doesn't mean Mexican or Puerto Rican; most Hispanics here descend from the first Spaniards who colonized this area four-hundred years ago. So, descendants of the people who first took this land from the Indians, then had it taken from them by the Anglos, are off exerting American power in somebody else's land.

You can see from the talk among the waitresses and the pleasant old woman behind the counter that the only ideology that crosses their minds is whatever they've seen on television mixed with a deep sense of purpose: the whole world has been swept up in an event in which this waitress, the cook and the sweet old woman are participating through those thirty-one men. What do you say about a place that is so enthusiastic about the prospect of losing so many of its male youth? What do you say of people who use this event in order to feel important? They seem nice enough, they are nice enough, lovely people in a place I've always liked. The question isn't whether they're right or wrong, nice or not, the question is: what's missing here? What hole in their spirit could possibly be big enough that they gladly offer thirty-one of their young to fill it?

Amarillo, Texas

On I-40 as you enter Amarillo a sign warns you that this is a route for "hazardous cargo." Nuclear weapons are assembled in Amarillo. Trucks come and go with plutonium. Just after this sign is the Cadillac Ranch—that line of old Caddies half-buried in a field by the highway. This time they're painted a bright sky-blue. I've seen them pink, yellow and green. So the plutonium passes the Cadillacs amid American and Texan flags that fly everywhere you look on the west end of town.

Seventeen years ago, only an hour's drive from here, some friends and I built an amphitheater. I'm told that recently a conquistador's sword was found a quarter mile from where we were, on the banks of the Salt Fork of the Red River, on the same route north as the cattle drives of the old West Texas cowboys. And all those signs for scenic Palo Duro Canyon? That's where the Cavalry killed off the last of the free Cheyenne. And I ask the gods of the highways, what do I do, what does any American do, with this crazy-quilt heritage? From the conquistadors to the Gulf War this heritage has never been about freedom, it's been about excess. Whether it's religious movements like the Puritans and the tent-preachers, or the youth movement of sex-drugs-and-rock-and-roll, whether it was how much television people watch or how big a bomb can be built, something about America craves excess. It's the theme that joins all America's contradictions. Can a place of such excess ever gentle itself?

Clarendon, Texas

I stay the night with George and Dixie, two of the builders of that amphitheater. We watch CNN. Will the ground war start tomorrow? Is Saddam still in control, or alive? Why does Gorbachev want a cease-fire? Why doesn't Bush want to stop the killing? What is the matter with Caspar Weinberger's eyes?

There he is, on *Larry King Live*, and after he finishes a sentence or so he will pause and fix his eyes straight at the camera in the queerest way. I've seen that look once before, from a man in a Brooklyn mental hospital who was asking about his mother. He wanted her phone number, he wanted her address. When he asked, "Have you seen her?" his eyes were like those of Ronald Reagan's secretary of defense. I don't know what that means, but I promise you it's the same look.

The wind is blowing strong like it always does at night in West Texas, and Bush has set his cowboy deadline: "World Awaits High Noon," the *Amarillo Daily News* will headline in the morning. And as I drive out at dawn I see a billboard on I-40:

STOP Helping Communism
Here, There and
Everywhere

And I think of a friend south of here in Lubbock. Her nine-year-old was sent home from the public elementary school with a list of Satanist signs and symbols that children are forbidden to wear or write on their notebooks. Among those symbols: the yin-yang circle, the Star of David and the peace sign.

The Arkansas State Line

They play fair in Arkansas. They let you know the score as soon as you cross over:

Speed Laws Strictly Enforced
No Tolerance

Palestine, Arkansas

"Where you from out in California?"

"L.A."

"L.A.?! That's where it's *all happenin'*."

Is he putting me on? No. He's getting a kick out of meeting some-one from L.A. The more you get out into America, the more you find it's a country where most people think it's "all happenin'" somewhere else. Sometimes I think this is the most dangerous feeling in America. To say it's all happening somewhere else is to say that nothing is hap-pening where you are. You are not a citizen, you are barely even a resident. You are something by the side of the road. If a television crew comes into town you know all the right words to say about how important family and flag and church are in your community, but what you *really* think is that everything important happens somewhere else.

So in Santa Rosa you will send thirty-one of your young men to some place that *must* be more important than Santa Rosa, and then fill the emptiness of your unimportance by emoting about those sacrificial men, sacrificed on the altar of your need to be important. And in Palestine, Arkansas, you'll humble yourself before a stranger. How much have you had to humble yourself every day to cheerfully and spontaneously shame your home?

Don't tell me this man is just talking light talk. It is automatic talk. Where you look for the secrets of a family or a country is in their automatic talk. Nothing is happening in Palestine, Arkansas. And to fill that vacuum thousands will die this weekend half a world away.

Tennessee

Across the great Mississippi and into Tennessee, the Big Sky coun-try is behind me. There's a rolling road through corridors of tall trees from here to Maine. I pass the exit for Shiloh, where 130 years ago many Americans died. Down the road a little more is the exit for Nathan Bedford Forrest State Park. During the Civil War, Bedford Forrest was a criminal who massacred 300 black Union soldiers after they surrendered; later he became the first Grand Wizard of the Ku Klux Klan. General Schwarzkopf has just finished saying that the Iraqis who committed atrocities in Kuwait City are not human like we are.

I've driven 800 miles since dawn and I can't seem to stop. The ground war has started. The speaker system in this Nashville restaurant is tuned to an Associated Press radio special; you can even hear it in the bathroom. There's a call-in-guy from Vermont. He's furious. Why aren't we trying to kill Saddam Hussein personally? "Five, ten years from now this guy'll be dropping bombs on New York City." If I had the time or mental energy I'd try to differentiate between all the different kinds of ignorance needed to make that statement. But it seems all I can do is drive, burning Eden with a vengeance, until finally, another 220 miles down the road, I start seeing the Little People.

It's always good to see the Little People. They must have come with all the Scots and Irish to these Appalachians. I think it was from the Little People that the old Irish proverb comes: "The most beautiful music is the music of what happens."

That's easy for them to say. To them, human history is a vast silent movie and they can step in and out of the screen as they please. Wisdom, I'm told, is to learn their dance and see the ways to step on and off the temporal screen. I'm working on it, but the music of what happens is breaking my heart. "A broken heart is the best musical instrument of all, of all!"

That was one of the Little People. I give thanks to him, and cry some, in the motel of a town whose name I never knew.

Near the Tennessee–Virginia State Line

The American flag is flying beside the McDonald's flag. It should go without saying that this is considered not sacrilege or satire but patriotism. Which may be a good place to add that McDonald's has the cleanest bathrooms on the road.

On I-81 on the Tennessee Side of the Virginia Line

At the Mini-Mart, a framed flag with the legend "These Colors Don't Run." And above the cash register:

Do Not
Except Foodstamps
'owner'
Ed Short

A poor speller myself, I haven't the right to feel superior to Mr. Short's use of "except" when he means "accept," nor to the odd grammar that makes the sign seem a command to the customers instead of a policy of the store. It's sad, though, that the flag-bragging and the stinginess are so close together. It contradicts the sign below the cash register: "Proudly American."

I-81 in Virginia

George Orwell once said to Arthur Koestler: "This is the end of history." He meant that from this time on all the records of historical events would be controlled by the state, and that after a certain point it will be impossible for anyone (including the state) to know what really happened. In this era of mass media, this will be the least-recorded war. There will be fewer actual accounts of the war than of any major conflict of the twentieth century. So a hole in the lives of the American people (who don't want to know) creates a hole in history spreading out from the Persian Gulf. Into that hole could drop the Bill of Rights, and any law that does not serve power. How do you fight a hole? You insist on meaning. I don't mean you insist dogmatically on what you believe; rather, you insist that things *mean*. You listen for the resonances. You speak and dance with your dying breath, if it comes to that.

Into Maryland and Pennsylvania

In West Virginia there's the exit to Harper's Ferry. John Brown's body lies a-moldering in the grave. Over the Potomac into Maryland, the first sign is "Antietam Battlefield," and on into Pennsylvania it's "Gettysburg 1 Mile." Stopping at a motel, I'm struck by postcards of the Three Mile Island nuclear reactors. "It's just up the road here," the young woman says.

"They sell any bottled water in this town?"

"I know what you mean. The fish are still floatin' in the streams, let me tell ya."

"What's happening with the war?" I ask.

"From what they say we're kickin' butt over there, but you never know." She's wearing a big yellow ribbon, but living in the shadow of Three Mile Island she doesn't need to be told that governments lie.

Harper's Ferry, Antietam, Gettysburg, Three Mile Island—American names from different eras share one thing: their memories are faded, their meanings all but lost.

I am suddenly in the world of Thomas Wolfe and Theodore Dreiser. The city of Wilkes-Barre is straight out of their era: no new buildings, massive old factories with tall smokestacks on the edges of town, church spires here and there rising high above the blocks of wood-frame one-family houses with peaked roofs. This city is the relic of an America that was trying to be something other than what we've become. Yet the writers who recorded such places with such love and concern already feared America was lost.

> Remembering speechless we seek the great forgotten language, the lost lane-end into heaven, a stone, a leaf, an unfound door. Where? When? O lost, and by the wind grieved, ghost, come back again.

Thomas Wolfe was calling for the ghost to come and guide him, and I am calling for Thomas Wolfe to come and guide me, to help me remember that we *never* knew, we were always searching, there was never any such thing as America. For the Founders the country was an experiment that they hoped would one day be America; for those who came later, it was a dream—bequeathed by strangers—that they were trying to remember, understand and live. And for those who came after those who came after . . . a confusion of ambitions, dreams and memories that have left too many holes, great stretches of emptiness not in the landscape but in our living rooms, kitchens, beds, holes in which the best of what we wanted goes adrift and is lost.

U.S. 44 in Connecticut

A two-lane twisting its way through hilly New England, huge trees on all sides, frozen ponds, and the houses white and large and old. No 7-Elevens. No mini-malls. Dignified signs as you come upon a cluster of homes: "Incorporated 1708," "1713," "1718." The kind of town Wilkes-Barre once represented, the blustery industrial town of the turn of the nineteenth century, was already a long way from, and deep betrayal of, what the people who incorporated these villages in the early eighteenth century dreamed, just as these villages were the beginning of the invasion of that ancient Hopi town at the top of First Mesa.

But my friend James in the hamlet of Thompson, whose water comes from his own well and who eats the eggs of his chickens, takes me on a walk through the local graveyard. He wants to show me the new thing in headstones. We walk past stones three centuries old, past the plot he has purchased for himself, to a row of new graves. Carved on one headstone is an RV, complete with television antenna. Carved on another, a bingo card, and above it the word: "Bingo."

Bingo

The war, or at any rate the fighting, is over for now. That is what they announce tonight. My friend and I watch the announcement. We are each wearing layers of clothes, as one does when there's real winter, for the houses are never warm. The snow falls. General Norman Schwarzkopf is playing with his charts.

He's so happy that he forgets himself and makes what he might call a mistake and what I call the truth. On the night of February 27, 1991, this is what he says: "Once the air campaign started we knew he [the enemy] would be incapable of moving out to counter [our] move, *even if he knew we made it.*"

The emphasis is Schwarzkopf's. He said it with great satisfaction. In other words, the press censorship was unnecessary from a military perspective. The enemy couldn't act on the information "even if he knew." The censorship had nothing to do with the enemy: its goal was twofold—to keep the American people ignorant of the realities of the war, and to keep the entire record of the war in the possession of the American military, so that no one (possibly even the American government) could ever know this war's true history.

In some places this would be called a coup d'état.

Still River, Massachusetts

General Schwarzkopf's show-and-tell exhausted the official version of the Gulf War both as history and as entertainment. Nothing can happen now but the obvious: a big power and its allies will dictate a consensus to various smaller powers. There will be all the trappings of political theater: men getting on and off planes, going in and out of doors making statements, modifying those statements, and modifying *those*; commentators commenting on each other's comments; and a quick return of just enough troops to make for a few good parades—seas of yellow ribbons and Stars-and-Stripes with the new American image of the raised fist.

And when all the men have gotten on and off all the planes, it will be said that solutions have been reached in the Middle East. The future will be presented like the opening of a new mall, everybody can get everything they want, there's plenty of time to pay, plenty of parking, big sale on "peace." It will be considered un-American to remember Thomas Pynchon's warning: "If they can get you asking the wrong questions, they don't have to worry about the answers."

For this has all happened before. The problems Bush & Co. will pretend to solve were caused by exactly the same process of large powers dictating a consensus to smaller powers. The very creation of Jordan, Israel, Saudi Arabia, Syria, Iraq and Kuwait as nations were brainstorms of the big powers. The real "problem" is that the region has a resource that the West wants to control, and the only way to control it is to keep the region fundamentally volatile so that it stays dependent on a constant transfusion of money and arms. This will be called a "balance of power," which really means keeping several factions poised for war. Whatever "solution" the West imposes will develop gradually into another war, which will require another imposition of so-called solutions. The details do not matter—not even for the peoples of the Middle East. While the specific objects of their anxieties shift, the underlying causes of their unrest will not change. Skip CNN, *Nightline* and all the newspapers for the next two, five, maybe ten years, then tune in on the next Mideast brouhaha a-brewing—you won't have missed a thing. Sooner or later a fundamental transformation *will* occur in the Middle East as it did in Eastern Europe, but it will not be imposed; the people will rise from the streets and create something genuinely different (maybe for the better, maybe not). Then, in the longterm history of the region, the Gulf War will be seen as just a high-tech version of the same old shit.

But in the history of the United States, the Gulf War is pivotal. Finally the elements of an American totalitarianism are both structurally in place and openly welcomed: the military, the media, the federal government and a hefty majority of the people have decisively rejected the values of the Bill of Rights. Americans are celebrating not victory but surrender—their utter and perhaps final surrender to the ideals of might and order. They are not wildly happy about beating someone else's army; they are joyously surrendering to their *own* army and admitting at last that the responsibilities of liberty have been too much to bear. Like anyone in the final act of giving up their integrity, they feel a giddiness of relief and release; like any sellout, they resent anyone who reminds them of what they've betrayed.

Meanwhile, in Still River, Massachusetts, the sons of Roben and David are baking apple pie. I wish you could have seen them, as they bickered over who made a better crust and who had a defter hand at apple-peeling, these three boys—the oldest in his teens, the youngest maybe eight, marvelously unaware of how much they love each other. It is a family ritual, the boys' baking pie (very good pie, too). The last time I saw Roben, her eldest was an infant. Today we walked the muddy roads around Still River, the landscape all grays and browns, the clouds low and slow, patches of snow in the forest, thin ice on the lake, gunshots far off. We talked our troubles and our dreams as we used to. Then dinner, then the pie, then I did her Tarot. I left at midnight, driving northeast. I have no idyllic vision of this family or any other, but I think I know the difference between an empty and a fulfilling ritual when I'm in its presence. Only a fool could be saved from the weight of history by an apple pie, but there are such pies, and I am a fool.

Maine

In Portland my high-school friend Carl invites me to go to an A.A. meeting with him. I've never been. Here is a war I respect, the struggle with one's own heart: all these meetings, all over the country, almost any time of the day or night, around this issue and others, with their potent mix of self-examination and camaraderie. But where is this energy in the politics of the country? How can the two things be happening at once, and on such a large scale? When in an A.A. meeting you hear people of very different levels of education speak with more intelligence, passion and generosity than any elected official in decades, you feel a kind of vertigo, the public life of the nation veering one way while the inner life of its people goes another. Yet the entities of "the nation" and "the people" overlap in so many places. These are the same people. It's maddening. Should there be, as James Hillman implies, 12-step programs to heal our dysfunctional ways of being citizens? Is that a tactic to get this energy one sees in an A.A. meeting out into our politics and history?

I go further north, to Waterville, to see my high-school friend Mark. I haven't seen him in twenty-one years, but as soon as I step out of the car I see it *is* Mark still. He says the same of me, how little it seems we've changed. And as we talk and drink and tell each other our lives over the next days, kept housebound by an ice storm, I think that this too is stronger than history: how something in us is impervious to the trends of collective thought, culture and politics—something which perhaps can be broken but can never be taken. In his novel *1984* George Orwell says this isn't so, says a totalitarian state can steal your psyche no matter how hard you struggle; yet Orwell has an odd way of proving it. In his novel it takes the entire power of the state to break one man's spirit. How strong, then, must the spirit really be? This thing within that is strong enough to keep us who we are through all the changes—that is the inner strength on which rests the ideal of liberty. In today's society many individuals have this strength; yet the collective, composed of those same individuals, does not. The question of our era becomes: Is there a way to heal that split?

The next day the motor that runs my windshield wipers shorts out. You can't drive in snow and rain without wipers, so where am I going to get a part for a twenty-two-year-old Chevy in Waterville? The Chevy dealer says he can have it for me in a week. But Mark's friend Rick thinks differently. He's a seasonal farm worker who lives with his wife and four children in a narrow trailer off a dirt road. He drives me all over central Maine, it seems, to find the part and install it while it's snowing, while not taking a dime for his trouble because I'm the friend of his friend.

Rick's thinking about going to Kuwait. He hears they're paying $9,000 a month for carpenters—plus room and board, so you can send your paycheck home. "I got the number of the Kuwait embassy. I'm going to do the paperwork and see what happens."

Boston

In 1959 Johnny Ertha came into my life. I was a street-kid at a summer camp, and he was my first real-life hero, the first man I ever wanted to emulate and live up to. It was Johnny who read us Orwell's *Animal Farm*, and it was from Johnny's mouth I first heard the words of Eugene V. Debs: "Where there is a soul in prison I am not free." We haven't seen each other since 1972. Sixty-odd years old now, he's heavier but he's still Johnny, still fiery, still coming out with things like, "You must let others be right, to console them for not being anything else."

At nine o'clock that evening we watch George Bush address Congress about his victory in the Gulf. We are preparing, according to

Bush, for "the next American century . . . Americans are a caring people. We are a good people. A generous people." Johnny, an African-American from Maine, lives in Dorchester, where many of Boston's people of color live. He teaches in the public schools. Across the street is such a school. There's money for war but none for these kids. They pass crack in the yard openly. Around the corner not long ago, somebody sprayed a few people with gunfire. In fact, as George Will reported in *Newsweek*, "During the 43 days of Desert Storm, violence in America killed many times more Americans than war did." It is safer to be a soldier fighting Saddam Hussein than to be a child on the streets of an American city. George Bush is able to ignore this, while smiling, gloating about a victory over an army that didn't fight back. According to him, this makes us great again.

The next day I go with my sister Joan to Lexington and Concord, where our revolution began—a fair fight, which we won against the most powerful military of that time. Across the bridge and up the hill stood 400 New England farmers; where I'm standing, a detachment of the English army. Ralph Waldo Emerson grew up in that house over there; it was he who would call this "the shot heard round the world." Thoreau would visit Emerson in that house; in a protest against our invasion of Mexico, Thoreau would coin the phrase "civil disobedience."

My sister and I drive back into Boston, to King's Chapel, and visit the grave of Samuel Adams. Adams was a tireless organizer and instigator, an inciter of riots and an uncompromising lover of liberty. These days he would probably be labeled a terrorist. After the Revolution he was the third governor of Massachusetts. When the Founders wanted to give us a constitution that did not specify our liberties, Sam Adams and his old rioters were among those who balked. He felt the Founders were betraying the Revolution and said so; then he maneuvered for Massachusetts—in those days, the most influential state— to demand a Bill of Rights. He hadn't fought for a nation so much as for a vision of liberty, and the canny old conspirator saw to it that this vision was passed on. They will tell you that liberty is defended with guns. Sometimes that's true and sometimes not. What's always true is that liberty is defended best by the exercise of liberty.

My sister and I stand quietly at Samuel Adams's grave. I say a prayer in thanks for all that he and his kind bequeathed, and think of something Johnny Ertha said the night before: "Just as important as what we do or what we don't do, is how we behave when we don't know what to do."

March 15, 1991

Standing at the Wall

In Washington, D.C., the day is cold, the air is still and the sun is warm. On afternoons like this, in late winter in the East, you can stand for hours in the light without freezing. I have stood a long time now, at this black wall. I don't know what I expected to find at the Vietnam Memorial. But after a Gulf War in which men who died behind the lines in traffic accidents were given heroes' burials, in which soldiers who met token resistance for 100 hours are called "greater" than those who spent months and years facing the fiercest guerrilla fighters of our century; and with President Bush pushing the notion that in Vietnam it was our loss, rather than our policy, that stained us, and that the Gulf War redeems that loss—it seems time to stand here.

But it seems shameful, too, to stand so inadequately, unable to think or feel, only to stare.

If you face the Washington Monument at the foot of the reflecting pond, then the Lincoln Memorial is directly behind you, up long flights of steps; the Potomac River is down a gentle slope on your right; the Vietnam Memorial is just on your left. The Capitol dome is not far in the distance and you can see the Jefferson Memorial, about a twenty-minute walk across the park. The last time I stood here was in the spring of 1970, in the huge demonstration to protest the bombing of Cambodia. A few days before, demonstrators like us had been killed at Kent State. It seemed possible that anything might happen; they might kill us all.

Squads of policemen on motor scooters (looking a little silly; the scooters seemed too small for them) drove forward on both sides of the pond, swinging their nightsticks to clear the area. I was afraid, trembling, but I was frightened even more at how I'd feel if I ran, so I stood, waited to be hit. But it was as though I was invisible—a formation of scooter-police drove straight at me as I shook, yet none of them looked at me, and the nightsticks they were swinging in circles never touched me. They passed, and I watched down the pond where they beat others. Then suddenly, it seemed I was the only one around. And I felt, at that moment, almost as baffled and useless as I feel now at this memorial. I don't mean in any way to equate my little episode with the experience of combat; it's just that here I was again, after another war we were powerless to stop.

"Nothin', all for nothin'," a woman in her sixties says as she and her friend slowly walk past me, looking at the wall. Another woman pushes a man in a wheelchair. He wears a jacket and tie, is about my age. The left side of his face is paralyzed, and he seems to have the use only of his right arm and hand. In that hand he holds a bouquet of flowers. The woman takes it from him and places it at the base of one section of the wall. With the flowers is a yellow piece of paper on which five of the more than 50,000 names are awkwardly printed. Quickly the woman wheels the man away. Perhaps the five died in the same action in which he was wounded. Perhaps this is the anniversary.

One of the vets who tends the wall comes with a ladder. With him are a gray-haired man and woman of about fifty with a redheaded boy of about twenty. The gray-haired man is apparently a vet too. The wall-tender goes up the ladder, finds a name and does a pencil-press of the name on a sheet of paper, then he comes down the ladder and goes to hand the paper to the gray-haired man. But the man gestures toward the boy and says, "Give it to him." The boy takes it. It is his father's name. Nobody knows how to act. They are trying not to be solemn. They take pictures. The real event is going on beneath their behavior; you can hear it in the strain of their voices.

A little later, at another place on the wall, a boy of about ten calls his mother over. "Mom! Mom!" She comes and shushes him. He covers one letter of someone's last name with his thumb. "Mom, if it's spelled like this, it's my name."

Only when I step back to photograph the wall do I begin to appreciate the genius of its creator, Maya Ying Lin. For you cannot photograph it, not really. There is no angle through which you can see it whole through a lens unless you're standing so far off that the picture would be meaningless. Even with advanced equipment, if you're close enough to see that the names are inscribed, you're too close to contain the whole; if you contain the whole, you can't tell from the photograph alone what it really is. So the wall defies deconstruction and transmission by any other medium. You can't take it home with you. You have to experience it to know it, and you can keep only as much as you've experienced.

It's not so much a tombstone or a monument as a grave. The top of the wall is at ground level. The path slopes down, so that to experience the wall you must descend. Thus, the wall coaxes everyone into the same ritual of descent, a ritual that the psyche can't help but recognize. American manners are becoming more crass and crude by the year, but here there is decorum—a decorum demanded by the wall itself. People speak softly here. They can do and say very private things in public while strangers gently project an acceptance that makes for no embarrassment. I cannot tell you what alchemy of design accomplishes this, but I can testify that it's like no other place in America. Here it's all right to cry. It's not threatening to stand beside a stranger. Even to talk to oneself. Nor is laughter out of place. The wall draws one into another ritual: almost everyone, at some point, can't help laying hands on its cool surface, feeling names like the blind.

Reminiscent, I suddenly realize, of the monoliths in *2001*, the wall takes all this in, absorbing the energy, increasing its power every day with every visitor. But the masterstroke is its sheen. It's not merely a wall or a gravestone; it's a mirror. Looking at the roll of Vietnam dead, you are looking at yourself—so clearly you could comb your hair or adjust your makeup if you chose. It reflects not only you and those near, but the Capitol dome, the Washington Monument, the lawn, the trees, the jets and helicopters taking off in the distance. On its surface death meets life, the past meets the present. What was, doesn't accuse; what is, doesn't apologize. But this is the one place in America where they face each other, like it or not, beyond cant, revision and lies.

Yet even as I am humbled and stunned by Ms. Ying Lin's creation, realizing that as an American work of art it far surpasses any other of my lifetime; even as the names of the dead seem to come to life in the reflection of my own face, my own body—I know that, through this wall, they are demanding of me a response, and I don't know what to say to them. I feel in my bones that they don't care whether or not I write about this, and perhaps they don't even care whether the country goes to hell now. History isn't their problem anymore. But it's as though they demand something of everyone who stands before them, and they demand it now, as you stand here.

And what can I give them? "Thanks for dying for bullshit"? "Thanks for being so good and brave and young that old men who never deserved your loyalty could deceive you unto death"? I feel like I'm insulting them just by standing here, and that is the last thing I wish. Is all I have for them simply whatever poor blessing one stranger can give another? I practically run from the place.

Then up the steps of the Lincoln Memorial, to stand before the gargantuan statue. It's hard to believe Lincoln would have approved of his sculpture. The only truly humble man ever to fill the presidency, he would not have wanted to be portrayed as a god on a throne. But they couldn't ruin his face. It humbles the place in spite of their grandiosity. Engraved on one wall is his second inaugural, and I stop at the sentence "The progress of our arms, on which all else chiefly depends, is as well-known to the public as to myself." Under Lincoln, this was true; it has never been true since. On another wall is his Gettysburg Address, words written to commemorate another era's dead soldiers. I had to learn it by heart when I was seven. I was supposed to recite it at a school assembly but was too terrified to show up. Funny how you can know some words all your life, then suddenly see that not only did you never get them, you hardly noticed they were there:

"That from these honored dead we take increased devotion."

The thought sinks into me as I repeat it: "We take increased devotion . . . from the dead. . . ."

I go back to the wall. We cannot promise to remember the dead, because memory is not reliable—we rewrite our memories every day. We may console ourselves that these dead have a place in history, but historical accounts are often contradictory, and historical perspectives shift so much from generation to generation that even "a place in history" is never fixed. Praise of the war dead is almost always self-serving. Grief can get too comfortable, can turn into a place to hide. But here, on the mirror of this wall, where the dead have borrowed our own eyes to examine us, the humility of Lincoln's "increased devotion" honors both them and ourselves. This is the song of the dead: that we deepen our reverence for life. It is that simple, that difficult.

As you walk away from the memorial, you do not see your reflection going in the other direction, further into the wall. You become aware, again, of the sounds of this terrible city. It's not a very long walk to some of the worst slums in the Western world, where children driven mad by America kill one another every day. In the *Washington Post* this morning (12 March), a front-page story began: "Higher food prices and rising need have forced government in the Washington area to stop providing food for thousands of undernourished children and mothers." But there's always the money to kill someone. It's not our culture that is crumbling, but our reverence.

I walk to the Jefferson Memorial. On one wall is a passage from the notes he wrote when the Constitutional Convention failed to abolish slavery: "Indeed I tremble for my country when I reflect that God is just."

March 29, 1991

A Stillness of Leaves

There's a woman in Georgia who looks at you and knows things. All the words for what she does have been twisted shapeless by the tabloids and the New Agers, so let's not call her anything. Can't name her, either—she wouldn't like that. But on the outskirts of Atlanta, following directions that either I always get wrong or are always given to me wrong, I manage to find her again. And again, as I sit saying almost nothing and she tells me almost everything, I'm stunned at what the psyche is, at how it walks around so naked that anyone with eyes can see it. As I'm leaving she tells me I should do a "sweat" if I get the chance. "Don't go in a white sweat lodge, go in a red sweat lodge."

"Give me a break, where am I gonna find an Indian who'll let me in his sweat lodge?" is what I think but don't say. She answers the question anyway, tells me if I'm open to it someone will come to me.

Driving the thousand miles between Atlanta and Austin, I consider everything she says except the "red sweat lodge" stuff. I don't give that a second thought. Then, backstage at the *Austin Chronicle* Music Awards, I keep looking at a Native American man who's looking at me. A few minutes later I forget about him. An hour or so after that, a woman I've known nearly twenty years wants me to meet someone. It's this same man. He tells me he is leading a sweat in three days. I don't know how to describe his look. Does it make sense to say it's both gentle and intense, both deeply concerned (with me, personally) and completely detached? He reaches out his arm, puts two fingers

172

on my heart, says: "You should come. The grandmothers and grand-
fathers have something to tell you."

I am so surprised that I completely lose the memory of his words
until my friend reminds me of them the next day. And then I'm doubly
shocked, even appalled, at having so blocked his words. The memory
comes back, I feel his fingers on my heart again, and I know I'll have
to go. And knowing that, I'm afraid. My friend laughs at my fear.
(She's been laughing at my fears for years.) She reminds me that nothing
can be revealed but what's already in the heart; that if it's a burden,
I've been carrying it all along, so what is there to fear? Easy for *her*
to say.

The man I sometimes refer to as "my Teacher" happens to be in
town. Our friendship, too, goes back almost twenty years. The most
extraordinary person I've known, his name is unknown to any except
his friends. He's said, pointedly, that only a fool seeks fame. That
people who become famous are doomed to repeat themselves for yet
more fools, and every time they're forced to do this they know less.
He says, "Language is not communication—language is a substitute
for communication." Then he adds, "Thinking is make-believe."

"I'll have to think about that," I say.

We take a walk by the Colorado River, which divides North and
South Austin. I never mention the sweat, the Indian or the woman
in Georgia. I don't need to. It's not that he knows without my saying,
though he sometimes does; it's just that he never interferes with a path
already chosen. We'll compare notes at the other end, maybe. He's
twenty or thirty years older than me (I've never been sure), and it is
enough to talk together, gossip about our friends, sass each other,
and know that the road is long. We'll walk together this way even after
one of us dies. We are both certain of this, without ever having spoken
of it, and we're walking alongside that knowledge as much as we're
walking alongside the river. At the end of our walk, for no special
reason, my fear has dimmed to simple nervousness.

That night at a club called Pontie's, Jimmie Dale Gilmore sings a
verse that will be on his new album: "*So good to be home on the
borderland/Where things are not what they seem/So good to be home
on the borderland/Between the dark and the dream.*"

Three days later I'm standing with about twenty others around a
fire as night comes on. Everyone has a towel. The men are in bathing

suits or cut-offs or shorts; the women are mostly in long, loose dresses. The Pipe Carrier, as his tribe would call him, is blessing the fire. As with the woman in Georgia, as with my Teacher, so with this: nothing is public about it; there are no ads and only the subtlest of signs; you find your way here through following something inside yourself that opens toward such things. So the Pipe Carrier blesses the fire and makes a gesture that includes all of us, saying, "This is not a game. We just come here to pray."

I feel strange telling you about this and didn't intend to write about it when I sat down at this typewriter, but the pact I've made with writing is: if it's demanding to be written, write it, no matter what. You start to say one thing, something else comes out. You follow where it goes, let *it* do the writing. Later, take the heat. Normally I would wait years to write of such things and then try to disguise them, not be so direct. If I'm offending anyone who participated in anything I'm telling, I ask their forgiveness. This is why I'm telling it:

Standing by the fire after the Pipe Carrier's blessing, I look up at the sky. Storm clouds are moving very fast on the wind. But down here, nothing at all, not a breeze. Even the smallest leaves are absolutely still. That's what the world feels like to me now. Gruesome things that we seem powerless to stop are happening all over the planet, and on every level of existence, like a monster storm, and yet there are places where the smallest leaves don't move, where blessings are possible. On the one hand, the country is going to hell; on the other, men and women everywhere gather in sacred ways.

In a small town near Augusta, Maine, a woman I haven't spoken with in many years tells me of gatherings of her and her friends, and they are just like the gatherings I know in Texas and California. The day after the sweat, 100 miles west on the Llano River, another friend shows me the shrine she tends, built with friends some years ago, and tells me of the days she spends beside the river alone, finding her way into her own rituals, which are so like mine, and those of other men and women I know. Clearly some communication is going on beneath language. Everywhere I go I run into people who are living like this.

The Western eye, which is expressed in a raw way by the media and in a more refined way by university-trained intellectuals, doesn't know what to do with this, because to enter this realm is to leave the West. Where it leads I can't say, and I don't know anyone who can.

Many things are coming together—old stuff, new stuff. Something is forming in a quiet way beneath the chaos. Whether it will have an effect on our history probably depends upon our courage, in the long run.

And maybe it doesn't mean anything. Maybe we're just a bunch of hysterics. Pathetic ghost dancers who think that if we dance till we drop the buffalo will come back. People so terrified of the new corporate order that we'll believe any slop that offers refuge. How did my Teacher put it? "We're so desperate we come awfully close to making fantasies work."

But standing by the fire, about to enter the sweat lodge, I don't think that.

This, then, is written in spirit from the clearing where the leaves don't move. Only to say that the storm is not all there is.

What goes on in the sweat is not for writing about, beyond what the Pipe Carrier said, that we've come here to pray. In the tradition of the Judeo-Christians, prayer mostly amounts to begging: "Please, God, give me this or that." In tribal tradition, prayer is the human power of blessing—something you never hear of in Western thought. And to bless with all your heart clears a space inside you where there, too, the leaves don't move.

The next day, looking at the world again, a Butch Hancock verse keeps singing itself in my head: "I asked my angel if heaven is near/She said, 'It's closer than it looks/But you can't get there from here'/Where can you go when you're already gone?"

Days later, on the banks of the Llano with the one I'll call the Shrine Tender, we talk about where you go when you're already gone. Crazy or not, right or wrong, pathetic or brave or both, somewhere along the road we've stopped believing in what the West calls "The World." I don't mean in our heads (which, actually, are the last things to go—intellectually, I can still get suckered by the West); I mean in our knees, in our hair, in our cocks, our pussies, our tongues, our hearts. We still have to pay our bills in that devastated world, and that may get real tiresome, but *that's* what feels like the empty ritual. And to give oneself over to that emptiness seems the only true mistake.

The Georgia woman and the Shrine Tender don't know each other, but they both spoke of the same deck of animal cards. The Shrine Tender had drawn the heron card, then sat on a rock by the river waiting for the image of a ritual to come to her. Instead, a heron came to her. Sat awhile, flew off. The day after she tells me this, 300 miles north in the Texas Panhandle, a heron glides across the road in front of me low and slow. I ease on the brakes and watch its passage. The last time I saw a heron hereabout, or anywhere, was seventeen years ago working with my Teacher on the Salt Fork of the Red River.

Call it what you like, I call it a sign. The storm is not all there is. The-world-that-calls-itself-"The World" is not all there is. I don't know enough tonight to give another clue. No one can go another's distance.

The next day my Teacher tells me, "When you start shedding some of the blocks, without fanfare, you meet with similar effort. 'Cause a man can't do this alone." A hard rain comes on as we speak. He laughs, "Hey! We're gonna talk it toward us, aren't we!" And later: "Others can only discover this as you've discovered it, by accident and effort."

April 12, 1991

Part Four

The Witness Tree

The Ability of Not Knowing

This picture, THIS picture—I don't give a FUCK what anybody says.
If you don't have time to see it, don't. If you don't like it, don't. If it
doesn't give you an answer, FUCK you. I didn't make it for you anyway.
John Cassavetes, after shooting his last scene in Love Streams

Las Vegas, eight years ago. It's the beginning of June and 110
in the shade. John Cassavetes is filming a couple of scenes of his last
great work, *Love Streams*. He has begun to suspect, and will soon
know, that he is dying. One day at dailies he says to no one in particular, "This is a sweet film. If I die, this is a sweet last film." For
the moment he chooses to take the possibility of death as just another
part of the atmosphere, significant but not central, in the creation
of his new work. "I set up an atmosphere, and the *atmosphere* directs
the film."

John's "atmosphere" takes place night and day, without letup,
whether the cameras are rolling or not, and now it's taking place at
a joint called the Tower of Pizza on the south end of the Strip. Several
of us are drinking wine and being loud, especially Cassavetes and his
cousin, the film's art director and John's staunch ally, Phedon Papa-
michael. They are driving the waitress crazy. Phedon wants absolutely
no garlic. Cassavetes wants to have a discussion with the cook. Phedon
is insisting that even a place called the Tower of Pizza shouldn't mind
preparing special, slightly exotic dishes that are not on the menu. The

179

waitress is barely restraining herself from throwing something not very exotic all over us.

Cassavetes eggs her on, because he likes her toughness. I've gotten used to this way of his, how he'll see a quality he likes in some stranger, even a negative quality, and he'll goad and push until he gets a good taste of it. If the food starts to fly tonight, he won't care. He likes flying food.

But as it happens, this becomes the only one-on-one argument I ever see him flat-out lose. The measure of John is that he's delighted to lose, digs the toughness of this woman, forgets all about wanting to talk to the cook, as Phedon forgets about a special meal, and both welcome the waitress into our impromptu gang as everyone enjoys the food anyway (which lets me off the hook—it's my hangout, I brought us here).

A young, beautiful actress in our party is explaining to John why she can't stand the character John is playing: "He's a creep with his kid." John comes back at her with something he loves to say and says often, that he understands everybody in the movie but his own character. Then John's eyes get brighter: he doesn't *want* to understand his own character, he doesn't want to understand himself either; on or off the screen, what people call "understanding" is goddamn over-rated. "I love motion, change, and I hate answers—because they stop change."

"You're a phony sonofabitch," Phedon says with the matter-of-fact familiarity of someone who's said the same thing many times.

"I'm phony?!" John explodes. Phedon has done his part, given John a hook for another riff, and now he sits back and watches the show, like the rest of us. "I feel sorry for *you*," John says with glee, "because *you're* phony, because you think you know what's right, what's good. I don't know and I don't wanna know."

"You put your life into the movie," Phedon tells him, "and then you say you don't."

"What?"

"You know. Don't tell me like you don't know."

A beat of silence—something rare in their exchanges. Then John says, "I'll put *everything* into the movie. What I know *and* what I don't know. And that's as far from phony as Kelsey's you-know-what." John doesn't give you time to know something important has just passed between them; he veers the talk another way, we finish the meal, and as usual he won't let anybody else pay. He stands up, cackles that laugh of his, and wipes the bill across his behind like a piece of toilet paper.

As we walk down the Strip back to our hotel, I'm thinking of another John-and-Phedon exchange a couple of months back during preproduction, an argument about the color of upholstery that went off into a discussion of love (a talk with John usually did, sooner or later). "That was the biggest discovery I ever made," John said at the time: "that love stops. Just like a clock. Or anything. Then you wind it and it goes again. 'Cause if it stops forever, then you die."

"Love," Phedon started to say, but as he paused to finish his sentence John interrupted with:

"I know what love is."

"You don't," Phedon said quietly.

"You know I know," John said just as quietly.

"And, if you know?"

"Love—is the ability of not knowing."

I was in the institution at the time. The institution of marriage, I mean. Testing in a real-life laboratory some quaint and/or self-destructive ideas about love. I heard "Love is the ability of not knowing" as Cassavetes' way of saying "Love is having faith." Which may be why his marriage lasted thirty-odd years (ended only by death) and mine six. For faith was the last thing on John's mind. He was talking about something far tougher: love between two people depends upon their ability to endure the unknown.

On the surface that sounds like faith. But when translated into our all-too-human terms, "faith" usually means spending a great deal of energy trying not to see what's staring you in the face. Even at its best, when faith admits there are unknowns it tends to tacitly assume that the unknown is on one's side, or is at least ultimately livable, manageable and therefore no match for the faith. Cassavetes had a dismissive shrug he reserved for ideas and people not worthy of his attack, and I can see him shrug that way at such assumptions. His films begin at the moment when a person has been forced beyond all that to the moment, as he put it, "when you can't find your way home." ("That's when I consider it's worth it to make a film," he added.)

And what if that unknown is impenetrable by love? What, then, can your bond with another human being consist of? When that bond is tested (for it will be), *what* will be tested? Cassavetes thinks that what is tested is what he called, in his peculiar grammar, "the ability of not knowing." How much can you allow yourself to feel, or share, or be, when you know you'll never know? When there can be no security, since anything that can serve as security, any promise or insurance, can be taken from you in an instant? When there is nothing but what you feel, what you sense the other feels and the unknown all round?

This "unknown" ain't passive. It moves you, buffets you, steals from you, infects you, wakes you up in a sweat, sweeps you away and throws you down, and finally eats you and we call that "dying." What if this is the way it is, beyond all the workshops, books, lectures, arts, therapies, all the palliative constructs? Welcome to the laughter of John Cassavetes.

That high, wheezy, witchy laugh that he let loose on film only twice, in short bursts during *Husbands* (1970) and at full force in the last moments of his last performance and last film, *Love Streams* (1984). A laugh that would end suddenly, as though he'd quickly stepped back from himself; then he'd give you a look that somehow was no less piercing for being gentle, and his eyebrows would arch a little, and his expression would seem to say, "See?"

Las Vegas, the summer of 1983, later that night, in John's room. The walls are colored puke green. "A perfect room," he says, "a room where lots of people have lost. Lost things important to them, not just money."

There are a few of us, we're quiet, it's the end of the night, the last drink. I'm thinking that it's incredible that his films, while so merciless, aren't depressing. They always make you feel more alive because they're so full of life, and that's because this man has the ability of not knowing. As the summer goes on it'll be clearer that he's dying, but we won't talk of it. Much later, a few months before his death, he'll say to me, "Is life about horror—or is it about those few moments we have?"

As always, he won't pretend the question has an answer. But now, in this terrible room which he really does relish, he's thinking about his art and he says, more to himself than to us: "What people *like* is different from what they want. You have to give them what they want, not what they like. They see insincerity and they hate it—but they don't say what they really feel. Why do people throw away all their mentality, all of what they really feel, in lieu of a promise—fake, made by the society—of how everybody's supposed to live?"

Goodnight, John.

May 17, 1991

In Defense of Alcohol

My mother and father didn't drink. A beer or Chianti now and then, maybe a 7 & 7, but they didn't *drink*. They rarely kept liquor in the apartment. Now that I think of it, I never saw them drunk. And I don't remember seeing any of my many relatives that way. Maybe a little loose on New Year's Eve, but never drunk. As for inebriated people on the street, it just didn't happen in the Italian neighborhoods of Brooklyn and the Bronx. In fact, the first up-close drunk I saw in my youth—was me.

Me and Dave, actually. Fifteen years old, in 1960. Dave lived in a modest house in Bayside, Queens, a couple of blocks from the not-yet-opened Long Island Expressway. A slightly older friend of ours had given us, as a Christmas present, a bottle of Four Roses spiked with rum. As we opened the bottle in the television room, Dave's mom sat knitting in the living room. The pedagogical theory was that it was better we get drunk in the house than somewhere they couldn't find us. A pretty far-out notion for 1960.

It had been snowing for days, big flakes floating straight down, huge snowdrifts, no cars on the streets, no one outside. Just outside the window, Dave's father had decorated a small pine with blue lights that made the snow blue, too. As we took our first drink straight from the bottle, Dave went though his brother's records and picked a new one with a funny title, *Mingus Ah Um*.

We didn't know from jazz—we just put it on for the title—at the hellfire first cut, "Better Git It in Your Soul." As Mingus and the whiskey

184

peeled dead matter off the cortex like a scouring brush, we felt suddenly alive in a way that we had never been. Something was being
said to us that had never been said, something of such urgency that
we were hardly prepared for the very different urgency of the second
cut, "Goodbye Porkpie Hat." Sensuous, slow, thoughtful, elegiac . . .
how could the whiskey go so well with both? After you git it in your
soul, the man was telling us, be prepared for the pain.

Where were we? Who were we? Dave and Speedy (that was my name
back then), who could say anything to each other, and who seemed
to know the same things at the same time, and were going to be great
adventurers, great writers, great *something*, live up to this man Mingus
somehow, use what he was giving us . . . a couple of boys who didn't
guess how hard it was going to be, just to be a man. Somehow Dave's
mother was looking the other way when we couldn't contain our energy
anymore and we took the bottle and walked off into the snow.

I yelled to the neighborhood, at the top of my lungs: "MIDDLE
CLASS SHITS!" and Dave said something equally polemical, and we
peed down into the empty Long Island Expressway, and we threw
ourselves in the snow when the cops came by, and lying in the snow,
laughing, loaded, already a little sick, loving the cold, loving each other,
and reciting the Dylan Thomas poems we knew by heart, yelling them
into the night—we *understood* Mingus, we understood everything and
the whiskey was part of it, and we loved the whiskey, too. God, we
were happy. You can't die bitter if you've had a friend like that, a night
like that. (It's worth adding that thirty years later we can still tell each
other anything, and the Mingus record just gets better.)

Most of what you read now about alcohol and addiction leaves out
how marvelous it can feel to be drunk—an omission that, as the addiction theorists would say, amounts to denial. It's as though they have
to deny the beauties of drinking or they couldn't make their point.
Is something wrong with their point, that it can't stand a little wild
beauty? (It was Rumi, the great Sufi, who said that wine gets drunk
with us, not the other way around.)

Didn't drink much in my twenties. Except when I was twenty-four—I
even drank in the morning that year. Otherwise it wasn't unusual to
go weeks or months without a beer. Then one morning I was twenty-
six, driving into the West for the first time. If you've grown up in the
East, your vision usually stops about twenty yards from where you

stand. Some wall, some tree. Space back there feels cramped. Driving 200 miles is a big occasion. But in the West, with its endless, beckoning vistas, I've driven 70 miles for a pizza, 500 for a party, 1,000 for a girl. This is not unusual behavior in Texas and New Mexico.

Anyway, the best day of my life was the first time I drove into that big sky. Driving across Oklahoma in a Pontiac Firebird on what was still called Route 66, horizon in front of me, horizon in my rear-view, horizon all around, great white clouds you could reach out and touch, it was more like flying than driving. Crossing into the Texas Panhandle. A huge storm to the south. It was as though, before I'd driven into that space, my mind had been a closed fist, and being in that wide, wide country for the first time—I can't tell you what it was, to feel that fist slowly open within my skull and reach out to the world.

Stayed in Amarillo that night. The motel room had a little porch. The wind kept the mosquitos off. I opened a bottle of VO. I didn't know what *real* whiskey was, couldn't have afforded it if I'd known. And that night VO was a gift from the gods.

But to understand that night, you have to understand a little about drinking alone. Drinking alone has a very bad rap. "Do you drink alone?" therapists ask you with a kind of squint. But there's a kind of drunkenness you can only feel alone. Sometimes it's a pain-drunk; the whiskey burns your throat and you feel like you're drinking pure pain. Now, pain is something we're *not* supposed to feel—on the Cosby show, in New Age thought, anywhere you look. Like the song says, "I haven't got time for the pain." Transcend it, elevate it to grief, do some damn thing with it, but get out of it. Most of the therapies and the entire pharmaceutical industry are based on "Don't feel pain."

And they say that all you're doing with alcohol is numbing that pain. And often that's true.

But sometimes it's not. And it would be refreshing to hear the theorists admit it. (Theorists have a hard time admitting the "sometimes" things. Afraid their theories will collapse. That's what's passing for "thought" these days.) For there are messages in pain, trying to be heard. So sometimes you don't drink to numb it. You drink to swim in it, to inoculate yourself with it, to go so far down into it that it holds no surprises for you any longer.

Whiskey, you see, is a mysterious fluid. In the Irish language, whiskey was called the "water of life." It can taste like pure pain or like edible fire, celebratory like all fire seems (even when it burns down your house). And there I was, drunk already on the land, the road and the sky, watching the moon come up, too dumb for lots of things but smart enough to know I was happy. I shared that whiskey with the moon.

The book I'd brought, John Steinbeck's *Grapes of Wrath*, was about other people who'd taken that highway a while back. And this, I swear to you, is the page I opened to:

> And always if he had a little money, a man could get drunk. The hard edges gone, and the warmth. . . . Sitting in a ditch, the earth grew soft under him. Failures dulled and the future was no threat. And hunger did not skulk about, but the world was soft and easy, and a man could reach the place he started for. The stars came down wonderfully close and the sky was soft. Death was a friend, and sleep was death's brother. The old times came back—a girl with pretty feet, who danced one time at home. . . . When was that? Ought to find a girl to talk to. That's nice. Might lay with her too. But warm here. And the stars down so close, and sadness and pleasure so close together, really the same thing. Like to stay drunk all the time. Who says it's bad? Who dares to say it's bad? Preachers—but they got their own kinda drunkenness. Thin, barren women, but they're too miserable to know. Reformers —but they don't bite deep enough into living to know. No— the stars are close and dear and I have joined the brotherhood of the worlds. And everything's holy—everything, even me.

About ten years later I was in a hospital in Austin, Texas, with most of my internal organs wired to television screens. My heart or my gall bladder or my liver—they never did find out for sure. (It *felt* like a heart attack, but apparently lots of things do.) A nurse had just come in and cheerfully said that, my, my, about ten minutes ago my brain-waves did a little flip, looks like a slight stroke. "But you *look* fine, don't cha?" And she just as cheerfully left. I was married at the time, and at the moment my wife looked about as bad as I did. We were trying not to wonder whether I was ever going to leave that hospital.

When I finally did leave, it was suggested that I stop drinking. A dear friend came down from Santa Fe. "I've driven 800 miles to tell you you're an alcoholic."

I asked my wife, "Am I an alcoholic?"

"Let's put it this way," she said. "Alcohol is a person in your life. A person who lives with you. With us."

Time for therapy, right?

Therapist: "Do you like to drink alone?"

Me: "No. I *love* to drink alone."

Therapist: "Then you're an alcoholic."

But after more therapy, it went something like this:

Therapist: "Hmmmm."

Me: "Hearing a therapist say 'Hmmm' is like hearing an M.D. say 'Uh oh.'"

Therapist: "Do you drink when you write?"

Me: "Never. I drink when I'm done."

Therapist: "You don't drive drunk, at least not anymore. You don't beat up on people. It doesn't seem to interfere with your work (though the damage is cumulative—behind your soulful eyes, your brain may be rotting). You're *too* responsible—you make up stuff to feel obligated about. The whiskey certainly doesn't undermine *that*. It's not good for your health, but your health is your business. You're a *moody* bastard, but so are lots of people who don't drink. So who am I to tell you to stop, except . . . hmmmmm."

Me: "Hmmmmm?"

Therapist: "When you might have a quiet moment with your own soul—I think that's when you reach for a drink."

Me: "The whole country reaches for the TV remote control when it's time to commune with their souls. I prefer whiskey."

Therapist: "We're not talking about the whole country, we're talking about you."

Reaching for Old Bushmill's instead of listening to my soul. She wasn't all-the-way right about that, but she was sometimes right. And "sometimes," as I said, fucks up a lot of theories (especially about yourself). On the other hand, *sometimes* I've got the right to tell my soul to shut up—a right which I think my soul supports. Which left me where? Paying a *lot* more attention to when I drink.

See, I pray every day, have prayed every day for years, and part of my prayer goes like this: "May our souls speak to us, and may we listen." I never pray for my or anyone's health, safety or the like. Just that our souls speak, and that we listen. That way, I figure, I'm not asking the gods for permission to exert my will over my own life or anyone else's. If the soul says something we don't want to hear, that's tough. But let it speak. Let us listen.

I do not want to live in such a way as to undermine my prayer. (Which may be a working definition of religious life.) So, having no intention of quitting the drinking I love, I've had to become more aware of the *choice* to drink. Am I drinking, at this moment, to shut off my soul or another person's? The question has become almost second nature. I don't pay attention to the answer all the time, but in general I drink less. Not every day, for instance. Which is a big change. And I feel my soul's gratitude at not being ignored as often.

I also feel its gratitude when Bushmill's on the rocks is exactly what the soul wants. I am attempting what the Buddhists call "right attention"—which doesn't necessarily mean moderation. It can also mean learning when to risk the immoderate. (After all, moderation *all* the time is an extreme, isn't it.)

A couple of things worth mentioning:

First, remember that white-male capitalism didn't invent inebriates. (Actually, the Goddess culture did.) Every society we know about seems to have had and used some sort of booze and drugs, from Day One. Booze and drugs aren't what's swamping our culture. Try meaningless work, enervating leisure, political powerlessness, education that leaves you stupider when you finish school than when you started, projecting what you fear onto other races and opposite sexes, and how everything—including what should be the sacred concept of "community"—has been sacrificed for profit. Our children have far less chance to pursue happiness than any generation in American history. People-abuse and planet-abuse make for lots of substance abuse. It's just denial to blame the substances.

Second, nothing I'm saying should be construed as polemic against AA, ACoA, or anything like them. I know people whose lives have been saved by those outfits, and while I might argue with their assumptions and even their methods, that's quibbling. Whatever saves your life is right, at least for as long as it takes to save your life.

I keep thinking of the brilliant thing my ex said about me and booze:

"Alcohol is a person in your life." A presence. A spirit. How that spirit relates to me will differ some from how it relates to you. And even the spirits themselves differ. The spirit of Bushmill's Irish Whiskey isn't at all the same as the spirits of Cuervo Gold or Chianti or Amstel or Dave's home brew (to which we still recite Robert Frost, Dylan Thomas, e.e. cummings—the poets we loved most in our youth).

I write this, then, in defense and praise of those spirits who have accompanied me into great happiness and serious misery. At times protected me, at times attacked. Spirits that have been straightforward and devious, loyal and treacherous by turns (usually in proportion to how I was acting toward myself). They have revealed great things, and hidden others; made some nights bearable, rendered some unbearable; brought me closer to some people, took me farther from others. And they have made a fool of me—sometimes gently, sometimes brutally. There is nothing simple about them. There is nothing simple about anything spirited.

I believe what the Sufis say: that something in you is already drunk, always drunk, and that this may be what is closest to the gods. And sometimes, as in tribal ritual, we drink to meet and wake that inner drunkenness. It's no accident that the 12-step programs are religious, for their task is to replace one door of the spirits with another. And it's no secret that anything touching upon spirits is dangerous. In the Bible, when angels appear even the prophets shake. "Take this cup from me" is no idle metaphor. And to raise a glass in another's honor is no idle gesture. It is a cup that's come down to us from our beginnings.

"Hmmmmm," my therapist might say. And now that the writing's done—the clean burn of Irish cooled with ice.

July 27, 1990

Every House on the Block

Do the words "alcoholism" or "addiction" fit the following cases?

CASE NO. 1: The X family. I'd left home at the age of thirteen and ended up in a foster situation in a small New England town. My neighbors were the X's. Mr. X was a professional man, reserved, intelligent and respected, a scholar who read Latin and Greek, wore a tie to dinner and loved to pun. Mrs. X was jovial and generous, had a raucous laugh, liked the blues and played viola in the local orchestra. (Her favorite film star was Harpo Marx, whom she slightly resembled.)

One of the X children, a boy my age, became my close friend, so I spent a lot of time at the X house. I soon learned that there were nights when Mrs. X was "not herself." She'd get bombed and gruesomely maudlin, become the cliché of the stumbling lush. Yet it was clear to me, even as a boy, that pain I saw reflected in his mother's face was beyond endurance, that it was crushing her, slowly and visibly. Her bouts of drunkenness were all that let it burst forth, like pus from a boil, so that in the exhaustion that followed she could find a little relief.

The X family, of course, blamed *its* pain on Mrs. X's drinking. Things would be all right if only Mom could dry up. But there was one little secret that only one member of the X family knew.

I learned this secret straight from Mr. X. I was especially vulnerable at the time because, being separated from my father, I longed for a father. And a boy without a real home is utterly defenseless. There's

191

no place, no person, to run to. Mr. X, probably sensing this, managed to get me alone on several occasions. ("Can I help you with your homework?" worked the first time.) He would lecture me about how the wise men of ancient Greece related to their students. Somehow this brought up the subject of cock-sucking, and would I pose for nude Polaroids? ("And if you have a hard-on at the time, that would be fine"—those words have remained in my mind like a bad smell.) I never did what he wanted, but was so afraid for my precarious security that I would listen, be polite and not tell.

I knew from what he told me that he and Mrs. X had virtually no sexual life together. And I am very sure that nobody in the X family—not even Mrs. X—suspected what would have been called, in those days, Mr. X's "tendencies." I can only judge from my memory of Mrs. X's face, but I don't think she would have let herself consciously know. Things are bad enough now; back then, most decent Middle Americans were reduced to a paralysis of horror by homosexuality. The X name would have been disgraced, the family's livelihood decimated. And in any case, Mrs. X probably blamed only herself for their long sexual hiatus, for the distance between their spirits. Hadn't she been taught that it was the woman's job to attract the man? And wasn't she the one who was being "bad" in plain sight? My heart cringes for that woman even now. Who, in all the world, was on her side?

In later years, I'd run into some member of the X family here or there, and they'd tell me, with a kind of desperate cheerfulness, how Mrs. X had stopped drinking, how one X child or another had also stopped. In the X family lore, alcohol was the giver of pain, and the absence of alcohol was peace. But I wonder if they knew how afraid they looked, even when they supposed themselves at peace.

What was the problem in this family? Alcohol? No. Homosexuality? No. The problem was that these parents were trying to live lives that had little to do with their true natures. They had, in fact, been trained from birth to sacrifice their natures. For what? What boon did they receive? Neither order nor peace, for on an open level they terribly feared the next bout of Mrs. X's "illness," while on a hidden level they sensed (as people do) the presence of a dangerous secret. Not to mention the fear of exposure that must have dogged Mr. X. Did the X's gain prosperity by their sacrifice? Some. Was money worth their frightened eyes, and the passing of that fear down to their children, who were even more in the dark about its roots?

And what would happen if this family went into therapy today? Few therapists would be gifted enough to see a youth-abuser in Mr. X, since his children were not the objects of his abuse. Many would call this an "alcoholic" family. Mr. X would be labeled a "co-dependent" and an "enabler." The X's would do a lot of therapy, express a lot of anger. The anger would be genuine, but the issues, to put it mildly, would be incomplete. Mrs. X and the kids would be in a 12-step program, the clinical fraternity would assure them that their problems were being handled—while the real dynamic would have gone untreated and unrecorded.

Far more importantly, therapists would probably not mention and certainly not attempt to treat the structural problem that goes far beyond this family: that Mr. X had become a kind of quiet fiend because he's been forced to repress his nature by threat of ostracism and poverty (nobody was on *his* side, either), and that Mrs. X was not allowed to live out her earthiness within the decorums and traditions of the only world she knew—a world she was bound to by training, love for her children and the strictures on women.

A societal war against their very psyches caused this suffering. The world that demanded their allegiance would not tolerate their natures, and the X family is multiplied by every house on the block. To frame such a problem in terms of "addiction" is shallow. It's clear their addictions were the only ways, however flawed, they found in which to express their natures.

What A.A. would call Mrs. X's "powerlessness" goes far beyond booze. A symptom, Mrs. X's drinking, could in some crude way be treated. And I'm all for that if it enables her to salvage a little dignity before she dies. But, my God, let's not allow ourselves to think a problem has been addressed, much less solved.

CASE NO. 2: The Y's, a working-class family in Canada. Mr. Y was shy, nervous. Good with his hands. A putterer, with a quirky sense of humor. Did shift work in a factory. Tried to breed a new strain of tomatoes in his back yard. Explained to his daughter—another friend of mine—that the way he fixed heavy machinery (his job) was to just sit and stare at it till the machine told him what was wrong.

It worked. He could fix just about anything, but couldn't make enough money to leave the upper reaches of the working class.

Mrs. Y was a survivor. She would teach her children to survive anything, at almost any price. She would educate herself, make a lot of money and live as she pleased. She was not terribly deep, but she was savvy. In every way, an impressive woman. Who, after several years and kids, decided (as was her right) that she was too impressive for Mr. Y and left him, taking the kids with her.

Mr. Y couldn't bear it. At least, not sober. The heartless world of making "real" money had frightened him, and that fear had lost him his family.

I don't think it occurred either to Mr. or Mrs. Y that his fear of the world might be a sign of depth or gentleness—something to be valued. Like most men, fear made him horribly ashamed. And like most women, she wouldn't live with a man crushed by his own shame. Yet who could blame him? It's natural to fear the merciless. And who could blame her? Money buys safety, so they say. Mr. Y could not move in the circles that dispense this illusion, and Mrs. Y needed it deeply.

Drunk, ashamed, afraid, Mr. Y grew more and more estranged from his children, unable to face them. When he wasn't distant and embittered, he was an embarrassment. He lied, he cried, he broke, he broke again. He reminds me of a Kenneth Patchen poem: "there are so many little dyings that it doesn't matter which of them is death." Yet Mr. Y still fixed machines by staring at them and still tried to breed that new strain of tomatoes.

Was Mr. Y's problem alcoholism? Or could you say that there was a gentle, unassertive soul, who might have been happy living on a small scale, and whose contribution would be machines that worked and a love of the tactile. But now he was judged—and judged himself— against a system in which he was not interested and for which he was not equipped, and he was forced by that judgment to live in daily shame down to the roots of his hair. Again, society condemned his very psyche.

And Mrs. Y—was she a "co-dependent," an "enabler," a "dominator"? Or was she a frightened child in a woman's body, tortured every day by some unexamined deprivation and seeking safety in the only terms her society supported?

Isn't the disease this: that most gentle, not terribly strong, modest people are denied their birthright in our world? Many lapse into numb, dead-end routines of wage-work and television. Are they healthy? Others, sensing that the pain of their deprivation may be the most *real* thing about them, keep their pain alive with drink. Are they wrong and diseased? Again, when I think of Mr. Y, I ask myself, who, who, *who* has ever been on this man's side? Who has respected this man's true nature as, year after year, he felt less and less a man? Oddly, the very people before whom he was most ashamed: the children he hardly ever saw.

They hated his drinking, they were disgusted by his boozy behavior (none developed substance-abuse problems), yet these children couldn't help but absorb what he really was. All of their lives took unique turns, quirky as their father's. Their mother had taught them to survive, and they loved her for it (God knows no one had been on her side, either); but it was their father's longing and originality, which he had not been strong enough to live out or protect—it was this that cued their choices, their paths in life.

A question, then. If Mr. Y had been as good as Mrs. Y at repressing his depths and being competent, what would have happened to the children? They very likely would have joined the legions of unthinking success-panderers whose natures are denied so young they can't really be said to *have* natures anymore. I submit that's a fate at least as bad as alcoholism or ACoAism. And I think what their father's drinking meant *and* communicated was: "The so-called 'normal' life is a lie. It breeds deadness of the heart. Avoid it at all costs."

Their father, to this day, wouldn't say these words. But his behavior did. His true nature, expressed through what the world would call his "alcoholism," taught them well.

August 24, 1990

The Corpse of the Eighties

Sorry, but I'm not quite finished with the eighties yet. Maybe we summed up that decade a mite too neatly. Something doesn't sit right about how all us cultural clerks (who call ourselves "critics") weighed the era, wrapped it, stamped it and shipped it express to what is now officially "the past"—where the forensic technicians of culture (who call themselves "historians") can cut it, test it, tag its toe and stack it in the freezer or wherever one puts something that can no longer fight back.

Being myself just another squeak in this clerical chorus, as intent as anyone upon stamping my initials on the dead decade's forehead— imagine my surprise when the corpse opened its eyes: "Not so fast. Don't you know that the past never dies?" Breathless, I awaited a cosmic exchange with the Corpse of the eighties—but it just wanted to bitch about us critics.

"With all the evils in the world, why pick on the critics?" I argued.

"Cause they've been picking on me," the Corpse shot back.

The Corpse of the eighties bade me consider other American decades, and the track records of *their* critics. The Corpse had a point. Peruse the intelligent publications of the thirties, for instance, and you'll find that John Dos Passos, John Steinbeck and John O'Hara were fussed over far more effusively (and sold lots more books) than quirky, murky William Faulkner. Nathaniel West was ignored, Henry Miller was banned, and it would be decades before one masterpiece, Anais Nin's diary, was even published. In other words, the Corpse insisted, literary critics and the informed reading public of the thirties had missed the most lasting, prophetic and influential works of their time.

The Corpse didn't let up: dig thirties music. Billie Holiday, our century's most original singer, had no champions in print—and compared to Bing Crosby, she didn't sell. (She didn't sell much even when *not* compared to Bing Crosby.) Benny Goodman got lots more ink than Lester Young, although Young was pioneering the future of harmonics. Goodman's drummer, Gene Krupa, is still a vaguely familiar name— but Jo Jones, whose drumming shaped every rhythmic innovation since, was and is largely unknown. Not to mention bluesman Robert Johnson, an enormously influential musical mind, a taproot of rock—he was obscure to the point of oblivion. (It took fifty years to find a photograph of him.) Faulkner would catch on by the end of the next decade, but the rest would wait twenty to forty years for fair recognition.

Critics of the forties didn't do any better. (The Corpse of the eighties still wouldn't let up.) What artist remains more contemporary than country singer Hank Williams? His records still play on jukeboxes everywhere, every night, and surely *that's* significant? As is the forties jazz idiom called bebop, out of which came the very spectrum of sound we now identify as "modern." Still, don't bother looking for bebop or Hank in the intelligentsia's favorite publications of '49.

"But," I entreat the Corpse, "we've been so media-saturated since the fifties that surely travesties like this can't happen anymore."

The Corpse grants that some things have changed. The abject failure of fifties critics to savvy rock & roll and television, and the way a rock & roll/television culture subsequently *took over* the sixties, smashing assumptions about everything from politics to painting—all this made the old criticism look pretty silly and changed the basics of cultural clerking. Now, afraid that the trivial might be crucial, critics vie over fleeting trends, inflating every balloon that just might be a work of art. And this process, for all its excesses, *is* accomplishing something great: it's breaking down the artificial distinctions between "high" and "low" art—distinctions that amounted to little more than a system of class prejudice by which the middle and upper could reserve "art" for themselves, unthreatened by the sensibilities of the lower.

"But is it possible," I asked, "that major artists, much less whole movements, could ever go unnoticed again? We're talking about *responsible* intellectuals, f'crissake! *The Village Voice*! The *L.A. Weekly*!"

"Says you," says the Corpse. "But how does this critical community get to *be* the critical community? Huh? Huh?"

The jig is up. The Corpse knows.

Knows that, whether "mainstream" or "alternative," our critics overwhelmingly are products of (or refugees from) the same formative experience: middle-class protection from birth; a suburban (or genteel urban) dilution of English-Scottish-Irish or Jewish roots; then a run through some university's obstacle course, scrambling over or crawling under virtually the same curriculums. Add "politically correct" left politics, accepted more through faith than a knowledge of history; the initiatory trauma of finally being on one's own in the big city, four to ten years after other sorts of people have had to be; and, as a group, living in the same neighborhoods, gorging on the same movies, inhaling the same magazines (much more than books), sampling the same television shows (and other drugs), and collectively wearing pretty much the same music both as fashion and identity . . . all in an atmosphere of highly charged "gender issues," i.e., sex, everyone simmering in a creamy but tart sensual soup that looks better than it tastes. For many there's also a year or so of travel (from student bohemian circles in, say, Boston, to student bohemian circles in, say, Paris). And for the real adventurers, throw in a period of odd jobs, "risky" nightlife and perhaps even some sort of activism. That's about it.

When virtually everyone in media shares the same general background, there can't help but be a sameness of vision. And it is the sameness that these critics often mistake for "culture."

Pause at that. It's the *atmosphere* of the intelligentsia's life, rather than what may or may not be bubbling out there in the world, that's taken for "cultural." Only when something penetrates this atmosphere is it judged worthy of in-depth consideration. To say that this is a drastic and artificial limitation on art and thought is an exercise in understatement.

Yet this subculture is the work-pool for the influential New York and L.A. publications. If they don't praise something, it doesn't exist. (Art usually needs a write-up before the broadcast media will touch it.) Stores don't stock the book, the film disappears, the song isn't heard. Not blending into this subculture's atmosphere is tantamount to cultural invisibility.

It gets worse. The total number of people who actually have decisive input into what gets covered—isn't many. A couple of hundred maybe. These busy folk rarely leave their office, much less leave town. Lots of *their* input comes from party and dinner talk—with people from the same old subculture. For information beyond their direct circle, they're as dependent on media as you are—media staffed by people like themselves.

Where does this leave a painter in Lubbock, Texas, a painter who *likes* Lubbock, Texas, who doesn't want to live in L.A. or New York or even Santa Fe, and hasn't the temperament to promote her own art? Maybe she's the greatest artist alive, but it'll be a couple of decades before *you* find out. A sculptor in Boise—or in Watts for that matter, since people of color are automatically a thousand miles away—is out in the cold. The critical subculture assumes that if you're *really* good, you come to the Big City. This is nonsense, but it's part of their belief system.

And say you *do* come to the Big City. Say you even entice some critics to your performance, exhibit, independent film. The Big City has maybe five, maybe eight, influential critics in your medium. In an audience, that's not many people. But in the media, it's everybody.

And people with similar backgrounds doing identical jobs tend to have few fundamental disagreements on content, fewer still on form, and hardly any on how the world works or what the world is. (Preferring left politics over right, or Woody Allen over Steven Spielberg, is an argument about what to do with the same elements; it isn't usually an argument about the nature of the elements.) So it's not surprising that the unknown's play, especially work by a playwright without backers from the critics' party-circle—it's not surprising that those critics might not like or relate to something that doesn't speak to their limited experience, isn't relevant to their insulated circle or wasn't included in their education.

In short, at least as much art falls through the cracks now as ever. It either stays home or goes home. Or, through an artist's doggedness or a particularly gifted publisher or producer (Columbia Records' John Hammond is the great example), the work gets out there—and is, as often as not, ignored. Excluded by a system of filters that doesn't only delete the incompetent (the function by which it justifies itself), but also siphons out what doesn't jibe with its assumptions or its mood. A system of filters that doesn't even *know* it's a system of filters—it thinks it's a smart circle of critics.

So nobody knows what the culture of the eighties *really* was. We only know what our culture-mill could assimilate. It will take years, even decades, for the rest, possibly the best, to get to us.

The Corpse of the eighties smiled. It closed its eyes. Now it could get a little rest in peace.

March 23, 1990

Blues for Stevie

Stevie told me once that he dreamed about Jimi Hendrix a lot. Jimi would teach him special changes in his sleep, but when Stevie woke up he couldn't remember the lessons. He figured that was justice. He looked this way, then that, then at me (a manner he had), and said, "There's no easy ways, man. You gotta learn the hard parts on your own, for yourself, over and over."

Another time, Stevie's then wife, Lenny, told me how he'd play till dawn, go to sleep, then play in his sleep. She'd get woken up by his fret-hand and pickin' hand moving so hard and fast. She'd look at him and see that his face was scrunched up tight like onstage when he was really into it. Usually she wouldn't wake him. "I'd just kinda listen, if you know what I mean."

If you want to know Stevie Ray Vaughan's roots, find a reissue called *Angels in Houston—The Legendary Duke Blues Recordings* (Rounder Records). Bobby "Blue" Bland gets first billing, while second goes to somebody even lots of blues people haven't heard of, Larry Davis. Larry Davis was a man who was too nervous to sing if he couldn't hold the microphone, so he had to learn to play his guitar with one hand. Circa 1960 he had a Houston hit called "Texas Flood."

Play the tune—it's *almost* Stevie's voice. Stevie is so close to the timbre, rasp and inflection of Larry Davis that some people can't hear the difference. I can just see Stevie as a wraith of a boy, a white-trash Texas kid even skinnier than when I first saw him in the mid seventies, intent as he always was, playing that record over and over because somehow Larry Davis's voice spoke to him with an intimacy no other sound matched. Some purists might say he "stole" that style. I'd say he couldn't resist its pull, and it shaped him.

An interesting note: virtually everybody who recorded for Duke records got robbed by its owner, Don Deadric Robey, and Larry Davis was no exception. It was a standard rip-off in those days for the record producer to steal the songwriting credit, and hence the royalty. Both on the original 45 and on the 1982 Duke reissue, "Texas Flood" is credited to producer Robey. But on Stevie Ray Vaughan's two recordings of the tune (also in 1982) it's credited to Larry Davis, like it's supposed to be. And he called his first album *Texas Flood*. Stevie Vaughan not only paid his dues, he paid his debts.

Like that time when MTV deigned to do a spot on the blues and interviewed him briefly. Stevie didn't talk about himself; he talked about Texas blues giant Lightnin' Hopkins. Played a typical Hopkins riff, smiled his wriest smile and said, "but that's just a white boy playin' Lightnin' Hopkins." He paid other debts as well, sponsoring and co-producing the influential Lonnie Mack's great comeback album, *Strike Like Lightning* (1985). And he had, of course, other sources, other guitar heroes. Not only people you've heard of—like Freddie King and Stevie's older brother, the Fabulous Thunderbirds' Jimmie Vaughan— but also people you'll never hear of, like Bill Campbell. All of them, knowns and unknowns, living it out night after night playing what Bill Bentley once called "the best music America ever forgot."

In Austin we first heard Stevie in the winter of '75–'76, with Paul Ray and the Cobras. *That* was a band. Paul Ray's supple voice over an infectious rhythm section, a sax and two lead guitars; Denny Freeman, who can still be heard at Antone's today, and who's still, for my money, the most original blues guitarist in Texas; and the skinny kid with the intense eyes and the mashed nose and the peacock tattoo, just nineteen or twenty, whose playing made you crazy. It really did. Some pent-up thing was coming out of him and it got *to* you. It was clear that this boy had made a secret pact with his guitar—a secret you could dance to. In 1977, while New York and L.A. indulged in disco fluff or the beginnings of mad-dog-rabies-is-good-for-you punk, the readers of the *Austin Sun* voted Paul Ray and the Cobras "Band of the Year."

It wasn't much later that Stevie started his own band, Triple Threat, with blues chanteuse Lou Ann Barton and singer-guitarist W. C. Clark. Mix cuts from Lou Ann's *Read My Lips* (1989, with Denny Freeman and Stevie's brother Jimmie) and Stevie's *Texas Flood*, preferably with tequila, and you get the feel of that band.

Yet, weirdly, even in Austin they played to pretty empty clubs. I know, because I was there almost every gig. Maybe Austin night people resented the breakup of Paul Ray's band, but whatever the reason, soon Triple Threat was shorn of Barton and Clark and became Double Trouble, the name Stevie's group kept till he died in a helicopter crash last week.

They say "the rest is history," but it's not. It's lost in a thousand "last calls." For instance, there's nothing but my half-dozen snapshots to record that night at Antone's in the spring of '81. Stevie had added the "Ray" by then and had married Lenny. I was honored to be one she'd call for donations when he needed a new used guitar. He was *real* hard on guitars, and rarely sat in with another band if he hadn't brought his own for fear he'd break somebody else's instrument—not break the strings, but break the guitar. (He never smashed one, he simply held the thing so hard that sometimes the poor babies would just crack.)

This night he played a long set with Double Trouble to a packed club of no-holds-barred revelers, then called a break, watched his band leave the stage and pulled out an acoustic twelve-string. I was sitting at Lenny's table, and her eyes were wide. "I never saw *that* guitar before!" Stevie jumped off the bandstand, asked someone for his chair, took it back up to the mike and sat down hunkered over the twelve-string. Closed his eyes. Played. Like he was all alone. The club was packed, but it got real quiet. And stayed quiet, while Stevie went deeper and deeper into that twelve-string sound. "Throw it all to the firewall," a woman near me said softly. I didn't know quite what that meant, but it sounded exactly right.

After a long while he gently put the guitar down. Nobody applauded, and few people moved. "It's like church," the same woman said. Stevie was back in a moment with the Fender that we'd chipped in on for his birthday. He sat in the chair again and played the pretty melody he called "Lenny," which was later the last cut on his first album. I have a snapshot of Stevie hunched over the Fender looking at Lenny, whose head is resting on her arms at the foot of the bandstand. There are others in the photo just standing, rapt, with eyes closed or heads down, the music taking them far into themselves. You can get some idea of what it was like on the *Texas Flood* version. What musicians would call his "ideas" were as elegant and intricate as a jazzman's, yet they never left the realm of blues-rock. But the album version goes on for only five minutes, while in Antone's it was timeless—not just longer, but in another world. Then he called his band back and rocked us home. He played that night non-stop for more than three hours.

I went back the next night. Something had happened. I never found out what, but he played with a desperation that was unusual even for him. Scary. I was still there after the place had closed. The chairs were up on the tables, and suddenly here was Stevie walking haltingly across the dance floor sobbing, sobbing and talking, talking quickly and to himself, about love. How important it was to him, that through his playing people would know that he *loved*. He loved *them*. That's what the music was for, it was for *love*. I cannot duplicate on the page the shudder with which he said the word.

I went back to my motel shaken. Inadvertently, just because I was there, I had seen the open wound, the raw and never-to-be-healed place that was the wellspring of his blues. The thing that was under the cockiness, the flashy hats, the drinking, the drugs and the later abstinence. The thing that both drove and sustained Stevie Ray Vaughan's extraordinary discipline and power as a musician. "Stare not too deeply into the abyss," Nietzsche said, "lest the abyss stare into thee."

That was all a long time ago, before Stevie cut his first record. After *Texas Flood* we lost touch, and I haven't seen him to talk to in years. Quickly he graduated to the big halls, the stadiums, the festivals. Not my scene. When it leaves the clubs, this music loses its versatility, its capacity to take the sudden turn into near-silence. Without just-folk dancers who reflect and extend it with their bodies, the music gets ever louder and flashier to cover for the audience's passivity. Oh, I'd go now and again out of loyalty and a hunger for the sound, and still Stevie would play brilliantly and passionately, but his new audience didn't want to be surprised, and when Stevie would try to do his magic, that stunning counterpoint of the fierce and the gentle that he did better than anybody, it would get lost in the commotion of a screaming crowd. He still sat in at Antone's, I heard, and would play after-hours with friends, play like the old days. But I haven't been to Austin in a while.

It's hard that you're gone now, Stevie. I always thought that we'd connect again. Remember that night you turned me on to O. V. Wright, and how many times we listened to his cut that went, "Are you going where I'm comin' from? Have you been where I'm tryin' to go?" I keep thinking of those lines now, I don't know why. And did you ever see the passage I wrote about you in my novel? It goes like this:

> He plays like an angel who's run with the devils, seen too many devils and seen through them to a music so fast and clean, so soft and harsh together, and piercing not because of how loud it was but because of what he played. I mean, one guy hits a note on a guitar and you hardly notice, you dance on, it's part of the scene; a guy like Stevie hits the same note and it goes right through you, comes out the other side, it's got blood and memories on it. . . .

September 7, 1990

Life on the Off-Ramp

Even horror can keep you alive . . . after love has only gotten you in deeper (which is, after all, what we asked of it); and after your work has stopped being part of the solution and becomes part of the problem; and after the demons from your childhood have appeared yet again, with even sharper teeth; and after therapy has petered out— for therapy is only something you can do when you can talk. And who wants to talk to therapists when you can't even talk to your friends, when the beauty in the eyes of one's friends seems meant for somebody who has nothing to do with you, when your friends don't even look like people anymore? When they look like memories fading even as they speak? After, in short, nothing gentle, practical or even human works for you anymore, *then* sometimes horror wakes you up, keeps you alive.

The problem, see, is that life is not rational, is not a rational phenomenon, and when people try to give you rational reasons for a fundamentally non-rational process like staying alive—well, both you and they feel frustrated, and a little silly. *They* know their reasons are lame. There is no "reason" to live, and there's certainly no reason why any one person, one race, one planet *must* remain alive. Life is its own reason. Until it's not.

But when all else fails there are horrors that peek at you and say: *Live—or else.*

That's a booby prize for having shed one's Western education. For it's been a long time since Western liberal thought—that predictable pastiche of male art, experimental science, middle-of-the-road psychology and left-of-center politics—has been enough to describe *my* world. It's been a long time since I have been able to discount the "mystical" experiences recorded in every culture in every age by people no less intelligent than we. Only our Amer-Euro brand of university-stunted intellectual is arrogant and silly enough to discount such a body of testimony out of hand. No, my friends and my family and I have had enough *direct* experience of "mystical" things, too much maybe, to believe for a minute that death is death.

And if death isn't death, suicide isn't suicide. Suicide is just another way to go through that door.

There is even a body of testimony to indicate that suicide sends you through that door in the worst way possible, that says suicide leaves you in far worse shape at the other end than you were here (though it's hard to believe I could be in any worse shape anywhere). So, believing this may be a real possibility, one sits on this side of the door, the side we call "life," half hoping for the worst of accidents or hoping that, at next week's doctor's appointment, the results of the tests will let one off the hook: perhaps one's symptoms *aren't* psychosomatic, but are a loophole, an excuse, something permissible, the gods saying, "Okay, kid, come on through, your time on earth is done."

But if death isn't death—then there's no rest. To die may be only to leave one set of difficult circumstances for what is almost certainly another set of difficult circumstances, because one of the oldest sayings we know of, dating back before the pyramids, states simply: *As above, so below; as below, so above.*

Trouble anywhere you look.

("Trouble—and beauty," I hear a trusted voice whisper. Yeah, sure, right, *beauty*—but can we leave the subject of beauty to another, less awful night? "Trouble and beauty are the building blocks of the universe." Will you give me a fucking break?)

I think of the great teaching-tales that have come down to us through Grimm, and the Arthurian stories, and all those shards of myth and miracle the world over . . . they insist on this theme: that the fairy queen, the prince of the magic kingdom under the evil spell, the talking horse that lives under the river in the Other World, when *they're* in trouble they come to *us* for help. Us! The message being that the Other World has needs, too, needs that only we can meet.

And the Hasidim say, "Give ye strength unto God," as though your strength is needed There—even desperately needed. And the Hopi would agree.

Talk about "trouble anywhere you look": an old Hindu text has it that "up to the Brahma world will the destruction of the world extend"—if we go, they go. And vice versa. As above, so below; as below, so above.

There are even those who tell us that *this* world is in such a shitstorm because we've forgotten that the Other World (worlds?) has needs only ours can meet, and that our world has needs met only in the Other World . . . hence both worlds (in this neighborhood, this slum, of the universe) are in chaos. And that the most important *political* act of our era is to remember this and rediscover the doors to the Other World and relearn, remember, how to open them, so that the Worlds may once again freshen each other.

Which would decrease the chaos, but not, if I understand correctly, the trouble. "Trouble and beauty are the building blocks. . . ."

All of which makes me amazingly tired.

On the nights—and they've been many, lately—that I've forgotten or ignored this stuff, my pain has yearned toward suicide with something that can only be called lust. I never had it before, never understood it. But I sure to hell understand it now. And it feels a horror to me that death is not an answer. Not even, from the point of view of the Other World, an option. (This stuff makes me feel so bad for Abbie—Abbie Hoffman, whom I knew a bit and liked a lot.) What horror to think one is going toward "a final rest" and to find instead that something of one's consciousness survives—survives in a turmoil that (because of the manner of one's passing) is even less manageable *there* than the turmoil one left here.

What a way to construct a universe: no outs.

If you've gotten this far then perhaps now I can tell you of "voices" and "spirits." Voices speak. Spirits intervene. They take strange forms. Strange because weirdly familiar. Like:

One night when I've been too shaky to leave this little one-room apartment even to eat, even for cigarettes, my neighbor knocks. But I don't know it's my neighbor. I don't want to open the door to one of my various loved ones with one of their various shrinks "intervening" on me, oh no, thank you very much. But this time it *is* my neighbor, a feisty Oklahoma woman about my age who lives across the hall with her little dog. She and her dog have locked themselves out. Can I help them get in? It's only the push-lock that's closed automatically, so I give the door a good shot and it opens . . . and with this minor but useful act of muscle I suddenly feel "well" for the first time in days. My voice sounds like mine. I can even work a little. There are even people I'd like to see.

And I walk around vastly amused for a time . . . why would such an incongruous little episode snap me out of that awful place? When nothing else could, and everyone else had tried? Oh, yes, it's symbolic as hell, busting through a locked door (what would I think if I'd dreamed it?), but the shrinks' theories (and they've got some pretty good ones) can only tell me why it *worked*, not why it *happened*. For that, I like *my* little theory: spirits intervene.

It's more fun believing that than not believing that, and fun is at a premium these days, in case you hadn't noticed.

Spirits intervene. And one can say no to them. I could have not answered the door. Or I could have spoken to her the way I've been speaking to the people I (supposedly) love—which is none too pleasantly. The people we love are too familiar, we forget *they're* spirits too. And anyway "love" is often nothing more than the password by which we admit people to our hall of horrors. But strangers—their spirit sides can surprise us, and it is always the spirit side of others (what we first loved in those we love) that works wonders.

But a little intervention like that, I grant you, doesn't last too long. It's just a stopgap till a tougher, more determined spirit grabs you by the throat:

I'm lying on the hard bed, but it doesn't feel like that, it feels like I'm dangling upside-down from a rope. The phone rings. Answer it, don't answer it. Haven't been answering it too much lately. What's the difference, answer it.

It's my brother, Aldo. A man I trust. Five years younger than me and his hair is grayer than mine, though mine's gray enough. A collect call from the mental hospital on Staten Island where he's been hospitalized for months now. (What a fucking family.)

Aldo asks me how I am and I tell him. And suddenly he gets very focused, starts talking quietly, forcefully, and, with my old writer's reflex, I get my notebook and try to keep up with his rapid-fire words.

Except for a few deletions, mostly for the sake of privacy, this is exactly what he said:

"Your wings have melted and you're on the ground and you don't like it. That doesn't mean you're having a nervous breakdown. But then you begin the merciless appraisal of all your faults. Yours and everybody else's. And that'll kill you, the ruthless eye of honesty you have. That doesn't mean it's *truth*. I think there's a difference between truth and honesty. There's cosmic truth—and our petty little honesty.

"And when you look closely with that so-called honesty there's the danger that you can magnify distortion. You look in the mirror, you see dark eyes, you see stubble, one too many drinks, one too many cigarettes. I suggest that, instead of turning all the arrows inward, you recognize that you *need*. And instead of punishing yourself, which you do, explore having people take care of that need. I don't mean like a baby looking for a mother. I don't mean anything out of the ordinary. I mean people taking care of business with people they love.

"The mistake you're making is isolating yourself. Grind your teeth, but don't do it in the dark.

"'Cause part of what you are, you don't own, you can't condemn. And that's why it's good you don't own it. And if you think your ruthless eye of honesty is seeing what you are, you're wrong. It's ruled by a coded pattern, it's selective, it digs into your weakest part.

"If you feel like digging a knife into your gut, realize: there's a part of yourself you do not own, you merely visit, and that's the part unsullied by the hand of man—which your ruthless selective honesty knows nothing about. You look at the decay, and you think you're looking at the garden. But the decay can be washed away. And then there's that part of yourself that you do not own, and it's *beautiful*. It's like meeting the most beautiful woman—but it's *you*."

He takes a breath. Then:

"Also—I need you. So don't fuck up."

June 2, 1989

The Queen of Cups

Everyone has many mothers, and they don't all die at the same time. The Clelia Rosalie Scandurra who stands in the wedding photo beside Michael Luciano Ventura—she died before I was born. That photograph could have been taken at any time from the invention of photography in the 1820s to the day they actually posed for it, in 1940. It was taken in America, though it doesn't look it. ("I don't think Ma ever *really* lived in America until she entered a mental hospital," my sister told me once.) The beautiful, dark, oval-faced woman of twenty-two in her white gown and the intense, handsome twenty-four-year-old beside her look innocent of America, innocent of many things. Innocent, especially, of each other. Their intelligence is apparent (she was the first woman in all the families of all our relations to graduate college, the only one of her generation, while he, to this day, writes me long letters analyzing books and dissecting politics); yet theirs seems a nineteenth-century intelligence, unsuited to their time. I was born only five years after that photograph was taken, yet Clelia would tell me, "By the time you were born I had given up on adult love." How many Clelias and Michael Lucianos had to die in order for her to speak that sentence?

She took a long time dying. Her Red politics started to die in the 1940s, along with some kinds of sanity; other kinds began breaking down in the 1950s; by 1980 her sweetness came only in flashes and her generosity was dead; then all that was left were the memories that fed her visions, the pride that kept her secrets, and her fierce and merciless Sicilian cunning. These, and her dignity—which I never saw her lose, no matter how insane, how afraid or how cornered she may have been. Even her panics were so formidable that her dignity was implicit within them: it could take four or five people to hold that little woman down. Then, when the "episode" was over, it was as though her composure had never been interrupted.

Like anyone of real dimension, Clelia (pronounced KLEL–ee–ah) was haunted less by others than by herself. Ideas, moments, emotions and even facial expressions of long ago would rise within her, displace her sense of the present, and play upon her mind and in her eyes. And always there was something of the little girl about her—not in a playful way, but with that mix of reserve and whimsy that you see in dark Catholic girls sitting stiffly in their first Communion dresses. That tiny woman, not five feet tall, walking down the street, looking like a little girl grown somehow suddenly old! Sometimes even strangers knew that you could ask her a question about God or the devil and she'd have an answer, for she'd spoken with both many times. "We speak with every cell," Clelia told me once. "Sometimes we don't know what it is, but we speak it."

Thirty years ago, when life demanded much more in the way of decorum than today, Clelia could take her blouse off on a subway platform and tell the crowd that anyone afraid to see a woman in only a brassiere "is not fit," then improvise (or rant) a kind of poetry about "an essence that combines beauty with venom," which led to the knowledge that "the Kingdom of Heaven is within you." She was about the age that I am now, and still quite beautiful. Perhaps her beauty was how she got away with it, that day, long enough for one of her sons to find her and lead her home. We, her children, were often frightened, but never ashamed. It never occurred to us not to be proud of her. Even if her "breakdowns," as she called them, hadn't had such grandeur, we had seen the years she held them off, struggling to keep her vision at bay, working crummy jobs to keep us together, trying to live a motherhood she knew she had no talent for—a motherhood that, in fact, her true talents worked against.

If I could have told her what she did to me sexually when I was little, she would have been amazed, surprised, shocked, hurt, disbelieving. The condition of some crimes is that they can be committed only if the perpetrator is unaware that they are crimes. "They call that 'abuse' these days, Mama," I might say, and her eyes might harden into brown stones and she might say something typically Clelia, something like, "What people call things, and what things really are, are not often the same."

And who can say she's wrong? Not I. Abuse, or initiation? Abuse, or baptism? To be submerged in a mix of sensuality and madness that opens a door into the Other World, the world where we *do* speak with every cell, and where the gods talk back—I call that both a baptism and an initiation. She opened that door for me, and it's remained open, and that's been worth whatever it cost. But, yes, abuse, too: a one- and two- and three-year-old does not know inside from outside; it feels a darkness coming at it from without as an inherent unfathomable black hole within; and, running from what it believes to be its own darkness, that child splits inside, and those parts grow up (if ever they do grow up) separately, at different rates, with different needs, even with different names. It is of such stuff that murders are made. Murders of others. Murders of yourself.

Comes a time, often at forty or so, that something within releases the lock on the memory. But the memory doesn't say "abuse," certainly not at first, not until you label it. The memory is just itself; it stuns in a way nothing ever has. When it hits it's like putting an ax through a beehive in your mind: you're filled with a maddened buzzing, the beating of so many tiny wings, the pain of so many stingers, the smell of fresh honey. Things shatter—marriages, friendships, jobs, ideas, whatever happens to be around. Or rather, the falseness in things shatters, and anything made of too much falseness shatters for keeps. Still, even falseness is a hard thing to lose, it gives such protection. And it's such a shock to find that all this time your mother, uncle or whoever it was lives inside you in the form of a sticky, stinging, too-sweet, terribly purposeful thing buzzing at the quick of your sexuality.

In these realms, phrases like "survivor of abuse," so popular in the new abuse-industry, sound hollow. It's harder for the spirit to survive a family that watches the American average of six to eight hours of television a night than it is to survive many forms of overt abuse. It's harder for the mind to survive the brutality known as public education, or years on a meaningless job. There *are* morally deformed parents who actively crucify their children; that's a deeper level of crime, and, with these, one may speak with accuracy of "survivors." But the beating, sexuality, abandonment, alcoholism and the like that's gone on in families for as long as we know about—it's so much a part of life that I've come to think it may *be* life: possible to redeem, perhaps, but not to prevent or cure. Light is the boundary of darkness, darkness the boundary of light, each cups the other, and from those cups we drink.

I read over that last sentence and think: if Clelia had said those words on a subway platform, with or without a blouse, or if she had talked about axes cracking beehives in her head, she'd have been hospitalized again, medicated, straitjacketed, electroshocked. I write them, and I get a paycheck. Even back then I sensed that both of society's responses, the hospital and the paycheck, were basically arbitrary. Later I would read R. D. Laing, Doris Lessing, James Hillman, C. G. Jung and others, and they would help me learn what I'd already sensed, what I'd even written down while still in my teens: that Clelia was a priestess (a Cassandra, was how I put it then), and that in another time and place, with another people, her visionary and sensual capacities would have been seen for the gifts they were, would have had a context, a purpose, a use, and she would have had no need to lavish them in such private ways upon a little boy. How did she put it one morning, during what the doctors called a "psychotic episode"? "This is legend, that they have forgotten! I bear a legend, a forgotten legend! I have a legend, it is here for the taking!"

Even now, with her dead two years and more, I feel her priestess power. And she comes in dreams to women who never met her, standing outside one friend's window and staring in, or asking another to intercede between us.

In the last eight years of her life I saw her for one day, and then, when I knew she was dying, for another five. A love that had once been measured by its closeness was, for those eight years, measured by its distance. That was the sort of thing Clelia understood in her bones, no need to explain between us.

There she was, a ravaged seventy. She'd often gone hungry, especially as a child. And as a mother she'd had the furious agony of seeing her children go hungry and be put in waifs' homes—for which she felt a crushing guilt, especially since she'd sacrificed the security of her family to her political activities. She'd seen the inside of jails and hospitals often enough; had, often enough, been interrogated by shrinks, bureaucrats, cops and even, on more than one occasion, the FBI; had lived to see her daughter graduate from one of the most prestigious colleges in the world, and had also lived to see her sons (whom she worked *hard* to drive crazy) in hospitals and prisons too, one handcuffed and beaten by the cops in her own kitchen, then taken away in a straitjacket. And never, not once, not ever, did she speak, act or feel like a victim. To have dignity is nothing less than to have the sense of being a full participant in your own destiny.

She'd disappeared utterly a couple of times, just walking the streets and sleeping anywhere, showing up sooner or later in some shelter, phoning one of her four now-grown children, going into another hospital, for weeks or months or years, getting out, getting another job—file clerk, nanny (I often wonder about those children), domestic. And she disappeared even more often into what I would call the Other World. I don't know what she called it, but she said, "Once in a while I trip, trip, trip, but then I come back, back, back—and the world . . . is a much larger place than we thought."

And hadn't she taken us to zoos, museums and the planetarium, over and over (back in the days when they were free), as though to drum into our heads that the universe was bigger than New York, and that the possibilities were wider than poverty? Hadn't she taught us to read and urged us to read everything, pressing on us books like van Gogh's letters (to help us understand *her*, I realize now)? Anything to get it into our heads that the streets, the television and school were nothing but tawdry fragments of a limitless world. If mothering is comforting, protecting, feeding, housing, she wasn't much of a mother; but she was a *great* teacher, and we were her class, her pupils, her disciples, loyal to her teachings long after we could no longer afford to be loyal to her.

The teachings came in many forms, like always telling me, when I'd show her my writing, "Remember, what's most important about words is their *music*." And like when she was pacing up and down that Decatur Street flat with a pot of water in her hands, screaming, screaming, and ten years old, I got on my knees and begged her to stop, and with a full swing she brought the water and the pot crashing down on my shoulder and said, "Don't you *ever* get on your knees to *anybody*."

I heard you, lady. Don't worry about it.

Ill, near death, sitting on my brother's couch, she said little, smiled occasionally, laughed now and then unaccountably, and sometimes got that closed, distant, almost angry, *somehow* urgent look that was impenetrable as ever—all this while listening to her beloved Caruso or watching the umpteenth rerun of her favorite show, *Star Trek*. And still, her oldness and illness were like a veil through which you saw so clearly a girl of maybe ten with hands folded on her lap, suspicious, bewildered, in a stiff, white ceremonial dress. My brother put words to our feelings when he said: "That's my mother, Mike. Nobody's ever gonna look at me like that again."

Happy birthday, Mama.

You're too fucking fantastic, as usual.

Thinking about you makes me tired. Don't take that personally. I mean, tired of our big, crude culture that has to simplify everything. The therapeutic community simplifies abuse and would classify you as a child abuser. Psychology simplifies and denies transcendent states and calls you paranoid schizophrenic and generally dysfunctional. The men's movement simplifies initiation (one of its doctrines is that a woman cannot initiate a man) and would say that I'd been sucked in by the Great Goddess; the feminists simplify the function of the priestess and matriarchy in general, speaking as though those things never cost blood. Only the FBI (of all people!) was accurate: it called you a communist, and you were—a Bible-reading commie who believed equally in Stalin and the Virgin Mary. To paraphrase Mr. Orson Welles, "It's a bright, silly world," and, as usual, the waters part before you, Mama. You were always larger than anything that tried to describe you.

And that's what you taught, with every cell: that we are, every one of us, larger than the things that attempt to describe us.

I wanted to die when you died. Tried to, as you did too on a couple of occasions. I got saved by two of my brothers, a lover and some friends. One of my brothers, who works with the dying for a living, who's sat by hundreds of them, told me, "Everyone—*every*one, Mike—doesn't wanna go alone. They wanna take somebody with them." And the other, our Aldo, said, "Mike, what you are you do not own, you only visit—and you do not have the right to end that." (What happened with the lover and the friends . . . we'll get to that some other time.)

Sweep the books off the shelves and stuff the diagnoses. I would have done better to reread your letters. Especially that one letter. How often, over the years, has its last line spoken to me? "Just live it, suffer it, delight in it." Over and over. Those words. That was twenty years ago, you and I were still in love, I had disappeared into the West, and we didn't speak by phone, couldn't afford it, but you sent me a greeting card that featured a wonderful shot of Jean Harlow's breasts (what were you trying to get across, Mama?), and you wrote: "All that's important is to have a dream and to give your whole life for it. Give your whole life for the dream." You had given your sanity, your children and the very clothes off your back for yours—so you had the right to say this. "You're not like me, you think too much. It's not so important to think so much about your dream. Just live it, suffer it, delight in it."

October 18, 1991

A Reader's Response

Dear Editor:
    Re: Michael Ventura's column "The Queen of Cups."
    . . . Clearly it is his own life, his own dream to live, to suffer, to delight in. However, to my mind, and my body, no adult—regardless of how unique, mystic, gifted or visionary that person may be—has the right to act out their sexuality on a child. That can only be the deed of an oppressor, one who uses power, knowledge and position to pursue his or her own interests at the expense of one less knowledgeable and powerful. What about each person's right to choose his or her own initiation? To decide for themselves when and how and with whom to cross the boundary between receding innocence and the experience of sexual completion? To rob someone of that choice is wrong, and no amount of romantic mythology can make it right.

Michael Ventura replies:
    The idea that there are such fixed rights and wrongs, and that choice

is ever so clear-cut, is "romantic mythology" in the extreme. More accurately, I would call such compartmented thinking the "psychological fantasy" that the abuse industry now sells. For instance, it is a simplistic fantasy to imagine that people who commit abuse are exercising much volition (not to mention "power" and "knowledge"). Most are driven by compulsions beyond their understanding and therefore beyond their control—compulsions they themselves fear terribly. In many cases, what they are doing is so shocking to *them* that their consciousness literally switches off during and after the act. Then the memory becomes as buried in the abuser as in the abused, and the truth of either is virtually impossible to know with certainty. When you factor in that in most cases (my mother's included) the abuser, when a child, was the victim of abuse as well—then you have to search high and low for your rights and wrongs, for you live in a world where the oppressed oppress the oppressed, where compulsions dictate the terms of choice, and where nothing is sure but that every human heart is torn and deserving of mercy.

The Witness Tree

Memoir of a Ritual

I give this record of my journey
not as a contribution to human knowledge,
because my knowledge is small and of little account,
but as a contribution to human experience

Henry Miller

Let me tell this story from the grave. Life, seen from the grave, looks like the negative of a photograph: light turns dark, dark turns light, the photo reveals secrets it didn't know it was keeping. This is a story, in any case, that leads to a grave, then proceeds from that grave, so it's best I lie in it and speak from it.

Fifteen years before the grave . . .

There is a damp, moldy bungalow, no better than a shanty, where Diane and I eke our way through a wet Austin winter—but compared to the grave it's a palace, and Diane and I are blessed. We know enough never to be lovers, for one thing, as we nurse each other through a season of breakdowns that would otherwise have left Diane (perhaps) and me (certainly) in mental wards. At the climax of my crackup I sit in a smelly green armchair without moving or talking for three days, three nights, "catatonic" they would call it, while Diane goes to work, comes home, tends me, tries to feed me sometimes, sits by

219

me, lets me know I'm not alone. It takes courage to watch a friend go through that without running to some authority to palm off the responsibility. As I begin to revive *she* starts to slip and I tend her. We do not analyze, we do not delve, it is both too late and too early for that; we simply do not leave each other in this dark wood. (I suspect this is an ancient therapeutic technique, however forgotten or unresearched today.) Toward the end of her crisis she looks at me wearily, she smiles, she says, "Thanks for going first." It is December, Merle Haggard has a hit called "If We Make It Through December," sometimes we can afford cheap wine and we get drunk sitting by the radio, listening to the C&W station, waiting for Merle's song, and when it plays we sing our hearts out to it, laughing like crazy.

From the perspective of the grave this behavior is proper and conservative: death is taken for granted, rather than taken as something that can be put off by earning money or making art; sanity is measured by friendship and compassion, rather than by order and strength of will; ambition, intellect, even sex are less to be valued than singing and laughter. And wasn't our suffering the suffering of acute vulnerability to our own hearts and the world's? And wasn't it a better suffering, seen from the grave, than that other suffering called "normalcy," which is the suffering of being closed to everything but one's own needs—or, as they say now, "priorities"? Looking back from the grave, that far-off time with Diane seems to me one of my saner Decembers.

Two weeks before the grave . . .

Fifteen years have passed, and I have earned a certain notoriety as a writer. *Which means nothing to the grave.* Diane has a respectable job, a house she bought herself, and a child. *The grave awaits them all.* My mother has recently died. *The grave accepts her happily.* So has my marriage. *The grave doesn't believe in coincidences.* I have fallen in love with another woman. *The grave knows the song.* But, even so, I want more than anything to join my mother. *Death being certain in any case, the grave is not impressed by my impatience.*

I can't get it out of my head that there is such a thing as forgiveness—not from God, but from people, both the living and the dead. Nor can I get it out of my head that the way to earn this forgiveness is to die.

I'm not even aware I'm thinking this, but I do think it, all day, every day. It doesn't matter that people I love insist I don't need forgiveness, and that, okay, if I think I do, then presto! They forgive me. But I don't believe them. I know—I have absolute knowledge (the most dangerous kind)—that when I am in my grave both they and everyone I have hurt will certainly and definitely and believably forgive me. *The grave knows better, but I am not there yet.*

It never occurs to me to forgive myself. Once a Catholic, always a Catholic. The Church robs one of the power to be one's own priest or priestess. (That's what the Reformation was about, taking back the power to be one's own priest, but that great intent got corrupted by Puritans.) I haven't been to Mass in twenty-five years, but I am a better Catholic than I know. For all my highfalutin talk about ritual and the gods, I cannot forgive myself because I don't feel the power to be my own priest.

The power to die is much more accessible. One needs nothing but sufficient desperation.

Let us slip into the past tense for a paragraph and ask why my mother's death so shattered my life. Suffice it to say that without a real Clelia in the world somewhere, a real person on whom (without knowing it) I still anchored my deepest feelings, the Clelia within me went wild, wilder than the real Clelia ever had, and my feelings of madness and abuse and sex and love—they burst the bounds of my life. For I had had a life, a craft, a family, a wife, and there was love there, however strained, subverted and flawed it had become. Terrible things had been happening within that life, but invisibly, in slow motion; Clelia's illness and death had spun the process out of control. The life I'd been living needed patience, care, moderation, dedication—but they were all beyond this spirit that now possessed me, this naked unstoppable hermaphrodite dancer.

Look at it dance, with my legs, my genitals, my middle-aging stomach, and Clelia's face, Clelia's breasts, my face, hers, mine, hers. . . . Look at it dance, ranting poems, seeing gods—it whirls and it has feet and hands, it whirls and it has claws and hooves, a hand and a claw, a hoof and a foot, a nose then a snout then a nose, hair then fur then snake scales then hair, and in this creature's lair is my writing, in this creature's nest is my sex, in this being is much of what is best in me, and I cannot let it dance away without me. I go where it goes, whatever the cost. It dances away from my family, so I leave them. It dances into the arms of another woman, so I revel there. And if it wants to dance me into death, where we can finally be forgiven—then let's die.

The grave is very patient with all this razzmatazz, as it is patient with everything. The living imagine there are distinctions between this death and that, but the grave turns all deaths into the same death and sees all existence only as a flurry before dying. My flurry was no better or worse than another's.

So. In April, on the same night that Abbie Hoffman (whom I knew only slightly) took his life, I almost go. And it's a first, a big surprise. Never *really* occurred to me before, I thought that it would be an impossibility—to do it myself, I mean. I'd said I wanted to die, but even I thought it was just a chapter in my usual melodrama. This night, however, I come close, so close. My brother Aldo stops me. He himself is incarcerated in a mental ward on Staten Island (as a family, we keep a lot of people busy), but Aldo senses something, calls me collect, talks me down. My shrink and my girlfriend Zee's shrink are both wondering about committing me. Hey, I'm not a crazy person, I'm a nice guy, a talented guy, a semifamous guy. This ain't like back in Austin, I've got money in my pocket now, what the fuck are you talking about? I had a little episode, it's over, I wrote a column about it, end of discussion.

Weeks later it's Zee's turn to save me. Then it's her turn *again*. Zee's as tough as Barbara Stanwyck (whom she slightly resembles), but a whole season of saving me is wearing her down. It's not her job to read my mind, a point she insists on with stubborn clarity, but she senses rather than knows the spirits she's *really* living with, sleeping with, the hermaphrodite dervish dancing out of control. Zee was glad to dance with it in my bed (my dervish's happy hunting ground and natural habitat), but how can she chase the thing, calm it, soothe it back to a place where it will at least not kill me?

And what if it decides to kill her?

It is a terrible thing when a brave person becomes afraid of you, even for just a day. It wakes you up. Then you see, truly, that, in Hemingway's great phrase, you have "gone beyond where you can go." It is unlikely you can save yourself, and unlikely that any one person—lover, therapist, friend—can save you. Your dervish has taken over. This thing, this fertile creature, this fecund freak, that had been your secret strength, your originality, the spirit who whispered your best thoughts to you—it's taking you over, finally, as you always feared it might, and you are dancing down into the grave.

I've used the word "possession," as in being possessed by a spirit. And that's true, but the spirit is not alien, like the Christians would tell you; no, it is of oneself. You are not one person, you are many people, you are a community of moods and selves under one name. Parts of you aren't even human, they're part mammal, part reptile, part rose, part moon, part wind. And life is a question of which parts of you are dominant—which, in effect, possess you. (I think most people walk around possessed by the dullest parts of themselves, and that this, the worst state of possession, is what's called "normal.")

The grave has absorbed monsters of every size, some fifty feet high, some no larger than a human heart, and it has sucked down every dancer since Salome, and before her, throughout time. The grave is unimpressed by any spectacle my poor psyche can offer. It is said that some have escaped the grave. The grave is amused that the two for whom this claim is made in Western tradition are Jesus and Oedipus. What ever could they have in common?

So. As I was saying. Fifteen years have passed since that damp shack in Austin. Diane and I keep close tabs on each other. After the time of "If We Make It Through December," each of us is committed never to let the other go down without a fight. This is a commitment that, as you've seen, I sometimes don't keep for myself, but I keep it for Diane, and she keeps it for me. There are a few friends I love as dearly, but there's no friend whom I allow to step into my life with the sort of authority I grant Diane.

Diane calls. I hadn't called her when my mother died—I still don't know where she heard it—and, in a way, that was like sending up a flare to tell her I've got trouble.

There is a difference between having problems and having trouble. You can talk or think your way out of a problem, but you have to *do* something to get out of trouble.

Diane, laying on her West Texas lilt a little thick, as she likes to when making a point, says, "Well, Mahkle. You ready to do some *work?*"

"Work?"

"Get your ass up here to Lubbock and we'll do some work."

The day before the grave . . .

Things get lighter now. Other people move more freely into my story. The grave breathes easier. For graves, as you've noticed, are rarely off by themselves. They like the company of other graves. This may say something that the existentialists did not suspect about death.

On the flight to Lubbock with Zee I am thinking of Diane's altars—wondering whether Diane realizes how much of a teacher she's been to all her friends in the matter of making altars and shrines and sacred places. It's more than ten years ago that she made her first altarpiece, or the first one I saw. It was almost as though she had made it for me, being that I'm her only Sicilian friend, for it was a kind of Aztec rendering of St. Lucy—the Sicilian saint who goes about holding a saucer on which are two eyeballs. It's part of my altar now, has been for years.

By "altar" I mean only: a small nook in my apartment that I've consecrated, where a candle always burns, and on which rest small objects from moments in my life that need the haven of this blessing-place where every day I say my prayers. In the last few years many have taken to doing this. I made one cross-country drive, and no one I visited had an altar; I made another a year or so later, and many did—and most didn't know about the others. (When I wrote a column about that, a reader sent me a wonderful note that ended, "Even the assholes I know have altars now.") It is all part of the long and uncertain attempt to become one's own priest or priestess—to officiate, as the Church would say, for oneself and for each other. A parish of friends.

The grave sighs. Every denomination has started out as a parish of friends and ended as just another Church feeding off its worshipers and its enemies. If this is some sort of movement we are unknowingly, or unconsciously, part of, then we are lucky to be like the early Christians, reckless with the devotion they discovered and unbound by any rules; for the grave knows that, like them, in a hundred years it's unlikely we'll be able to recognize or stomach what we've had a share in starting. The grave has heard too many prayers to care about the details. Only the ground note of holiness matters.

Thousands of feet in the air, at hundreds of miles an hour, Zee and

I hold hands and pray. Not out of fear. I have never been able to bring myself to beg the gods for safety. No, we pray both because we love to pray together, and do it often, and because praying opens a window between this world and the Other World, and those worlds freshen each other. Life, in prayers, does not run from death; nor, in prayer, does death exclude life—for, as a great *zaddik,* the Rabbi Pinhass of Koretz, once said, "Prayer unites the principles." *The grave is this fact.*

But why, with all this prayer, am I still so crazy? I ask myself that sometimes, then get embarrassed at the silliness of my question, for people have been praying for eons, at every level of faith and devotion, and the history of those eons makes it clear that, whatever prayer does and is, prayer is not about sanity. *"What does Eternity care about sanity?" So mocks the grave.* Prayer is about having both the need and the courage to spend some moments open to Eternity. Which is just as likely to make you crazy as to make you anything else.

Which may be why Diane's father once told me, "If prayer is cut out to be what I think it is, it oughta have a touch of humor in it."

It's a bright autumn day in the Texas Panhandle, where the wind never stops, and its sound is part of every noise and every silence. Diane has a large back yard, the garage is her studio, there's a patio with chairs and a superb tree under which is a fire pit. A high plank fence makes it private. We sit on Diane's patio, drink beer, smoke cigars and cigarettes, listen to Butch Hancock and Joe Ely, Patsy Cline and Hank Williams, whiling the day away. We talk about God and about who's fucking whom, and it's so strange, to feel so good and at home, and at the same time to be this other Ventura who can't be trusted to stay alive. Can't be trusted for anything.

Zee and Diane look into each other's Celtic eyes and know they will be friends. Some warrior-witch signal of trust that no man is fast enough to catch passes between them. Then Spider and Lora come by—no need to call first, they just come by, that's how it is in this part of the world. Spider is tall and wiry, funny, gentle, but with a toughness you wouldn't want to challenge—and Spider's always thinking, *really* thinking. Lora looks like Patsy Cline sings—meaning, if I'd never seen Patsy's picture I'd expect her to look like Lora, with Lora's sad laughing eyes. She and Diane are best friends, and I've known Lora for as long as I've known Diane—we're what I call "close from a slight distance." Lora and Spider have been together for years, they live in a little West Texas town where they earn their living (or not, depending on luck) carving exquisite art out of wood.

A grave is growing in that back yard, and I don't know it.

Then James comes by. I don't know him. He's a new friend of Diane's, a hard man to read, and I think he likes it that way. I learn he's about my age, a 'Nam vet, loves guns, often carries one—not that I think he needs it, with the way his eyes pierce and how well he carries his solid weight. I trust him not only because Diane does, but because trust is the body's judgment, not the mind's. My bones trust him.

We know more about what pries people apart than what brings them together. Actually, we know practically nothing about what brings strangers together—a rather fantastic fact when you think about it. Zee knows no one but me, Spider and Lora don't know Zee or James, James doesn't know me or Zee or Lora or Spider, Diane doesn't know Zee. I don't know James—and no one knows the alchemy by which we talk as though we've all known each other a very long time. *It's possible even the grave doesn't know. This may be beyond its field of expertise.*

Diane and James, and another man, and two other women had gone into the badlands of New Mexico, for some days, to do what they called "work." "The prayer is in the *doing*," James says several times that afternoon. "It is not in the thinking about it." (He can't know he is giving Zee and me one of the sentences of our time together, a sentence that will pass between us whenever we need it: "The prayer is in the doing.")

Before they went to New Mexico, Diane, James and the other man and two women (none of whom were sleeping together) had come to some audacious conclusions: that helpful as therapy is—and philosophy, and religion, and booze, and art, and rock & roll, and whatever gets you through the night—as helpful as all that is, they had need of some hands-on ritual. What is ritual? Ritual is: to *enact* the metaphor. You get an image, and instead of thinking about it or writing it down or forgetting it, you *do* it. Enact it. Put yourself through the metaphor that the imagination offers. With a little help from your friends.

And yes, that's why sex play can be so intense: it follows the basic forms of ritual, it enacts the metaphor. Religious fundamentalists hate pornography not because pornography is evil, but because it's a rival; pornography is a form of religious fundamentalism. The basis of any fetish is that it's a metaphor that you can enact on your own, that you can *do*, and, if you do, the result (so you hope) will be transcendent. The object of religion and the object of sexual obsession are the same: the transcendent moment. The fundamentalists include sexuality in their religion by obsessively opposing it, the way the sexually driven include religion by offending it. Everybody's happy. *Religion and sex being, as we all know, so concerned with death, even the grave is happy.*

It is precisely this relationship between sexuality and ritual that is one of the highest barriers to becoming one's own priest or priestess. Ritual unleashes enormous energy. That's why most religions put so many strictures on their priests—to make the priests contain that energy, to keep it in control, focused. So when a few ordinary people take it on themselves to create ritual in their lives, they are playing with the religious history of their race. They are standing at the crux of what that history has been running from for centuries.

So the air becomes charged as Diane and James tell us about the work, the ritual, about how five people put themselves through three-dimensional metaphors in an environment beyond the law, in which anything could happen. They didn't say pretentious stuff like "We are going back to the roots of religion," or "We are rediscovering the origins of theater," or "We're back at the threshold of sex" (though there was no sex involved)—that's not their style, and, anyway, they were just trying to heal themselves and help each other. And more than that, like us, they were flying blind, they didn't really *know* what they were doing. How could they? How could we? They knew only what moved them, and they had made a pact to trust that.

It involved a lot of confusion. They made their campfire and, as they had learned from the Indians, blessed the four directions—and then they noticed that the fire cast their shadows on the canyon wall, and that their shadows looked like ancient petroglyphs.

"And it was *not* unfamiliar," James tells us.

"We didn't have a clue about what we were doin'," Diane says. "It was, 'Let's pretend.'"

At one point they could only scream. James says, "We taught the coyotes all *about* screamin'."

And then something unexpected happened to them. It's not my place to say what—and it really doesn't matter what, it would be different with different people. But it happened, and Diane felt a shift. They all did. She tells us in her back yard: "And then I said, 'This is the opening—this is the opening we've been looking for.'" And their healing work proceeded from that opening.

Is this the kind of audacity I'm supposed to be capable of? As Diane used to say, "Do you know how to spell 'fat chance'?"

The talk in the back yard goes on—beer, cigars, jokes, God, who's fucking whom—and the work, and the thoughts that come from *their* work. James says something that burns out a few synapses in my brain: "Jesus was trying to bring tribal society into the present." Oh yes. It's becoming clear, though it's never said, that James, this man I've never seen before, has been, in effect, selected by Diane to lead my work. Speaking of the world in general, he says, "Core values that have been hurt have to be healed." But he is also speaking of me. "And to do that," he goes on, "we are calling on the healers of all time."

I venture a question about preparation and James says, "Number one, share the intent. Number two, be prepared to share it." I am amazed at the depth of authority they have acquired from their experience in the badlands. "You have to be invited with full consent, full informed consent, to work on the mythos level." Oh. *That's* what this afternoon is all about.

The day of the grave . . .

There are graves suspended in air. The people who once hunted these high plains, the Comanche and the Kiowa, like the Apache and the Navajo to the west, and the Sioux and the Paiutes to the north, raised their graves above the ground on poles. In a wind-sheltered dip in the land, or in a small box canyon, their "burying ground" would be a cluster of platforms—graves, as I said, don't like to be alone— on which the dead lay, decked out in their finery, with some tobacco, and with whatever tools and jewels they would need in the Other World. The weather and the birds did for them what the worms do for us. All graves partake of each other. If a grave can just as easily hover as burrow, then perhaps the graves beneath the earth are straining upward, and the graves that hover don't mind sinking.

The morning is pretty and fresh. We eat a big country breakfast

at a table in Diane's back yard—the same people who were there yesterday. I am more calm than I've been in a very long time. I'm not thinking of "the work" at all, it's not real to me that it's even going to take
place, and maybe I'll decide not to do it and we'll just have another
afternoon of good, far-ranging talk.

Talk and music. All Diane had told me to bring from L.A. for the
work was music. I didn't give it any thought, just took the three tapes
that struck me as I was about to leave. The one we play through
breakfast I've labeled *Dreaming With Django*. I'd taken Django Rein-
hardt guitar solos and duets off several records. The depth of tone
of his Gypsy jazz, recorded half a century ago, goes just fine with
the sound the wind makes in the leaves. The two other tapes are Miles
Davis's *Sketches of Spain* and a tape that combines k.d. lang's *Shadow-
land* with her *Absolute Torch & Twang*.

Where has my dervish gone? He/she's talking, but I don't know
it. I'm told later that all through breakfast I didn't speak but to tell
stories about my mother, her life, her death—the dervish dancing on
the tip of my tongue and I can't remember a word. The others talk,
too. Zee disappears into the house, comes back with something
wrapped in a napkin (there's a golden flower on the napkin) and hands
it to Diane. Diane opens it. It's Zee's necklace from Fiji, a marvelous
thing. This, I think, is what Diane would call our "opening." Diane
is so moved she starts to cry. I put my arms around her. For some
reason we're all suddenly crying, even Spider. Nobody knows why.
We kind of laugh about it, but our eyes are still wet.

What just visited us, through Zee's giving? We cannot say, but it
feels as though spirits have arrived, gentle ones, here for the work.
I'm not even frightened. Diane puts on the necklace and says, "Well,
Mahkle—it's that time."

Spider and Lora hadn't even intended to stay! They were just having a meal and saying goodbye before driving the two or three hundred miles to their town, they weren't intending to be part of the work.
But something in that visitation has decided for us all. They have no
intention of leaving now. Somebody says something about calling in
sick, and Lora says, "Let's call in *well*!"

The darkness within me is baffled at this light. I make a note to
tell Zee later: "Love needs shadow, work needs light." It's like a little
chant in me. The words stay awhile, then go away. *A grave is open-*

ing up, not like I thought it would, but gently flowerlike. I should have known that graves like light.

Diane tells me to choose my music. I'm walking as though in a daze, a strange viscous atmosphere has descended on us, as though time is being pulled like taffy. Little things, like putting the Miles Davis tape into the machine, take a long time. The machine eats the tape, but somehow doesn't damage the tape. I put the k.d. lang tape in, but I don't turn it on. I'm in a strange state of waiting, aware that the others are doing things, but I don't know what.

Later I will learn that they all went to their tasks as though they'd rehearsed them—this, though they hadn't so much as a discussion. It's impressive, what James calls "the power of shared intent." Months later I will tell this to the man I call my Teacher, and he will say, "If you're able to go up with three or more people in multiple belief you can do incredible things." And he will say: "You have to learn to do ritual for yourself to survive. You have to have it to save your ass. Ritual has to be moved from the area of the special to the commonplace."

There is much I'll relate now that I learned later, when we all compared notes, but I'll just tell you how it happened.

While I am drifting in a kind of slow-motion state, not aware of the others, they are preparing as though for a sports event, stretching, breathing in deep, doing neck exercises. In the house Zee lights a candle and says the names of my brothers, my sister, my father and my mother (none of whom she's met), invoking their spirits to help me. "I thought your blood should be there," she will say later. Diane tells Spider, "Don't use your head, use your heart. I want you to watch him. If you need to wrestle with him or dance with him, it's all right, just do whatever."

They unroll a long white sheet maybe ten or fifteen yards down the middle of the back yard. Which sounds like nothing. But an atmosphere has come upon us. As though if you say something it will echo in the Other World. Which perhaps is the definition of "sacred space," "ritual space." As in an outdoor movie set where, when the spots are turned on, the sunlight and the electric light blend into still a third light—the mood is like that, as they unroll the sheet, and set up a tall wooden column, and ask me where I want to stand. By the power of our shared intent, it is all happening in some strange third light.

I choose a spot. They ask me where I want them. I arrange them in an arc in front of me, except for Zee. She I place a little behind me and to my right—"flying my wing," I say. Protect me, my eyes tell her. I will, her eyes say.

"I am all the protection you need," whispers the grave. (Graves lie too.)

Diane asks me to talk. I am relieved that talking can be part of it—until I hear what I'm talking about. Then I'm frightened and disgusted, frightened at the nakedness, disgusted at the self-pity, my god, *listen* to me, have I been walking around this way for months? I'm ashamed of my pain, ashamed to be standing in front of them. I feel stupid to have consented to this.

Okay, so I'm talking. Fuck. I'm talking about writing. (Always a bad idea.) I'm being paid to write a screenplay about a writer who's going through a transformation, but *I'm* a writer going through a transformation, and I don't want to, I'm *afraid* of how I'm changing, so I can't write the thing.

"You'd rather die than write the screenplay?" James asks sarcastically.

"Yes."

And James's voice changes. His West Texas voice starts to sound like Clelia's, my mother's. He's taking her part. He's yelling at me. I want to kill him but I'm paralyzed, drained. What is *she* doing here? *("She's only in the grave," the grave says, "and since the grave is everywhere, that's where she is, stupid.")* I was so happy such a short time ago. Now I'm crying (something I say I don't do often, but apparently I do it more often than I know). I'm talking about how the mission of my writing was to save my family, save them by justifying the pain, justify it by making something of it, so our poverty and insanity and failure as a family won't have been for nothing, so we won't have been defeated. But all I have to show for that is a book of rather careful essays and a dirty novel, and no one's been saved. *The dumb bastard can't decide if he's Oedipus or Jesus. Somebody change the channel.*

James is still Clelia. He's still haranguing me: I've failed, damn right, I'm not good enough, I deserve to die. I haven't lost all my brains in one afternoon, I know he expects me to come back at him, fight Clelia through fighting him, but if I did I'd be acting, and I don't even have the strength for that, I just can't. I let him say it and say it. And the dervish inside me grows so much bigger and stronger that I'm starting not to exist. It is so strange to stand there and not exist. I'm weeping. And I hear myself saying, "I've done enough, Mama."

I've done enough, Mama. Do you hear me? I've done enough.

James-Clelia is still yakking at me, but I am saying this over and over, to myself or out loud, I don't know, but this isn't a breakthrough, it's the final step down and I know it, I am raising the white goddamn flag. "*La commedia finito*," or however you say it in goddamn Italian.

There is talk of my wife, talk of Zee, there's James-Clelia asking why she doesn't have grandchildren, fuck-all!

"Where are your children?"

"Safe. They don't exist."

How did this yard, in this strange light, under this sweet wind, fill with so many swarming words, like gnats you have to keep brushing away from your face? I look at Diane. For the first time in twenty years I can't read her expression. I look at Lora. Her eyes are so kind. Spider seems transfixed, both shocked and fascinated. Zee is crying. Strong tears. Clear-eyed. Just looking at me.

Life is turning, turning, something must happen here. I may not have any courage, sense or dignity left, but I have not gone this far only to deflate. Something *must* happen, and I will wait in this yard, this awful place, till by force of nothing but waiting I make it happen, even if it's my death, how do you like that, motherfucker-James, what are you gonna say to the cops *then*?

Your Indian grave has floated from its hovering place to rest upon the surface of the ground. Your white man's grave has risen from its buried place to rest upon the surface of the ground. Don't be surprised that the ground itself, this lawn where you've known such love and care, is only a grave in disguise. Whitman told you about the leaves of grass, that every lawn is a grave, you knew that, or said you did, and read his line about "carrying the crescent child that carries its own full mother in its belly." Here is your grave, lie down.

Spider and James are so physically strong. Holding my arms they don't force me but guide me to the place on the lawn. The sheet is there. I *see* a grave.

James-Clelia won't shut up, the whole way to the grave he/she is taunting, taunting. I expected Mama to be sorry for me when this happened, I didn't expect her to be cackling with victory. It's a little hard to take, but I just don't have the energy to protest.

So they bury me there on the lone prairie. *Welcome, says the grave.* A sheet above, a sheet below, like an Indian but on the ground; then heavy things, I still don't know what they were, they felt like logs but were probably pillows, but really, they felt like logs, I couldn't move. It was very dark in my grave. Well, what would I expect but darkness there? And I got very cold. And I felt very silly.

I have come a long way to play an embarrassing game, it's not going to make any difference one way or the other.

You should know better. The grave always makes a difference.

I hear weeping. Zee is weeping. So are Lora and Diane. Spider's all choked up. They're not acting, they're weeping. Spider's saying he's always admired me, and I had to go and do this. James is calling me a chickenshit. "Everything I heard about this guy, and look at him, he didn't even protest, he didn't even argue, he just let us lay him down. Chickenshit to the max."

It may have been a game, but my chest constricted in shame and grief. Wasn't anybody going to forgive me? That's why I'd wanted to die, so my wife wouldn't hate me anymore, so my stepson wouldn't think I was a failure anymore, so the dervish would go to the Other World (where it had always longed to go), so everyone would see how hard I'd tried. Wasn't that the deal I'd meant to strike with death? *Death doesn't deal.*

I know I had to go a long way, through lots of Sturm und Drang, to find that out, but my friends were teaching me that this sort of suicide was the one thing no one I loved would forgive me for. They would be angry at me for this for the rest of their lives. All my other failures and sillinesses, even my betrayals, were just life, and, since they know life, they could ultimately forgive me, as I would forgive them. But this—about this their anger would be implacable. Even if they didn't want it to be. Slowly their anger would eat away at their love. If this was all it was going to come to, I wasn't worth so damn much trouble.

But where have they gone? It's absolutely quiet except for the wind. And dogs barking. Where have they gone? What am I supposed to do?

Nothing, dummy. This is the grave, remember?

They have gone out of hearing range is where they've gone, and I will learn that they, too, are wondering what to do. Zee is crying. Lora is holding her. Diane says, "Let's dance." She puts on the k.d. lang tape.

I can't tell you how funny it seems, suddenly to be listening to k.d. lang from the grave. But the song is so touching, the voice so strong, so alive. "Out of nowhere this gust of wind," she's singing. And then that delicate mournful song about the abused child. This isn't funny anymore. I'm *in* her voice. In the middle of it. There's nothing but the dark and that voice.

The others are dancing quietly, each of them alone. Then, one by one, they stop. "How long do you think he'll stay under there?" James says. "I dunno," Zee says, "he's pretty stubborn." "Maybe we should go to a movie," says James.

Lora says, "He shouldn't be alone," and, unknown to me, goes and sits in a yoga position near what has become my grave.

I can't move. The grave of my imagination has blended with the grave they have created into something frightening and strong. Something rises in me that I cannot identify. I hear a stronger weeping, my own weeping, and I tell my mother, and my wife, and everyone I've failed or betrayed, including my art, that I've had enough, that my begging for forgiveness is done, that I'm no longer willing to die for it.

Of course, my actual mother, my actual wife, my actual lost friends would say, "What makes you think we wanted you to die, anyway? We're not interested in your goddamn histrionics. Go muck about in the back yard all you want, but leave us out of it." Yet is anyone entirely innocent of the way they exist in another's heart? Every interaction is part conspiracy. Afterward, each person is both more and less than they were, and none of this has happened without some intent, however unconscious that intent may be.

Now I feel a lightness in this grave, a sweet lightness. R. D. Laing is talking to me! R. D. Laing, k. d. lang, maybe that's the connection, she's singing, he's talking, and I hear one of his sentences whole and clear: "There are sudden, apparently inexplicable suicides that must be understood as the dawn of a hope so horrible and harrowing that it is unendurable."

Hope?

And I start to laugh. Laugh-cry, cry-laugh, I have been such a *dope*. I ALMOST KILLED MYSELF SEVERAL TIMES and I didn't even know that I was suffering not from despair but from *hope*. That's what this has been all about. A germ of hope—no, make that a wild hair—that would, if followed, invoke changes in my life that terrified me, and this terror was enough, almost enough, to kill me. Jesus H. Oedipus on a crutch. Did I really just almost die of *hope?* A hope I was afraid to live out? That would have been a weird thing to write on my death certificate. k.d. lang is singing, "Are you getting scared, my dear?"

Less of some things, more of others, but it's at least nice to know what I'm *really* scared of.

Meanwhile, back at the patio, James asks Zee, "Are you angry?" "No," she says. "You don't have any anger about how he's wanted to die." "Yeah. I have anger, yes." "Why don't you go over there and kick him?" Spider chimes in with: "I want to get that dirt over there and put it on him." "Well, go ahead and do it," James says. "I'll help," says Zee.

In fact, they're all angrier over my foolishness than they'd realized, they all seem to think shoveling dirt on me is a high idea, and they get shovels and such and walk over to a pile of gravel.

If you're under a sheet, and weighted down with things for the whole length of your body, it is a strange thing to feel the weight suddenly get weightier, in sharp hard bolts as something, you don't know what, hits you and makes a strange sound. Gravel weighs a lot. And then, quite painfully, a large pack of it smacks into my face—Zee, really mad now, scooping a whole shovelful and not caring how hard it hits.

Enough is enough. I'm going to get up now. Or am I? What makes me linger a little longer is that I have grown to like this grave. It has taught me what I didn't know how to learn from any teacher, friend, lover or therapist. I start to rise, but it's almost too much, there's too much weight on me. I get a little panicky, which gives me the strength, and I rise, lifting the dirt and the other things off me, and the light hurts my eyes.

The Indian grave rises back into the air, the white man's grave burrows back into the ground. I will visit Diane's again and again in my life. I will stand at that place. I will think, "What a fine day that was.

How willing we were to risk any awkwardness to reach each other. What a strange, funny, lovely day, when my friends helped me get my life back. What enormous power raw ritual has."

As my eyes adjust to the light I expect my friends to be glad to see me. They tell me later that I was crying at this moment, but I'm not aware of it now. I'm just aware that they don't seem glad to see me. James growls and charges me, yelling, "Stay down there!" Spider too, then the women (none of whom is a fragile flower). On a normal day neither Spider nor James would have much trouble taking me, but at this moment my feet plant themselves so solidly that it takes all five of them to get me down, and by then we are all laughing as we all fall, like children, patty-cake, patty-cake, all fall down.

It's amazing how much silliness you have to endure in order to learn something about yourself.

We lie there all entangled, Zee with her head on my legs, holding my hand, my head on James's chest, and I'm crying again. I would have thought that it was over now, but Diane has disappeared, and Miles Davis's "Sketches of Spain" fills the yard. "Zee doesn't want to come home to a little boy anymore," James says. (Alas, the grave hadn't addressed that and I couldn't change fast enough.) Diane appears again. I'm supposed to dance.

Alone? In front of everybody?

But I find myself dancing. I don't care if it's alone and in front of everybody. The body that has tasted the grave needs to dance, quite apart from whatever bullshit I happen to be thinking. How strange for my body to be doing this, to not really care that I'm embarrassed. It's really trying to get inside Miles Davis's tone and move there, it doesn't much care about what it looks like. I feel electrical charges run up and down my arms, across my shoulders, across my forehead, up and down my back.

Diane tells Zee, "Go dance with him, mirror him, make him mirror you." So Zee and I dance. Spider and Lora dance around us, holding that long thin white sheet, and they begin wrapping it around us. Finally, we stand still, Zee and I. We talk softly. The others seem to have gone away. But they haven't, they've just stepped out of our line of sight. When we turn toward them they're standing under a tree.

I'm a city kid, I don't know from trees. It's about three stories tall and bends over the yard making a wide shady space. There's a song

Zee and I love, a Robbie Robertson song with the line, "I will meet you by the Witness Tree." That is the species of tree this is. A Witness Tree. There are new religious feelings happening, new in the sense that anything is new: a recent combination of ancient elements. It may be necessary for survival. And this is what is being witnessed now. By James, Diane, Spider and Lora, standing under the Witness Tree. They are asking us to join them. And the manner of their asking reminds me of a line in Robert Bly's translation of a poem by Tomas Transtromer: ". . . a biblical saying never set down: 'Come unto me, for I am as full of contradictions as you.'"

James blesses the four directions, as he's learned from the Indians. Spider takes my boots and socks off. Holding me strongly, he leads me into the fire circle. They have made concentric circles in the ashes of last night's fire, the ashes are still hot, they sting my feet. The stinging feels good.

James says, "Standing in the circle, you're standing on the shoulders of your ancestors."

I have not had many visions in my life, but at this moment I have one. That's why I am here to tell you that this ritual stuff is for real. As James speaks of ancestors and descendants both of blood and of spirit, and asks whether I promise, in this company, to be responsible to those ancestors and descendants and our spiritual kin for the rest of my life, and as I promise, this is what I see:

I see my mother's face enormous in front of me. But when James says the word "ancestors" her face gets smaller, gets human-size, and I see Clelia at about age fifty-five, in her favorite house dress, her hair in bobby-pinned curls, smiling seriously, gently, and moving toward a crowd, a quiet but very very large group of people who stand attentively awaiting her: our ancestors.

What a wave of comfort comes from them to me in this moment. Even the meaning of that comfort comes to me, though not in so many words: that your mother is your mother, your father is your father, and they can't help but have a mythic dimension in your psyche, but— they are only two of many, many many many, who go back in time, and whom you will someday join. No agony of mine can buy peace for Clelia, but no agony of hers is too much for the touch of all our ancestors to soothe. In this realm, mother and father are not immense presences overwhelming the psyche—they are not alone in the Other

World, so they are not alone in your psyche. They are accompanied by the ancestors you share with them. As a Western person, you have to look for those ancestors, you have to go way out of your way sometimes for them to appear, for you to feel their great soothing presence, but they are there, and they can welcome your parents and soothe them the way you tried to and never could because no children can. And, with all their shared experience, they can understand you, too.

I feel the smiling of my ancestors around the Witness Tree. I see my friends smiling. I feel more fortunate than I can say.

Zee joined me in the circle. We had felt from the first day we met that somehow we'd come from the same family, and that feeling was strong as we stood on those ashes. A cup was passed around from which we all drank. My ancestors made a larger circle around us, which the others couldn't see, which I could no longer see, but I felt it so strongly. The spirits that had welcomed us when Zee gave Diane the Fiji necklace, and that had helped us begin, seemed to be back, the air had their gentle quality and we all sat in chairs around the fire pit, smiling wearily, thinking it was over.

It wasn't, amazingly enough. We thought we were finished with the ritual, but the ritual wasn't finished with us. We began to speak of what had just happened, the way you speak of a storm after it passes. I learned that the images Diane and James had conceived for me were that I go into a grave, and if I chose to arise from that grave, I had to dance. But the manner in which this would happen is left to the moment. The progress of going through these images gave me my vision. As we continued to speak of the ritual, assuming it was over, the ritual sought out Zee. She began to speak, we began to react, and to everyone's surprise the ritual resumed. It was now *her* work—but that's not my story to tell.

As for me, I was cured of suicide. Not of crackups—I crack up pretty regularly, and probably always will. That's just life for some of us. I've had some bad ones since, and that's how I know the day of the Witness Tree cured me of suicide, because no matter how bad the crackups have been (and one was a doozy, believe me), suicide is no longer a possibility. I don't think it ever will be again. I gave my word in that circle to my friends and my ancestors and my descendants— which means that my entire psyche, every level and cranny of it, heard that promise. And I had been stripped down enough so that my word was not (as it so often had been) a pose. It was all I had left. I am a stronger priest now, for myself, for my friends.

And on that day my mother and I began to love each other again, truly—she from the Other World, me from this one. Now we talk again, laugh again. She's there in the Other World to be called on, a powerful helper. I bless her, and she me.

And the dervish—still does what it does in me, and that's as it should be.

October 25, 1991

Coda

Solutions to Everything

It's happened once too often. Somebody says or writes to me, "You talk about what's wrong but you don't offer solutions," or "My girlfriend-boyfriend-lawyer-therapist says you should suggest solutions, not just talk about bad stuff." And maybe they're right. Maybe to detail one's vision and let readers take it from there if they feel like it just isn't enough. Maybe there *are* solutions, and maybe I *should* know them.

So I sat down and thought real hard, and here, numbered for your convenience, are my solutions to everything.

00. Indulge in secrets. Without one or two *major* secrets, your life will surely fade. (If you're over forty and don't understand this . . . you're in big trouble.)

A conundrum: secrets aren't lies—they're mysteries, havens, passage-ways. Lies wreck your life; secrets can save your life. But sometimes you have to lie to keep the secret. Uh-oh.

1. Make mistakes. As Coleman Hawkins said, "If you don't make mistakes, you aren't really trying."

2. Stop lying about yourself. To yourself. To your friends. To your family. To your business associates. Maybe even to your enemies. (Your enemies oppress you as much by your fidelity to your own lies as by anything else.)

3. Stop tolerating in your leaders what you wouldn't tolerate in your friends. But . . .

4. Tolerate impurity. Trying to be pure about *anything* is a way

of setting yourself up to fail. Asking other people to be pure is a way of setting them up.

5. Read one book a month—a book that you didn't find out about in a magazine or newspaper. Browse an independent bookstore and wait till some book says, "Read me" and read it.

6. Listen to the voices. The wee inner voices. Even if they don't speak, even if they only breathe a little, like dirty phone calls. Do anything they tell you to do except rape, kill or pillage. (The voices make mistakes sometimes, but they don't make *boring* mistakes.)

7. Leave people alone when they tell you to leave them alone. If they mean it, they need it. If they don't mean it, they're trying to manipulate you, so fuck them. (Note: This rule applies to grownups only.)

8. Don't make the "sophisticated" error of thinking that a negative voice is automatically smarter than a positive voice.

9. Eat real food but don't be a fanatic about it.

10. Don't be a fanatic about *anything*.

11. Do only exercises that take you somewhere. Walk, ride a bike, roller-skate, swim. All other exercise is ego- and/or fear-driven, and if you listen to ego and fear you will drown out the voices you most need.

12. Don't run. Really, *don't*. America likes to run because running from (fill in the blank) is what we do best. Everybody who runs is running down an alley away from something terrible. Stop running and find out what's behind you.

13. Don't dye your hair unless you're a woman over forty and you dye it the color of my obsessions. Even then, don't cover up all your gray. Gray is gorgeous. And if you're a man, then *really* don't dye to cover gray. Dig it: EVERYBODY KNOWS. And they talk about it in a snide way behind your back. I'm not kidding.

14. Eat Italian food. Italians went from being oppressive Romans to being the inefficient, wonderful Italians they are today. It's probably the food.

[15. No longer applicable.]

16. Given that you're living in a city where driving is necessary, learn to drive. You may think you know how, but my experience of the way you drive is that you probably don't. So here's how:

Drive for space, not for speed. Space in front of you is the safest thing you can have with a car. Darting in and out of traffic doesn't change anything, it just makes you older. You can't beat the average traffic flow on any given street or freeway by more than five minutes, which only makes a difference if you're having a baby. And don't you feel like an idiot when you've passed six cars and they pull up beside you at the next light? They're laughing at you. And they hate you. Which isn't good for you. Drive for space.

If the move ain't smooth, it ain't right. There's no excuse for a jerky turn, stop or acceleration. It's hard on the car, it's hard on the other passengers, it confuses other drivers, it's not aesthetic. Such moves are for emergencies only.

Ninety percent of the time you drive with your habits, not your head, so figure out what your bad habits are—gunning it through yellows? not signaling? tailgating? Your worst habit will turn into your worst accident. So stop it. Drive for space. End of lesson.

17. Dance. Jesus said, in one of the Gnostic gospels, "He who does not dance does not know what happens."

18. Don't worry so much about being fat. Fat feels great in bed.

19. Have at least one other living thing in your abode. Rhododendrons, for instance, are fantastic creatures. They give much, ask little, have marvelous names, and they don't shit where I walk.

20. Look into people's eyes when you talk to them.

21. Call your parents by their real first names the very next time you see them. Try it. Watch their faces. Then do it at least half the time you talk to or about them from now on. (If people all over the world did this, nations would cease to war.)

22. Have candlelight in your life. (If you should get into rituals, it'll come in handy.)

23. No matter how rushed your schedule is, spend at least five minutes in the morning quietly in bed with your loved one just being gentle together. Perhaps drinking tea.

24. Tell your mother and father, individually—and your children, if you have children—what you *really* think. Once a year, minimum. If more people did this, it would save more lives than arresting drunk drivers.

25. Do not avoid the eyes of the homeless.

26. If you think something's wrong—at work, in your family, in your self, in your country—agitate for change. If you won't do that, it doesn't matter how tan you are.

27. As regards No. 23: Assuming that you want a loved one but don't have one, my bet is it's not because you're fat, ugly, crazy, old, a failure, a drunk, a ninny or a clod. Lots of fat ugly crazy older failing drunk ninnying clods have loved ones. Lots who don't have lovers want one, and would probably even put up with you. So there's some lie at the heart of your loneliness; being with someone would reveal the lie, and you don't want that.

28. Tape this to your bathroom mirror:

> One can only face in others what one can face in oneself.
>
> *James Baldwin*

29. Work is a sacrament. Don't despise anyone's.

30. Don't talk down to kids.

31. Don't chicken out about sex. Given that you're with a consenting adult, do whatever you fantasize. This is much more important than quitting smoking.

32. Watch at least one black-and-white film per month.

33. Regarding No. 6: Entertain the notion that there are . . . voices. Some come from within, some from the plants and objects and such around you, and some come from what I call, for shorthand purposes, the Infinite. If you don't listen for them, your life will be more difficult than it has to be.

34. Pay more taxes—and insist that those taxes, and the taxes you already pay, go for education. Giving the young a lively, thorough, truthful education is the most important *environmental* issue today, even more important than acid rain, tropical rain forests and ozone holes.

35. Let me make that a lot clearer. Recycling and shopping ecologically are almost pointless when one-third of California's high-school students drop out, and most who graduate can't read much and have no skills to speak of. How can these people inherit a world? Even if we give them a greener world, are they equipped to keep it that way? You want a solution, so here's a solution: Take to the Streets for the Education of the Children.

36. Pray.

37. Stop looking for other people to supply the solution. *You're* the solution. If you're not, there is no solution.

38. Be aware of the Network. We live by a network of connections and links. Your connection to yourself, to your intimates, to your place, to the collective, to the planet, to the Infinite. (Each is a distinct connection.) Equally powerful are the collective's connections to you (not at all the same as yours to it), to groups of intimates, to itself, to the planet, to the Infinite. Finally, the connections of groups of intimates to one another, to the collective, to the planet, to the Infinite. All these levels and connections interweave. *All are equally important.*

All the links or connective points of this network (call them the acupuncture points of our universe) both take and generate energy. Any link out of sync weakens the others. (The West, for instance, has concentrated too much on the individual; the East, too much on the collective; both approaches have been catastrophic on every level of the network.) This network, from you all the way to the Infinite, is a living whole, ceaselessly changing. Some of these changes take millions of years. Some happen instantaneously.

May the links of the network shine.

March 9, 1990

The State of the Culture:
Religion, Men's Issues, Deep Ecology . . .

Santeria • Luis Manuel Núñez
A Practical Guide to Afro-Caribbean Magic

Though Santeria worship claims millions of participants in the Americas, its rituals are a major assault on the Western mind, long accustomed to a distant God and to orderly liturgies. Messages from Santeria oracles, its sacrifices and body-healings are as immediate as our blood, sweat, and the heat of sex. This book presents the Gods, oracles, spells, and ceremonies of a growing underground religion. (163 pp., ISBN 0–88214–349–2)

Return to Father • Gregory Max Vogt
Archetypal Dimensions of the Patriarch

This manifesto for the new patriarch restores historical and archetypal substance to the impoverished male psyche and body. Vogt challenges each man to revive in a new way the great patriarchal tradition of hunter and builder, lover and philosopher, protector of society and visionary. "This is one of those books that can make you feel good about being a man."—*Seattle M.E.N.* (169 pp., ISBN 0–88214–347–6)

The Greening of Psychology • Peter Bishop
The Vegetable World in Myth, Dream, and Healing

Revives the fertile but deeply downward and uncanny roots of our vegetable soul, thereby radically dislocating our usual assumptions about consciousness. Explores the vegetative nervous system and its symptoms (reading anew Freud, Jung, Reich), addictions to plant concoctions (cocaine, coffee, sugar, etc.), social rootlessness, the worship of growth, and the fear of rot. Illustrations, index. (237 pp., ISBN 0–88214–345–X)

Inter Views • James Hillman with Laura Pozzo
Conversations on Psychotherapy, Biography, Love,
Soul, Dreams, Work, Imagination, and the State of the Culture

Extraordinary, yet practical accounts of active imagination, writing, daily work, and symptoms in their relation with loving. The only biography of Hillman, the book also radically deconstructs the interview form itself. Wm. Kotzwinkle: "*Inter Views* is a lens focused by the bright gods, the archetypes, with whom Hillman is in creative rapport." (198 pp., ISBN 0–88214–348–4)

Write for a complete catalog:
Spring Publications • P.O. Box 222069 • Dallas TX 75222
or order directly from Publisher Resources: 800–937–5557